RESEARCH UNIVERSITIES
AND THE PUBLIC GOOD

INNOVATION AND TECHNOLOGY IN THE WORLD ECONOMY

MARTIN KENNEY, *Editor*
University of California, Davis and Berkeley Roundtable on the International Economy

Other titles in the series:

RESEARCH UNIVERSITIES AND THE PUBLIC GOOD

Discovery for an Uncertain Future

Jason Owen-Smith

STANFORD BUSINESS BOOKS

An Imprint of Stanford University Press · Stanford, California

Stanford University Press

Stanford, California

©2018 by the Board of Trustees of the Leland Stanford Junior University.
All rights reserved.

No part of this book may be reproduced or transmitted in any form or by any
means, electronic or mechanical, including photocopying and recording, or in any
information storage or retrieval system without the prior written permission of
Stanford University Press.

Special discounts for bulk quantities of Stanford Business Books are available to
corporations, professional associations, and other organizations. For details and
discount information, contact the special sales department of Stanford University
Press. Tel: (650) 725-0820, Fax: (650) 725-3457

Printed in the United States of America on acid-free, archival-quality paper

Library of Congress Cataloging-in-Publication Data

Names: Owen-Smith, Jason, author.

Title: Research universities and the public good : discovery for an uncertain future /
Jason Owen-Smith.

Description: Stanford, California : Stanford Business Books, An Imprint of Stanford
University Press, [2018] | Series: Innovation and technology in the world economy |
Includes bibliographical references and index.

Identifiers: LCCN 2018008488 (print) | LCCN 2018018764 (ebook) |
ISBN 9781503607095 | ISBN 9781503601949 (alk. paper)

Subjects: LCSH: Research institutes—United States—Social aspects. | Universities
and colleges—United States. | Academic-industrial collaboration—United States. |
Federal aid to research—United States.

Classification: LCC LB2372.3 (ebook) | LCC LB2372.3 .O94 2018 (print) |
DDC 378.007—dc23

LC record available at https://lccn.loc.gov/2018008488

Typeset by Newgen in Minion Pro 11/15

Cover design: Preston Thomas, Cadence Design Studio

This book is for Jenn, Connor and Audrey.
I left off that Oxford comma just for you.

CONTENTS

ACKNOWLEDGMENTS

As befits a book that is all about academic research networks, I have incurred too many debts to comprehensively list. I'll try to do some justice to the people, places, and events that have shaped my thinking, but I'm certain to miss things. I apologize. Regardless, the people and organizations listed here bear no responsibility for the content of this book.

Many colleagues and friends have helped me in ways large and small during the many years this book has gestated. At Michigan, conversations with Barbara Anderson, Renee Anspach, Elizabeth Bruch, Helena Buhr, Mariana Craciun, Jerry Davis, Becky Eisenberg, Russ Funk, Felix Kabo, Howard Kimeldorf, Kristina Ko, Maggie Levenstein, Tim McKay, Mark Mizruchi, Marvin Parnes, Maxim Sytch, and Mayer Zald have shaped my thinking. Michael Cohen and Rick Price taught me much about how to navigate and thrive in an interdisciplinary university, for which I remain grateful. Mitchell Stevens, Andrew Nelson, Victoria Johnson, Jeannette Colyvas, and Elizabeth Armstrong were instrumental in helping this book take its current shape. The whole project has benefited from the work of a large group of talented graduate and undergraduate research assistants.

The Interdisciplinary Committee on Organizational Studies (ICOS) has proven to be exactly the kind of rich intellectual environment that features so prominently in my arguments about what is best about universities. The University of Michigan itself has been an inspiration, a source of support, and a living case study. Much that I've learned in all my roles there can be found in these pages. The opportunity to serve as director of the Barger Leadership Institute and the many interactions it has allowed me to have with staff, students, and alumni from around the country, including Crystal Ashby, Dave Barger, Barry Blattman, Leslie Bond, Jonathan Carson, Dan Denison, Jeff Hall, Joe Kaplan, Dave Korus, Andy Lansing, Lisa Miller, and Jamie Sprayregen, have also helped me see the institution in a new and valuable light.

Further afield, Richard Arum, Pierre Azoulay, Steve Barley, Henry Brady, Ron Breiger, Ron Burt, Bruce Carruthers, Lis Clemens, Nosh Contractor, Jennifer Croissant, Gili Drori, Wendy Espeland, James Evans, Lee Fleming, Neil Fligstein, Scott Frickel, Danny Goroff, Neil Gross, Ed Hackett, Heather Haveman, Mike Hout, Michele Lamont, Jim March, Doug McAdam, Jennifer McCormick, Miller McPherson, Kelly Moore, Cal Morrill, David Mowery, Fabio Pamolli, Chick Perrow, Massimo Riccaboni, Hal Salzman, Marc Schneiberg, Andrew Schrank, Chris Scott, Susan Silbey, John Skrentny, Laurel Smith-Doerr, Toby Smith, Paula Stephan, Diane Vaughan, Marc Ventresca, John Walsh, and Josh Whitford require thanks for many rich discussions and the occasional provocation.

Presentations and discussions at universities too numerous to list have played an essential role in all this work. A conference at NYU and conversations that followed helped me to first articulate what it means to call a university a hub. Another, at the Wisconsin Institute for Discovery, led to a significant change in the direction of some of my arguments. The network sensibility that animates my thinking benefited immensely from summer weeks spent at the Santa Fe Institute and my participation in a working group organized there by John Padgett and Woody Powell. That group included Ken Koput, David Stark, Brian Uzzi, Doug White, and a rotating cast of scholars who helped my thinking in ways large and small.

More recently the work of conceptualizing and founding the Institute for Research on Innovation and Science (IRIS) has crystalized many themes you will find here. My collaborators in this effort, Barbara McFadden Allen, Ron Jarmin, Julia Lane, and Bruce Weinberg, have introduced me to many challenging and rewarding ideas and taught me much about navigating the complicated and rewarding world of data and institution building.

The work of IRIS has also brought me into contact with university associations such as the Association of American Universities, the Association of Public and Land Grant Universities, the Council on Government Relations, and the Big Ten Academic Alliance, where I have had the opportunity to see institutions like mine in a different and challenging light. Conversations with administrators and faculty at the many IRIS member institutions have added immensely what depth is to be found here. An opportunity to serve on a National Academy of Sciences Panel chaired by Dick Celeste forced me to think and talk in new ways about the university and the research enterprise it anchors.

At Stanford University Press, Martin Kenney, Steve Catalano, and especially Margo Fleming were essential sources of support and editorial wisdom.

My sociological groundwork was laid at the University of Arizona and expanded at Stanford. In both places, a long-standing and incredibly rich collaboration with Woody Powell has done much to define the ways I think and write. I've learned an immense amount from him over the years. He's not to blame for any of this, but his fingerprints can still be seen. One way that happened was through the "lab" he ran at Stanford University, which included Kjersten Bunker Whittington, Jeannette Colyvas, James Evans, Stine Grodal, Andrew Nelson, and Kaisa Snellman. Very early instances of some of these ideas were first aired and improved there.

There are also many people who have contributed their time and insight in interviews, in allowing me to observe their work, and in otherwise taking the time to educate me about their worlds. I cannot name them for a variety of reasons, but they helped to shape my thinking in important ways beginning almost twenty years ago.

Finally, I would be worse than remiss if I didn't acknowledge the financial support that made much of the this work possible. Several programs at the National Science Foundation have supported my work over the years. These have included grants 1158711, 0545634, 0724675, 0949708, 1240409, 1560987, 1262447, and 1535370. The Alfred P. Sloan and Ewing Marion Kauffman Foundations and the University of Michigan have also supported key aspects of this work.

RESEARCH UNIVERSITIES
AND THE PUBLIC GOOD

INTRODUCTION

Knowledge, Infrastructure, and the Need for Change

RESEARCH UNIVERSITIES ARE KEYSTONES in the nation's "knowledge infrastructure"[1] and the core of what former Google CEO Eric Schmidt and prominent geneticist Eric Lander call "the miracle machine . . . powered by federal investments in science and technology." There's a problem, though: "too few people—in government or in the public—understand"[2] how that machine works. This book seeks to change that by describing how public investments in research-intensive universities create and sustain a system that helps keep our nation and our world poised to shape and respond to an uncertain future.

Research universities are a kind of social insurance: "Pay the money in and if nothing happens, great! You get to know more about the universe. But if something does you are ready."[3] They help insure our future because their history, their organization, and the public support on which they depend make them *sources* of knowledge and skilled people, *anchors* for communities, industries, and regions, and *hubs* connecting all the far-flung parts of society. The chapters that follow elaborate on these three metaphors to explain how research universities keep us ready to take advantage of opportunities and to address problems we don't know we have yet.

The ideas presented here are meant to help us think and talk more clearly about how our research institutions increase well-being and keep us prepared for a complicated future. That's important because the language we are currently using—a rhetoric that emphasizes market responsiveness, productive efficiency, and individual returns on investment for students—is profoundly unsuited to accurately explaining the true public value of research universities and their need for ongoing public support.

This book is about a very small slice of higher education that does an immense amount of important work. I focus my attention primarily on the research component of the university knowledge mission, which also includes transmission through teaching and learning and dissemination via public service. It's hard to know where precisely to draw the line between research-intensive and more teaching-focused campuses, but consider the fact that the U.S. Department of Education identified 5,071 degree-granting higher-education institutions that awarded federal financial aid in 2015.[4] About 2.8 percent of those colleges and universities (141) did at least $100 million of research and development (R&D) in the same year.[5]

Those 141 campuses accounted for just over 89 percent of all academic R&D in 2015.[6] They are located in forty-five states and the District of Columbia. This group offers one important proxy for what I mean when I talk about public and private research universities.[7] The academic research enterprise in the United States is largely defined by work that public investments support on about 3 of every 100 college and university campuses. Because I begin with research, I emphasize this small but unique class of higher-education institutions.

It is not really a good time to be one of those universities. Institutions that combine teaching at all levels with public service and substantial research are expensive, complicated, and hard to understand. They are also flashpoints for political and cultural conflict. In the last thirty years public research universities have faced state divestment, which has accelerated dramatically since the great recession. The result, in the words of Louisiana State University president F. King Alexander, is that institutions like his "have taken a decade's worth of hits."[8] Declines in support from states go hand in hand with increasing tuition and fees.

In the same time period, federal support for research has declined in real terms, again striking our public research institutions. Prosperous private institutions also feel the pinch as federal grants fall short of covering the full cost of the research they support. Universities generally receive far less than the overhead reimbursement rates they negotiate with the federal government. At MIT, for instance, vice president for research Maria Zuber notes, "We lose money on every piece of research we do."[9] The result on both public and private campuses is the need to cross-subsidize the costs of the research and teaching aspects of the university's knowledge mission.

In 2005, federal grants accounted for just under 64 percent of science and engineering research expenditures at academic institutions; by 2015 that number had dropped to just over 55 percent.[10] States, corporations, and private foundations are not rushing to fill the gap. Instead, universities themselves are making up the difference, sometimes with the help of philanthropically minded individuals. In the same time period, the percentage of science and engineering R&D funded by universities themselves grew to nearly $1 of every $4 spent. But the possible sources of funds that allow universities to directly support academic research are limited.[11] Among the universities that are members of the Association of American Universities (AAU), for instance, research grants are the largest source of revenue followed by tuition and fees.[12] For both public and private universities, instruction and research are the number 1 and number 2 costs.[13]

The result of all of this is that research-intensive universities find themselves in a bind because of their dual focus on research and teaching. The situation is worst on public university campuses, which educate the plurality of four-year students (28 percent, more than 3.5 million).[14] Private universities are also under pressure. But because they never relied on state appropriations, because they enroll far fewer students, because they tend to have more substantial endowments, and because they face less scrutiny over their tuition charges, their situation is somewhat less dire.

Regardless, the decade since the great recession has accelerated financial trends that put significant pressure on our nation's public and private research universities. These circumstances "create unprecedented challenges in managing finances at research universities and are legitimate threats to the nation's basic research capability."[15] The situation seems likely to worsen as a new federal budget unveiled by the Trump administration proposes drastic cuts to research funding.[16]

In defending a nearly 20 percent proposed cut to the National Institutes of Health, then secretary of health and human services Tom Price took aim at already insufficient indirect-cost reimbursements.[17] Secretary of education Betsy DeVos issued a clarion call against "the education establishment" that seems to be borne out in significant cuts to higher education.[18] In defending proposed budget cuts, Office of Management and Budget director Mick Mulvaney said "one of the questions we asked was 'Can we really ask a coal miner in West Virginia or a single mom in Detroit to pay for these programs?'"[19]

Mulvaney was speaking explicitly of the Corporation for Public Broadcasting, the National Endowment for the Humanities, and the National Endowment for the Arts. All three of those support work on many university campuses. Regardless, the drastic cuts proposed for science agencies that fund the bulk of academic research and for student aid suggest that many policy makers feel that research universities and their key activities are not things we can and should ask taxpayers to support.

That belief is wrong and deeply destructive. Understanding why that is and how it matters requires that we shift the typical focus of books and commentaries on the state of higher education. I do that in three ways.

First, I am concerned only with a very small but exceptionally important part of the entire ecosystem of higher education: research-intensive universities. Second, where most analyses of universities start with students and ask why we should do research in institutions devoted to education, I flip the question to begin with research. In so doing, I ask about the benefit of educating large numbers of students in organizations dedicated to creating, conserving, interpreting and adapting knowledge. Finally, I shift focus away from the private returns that individuals realize from their education or that funders see from particular grants to a collective calculus that emphasizes our universities' contribution to the general welfare of the nation and, ultimately, the world.

Consider a small sampling of recent books about universities, which all emphasize the need to increase private returns and propose moves to (1) unbundle research, teaching, and service and even the components of degree programs; (2) streamline the organization of universities to address current market needs; (3) reduce or eliminate programs that don't have clear and immediate applications to the problems we know we have now; and (4) make the whole institution more responsive to market discipline.[20]

These proposals are mind-numbingly wrong because they make two fundamental mistakes. First, they fail to distinguish institutions that do significant research and graduate training from those whose primary or sole purpose is education. In so doing, these proposals threaten to damage the national capabilities for discovery and innovation that have grown up within and across our research universities since the end of World War II.

Second, they mistake the value of research universities for the return on individual investments in them. Doing so reinforces our knee-jerk reliance on the language of markets and market return to explain and justify investments in an institution that is valuable because it is a public good and produces them. The tendency to emphasize individual returns is also apparent in political discourse pertaining to both research and education.

In the former case, congressional action has pushed the need for the director of the National Science Foundation (NSF) to justify each individual grant in terms of its contributions to concrete national interests.[21] In the educational realm, a bill recently reintroduced into the Senate authorizes income share agreements (ISAs), which allow private investors to pick up the costs of an individual student's education in return for a fixed percentage of their later earnings.[22] Both of these moves exemplify destructive tendencies. One reduces the value of research to the return expected on individual grants at the time when they are funded. The other reduces the value of education to the earnings potential of individual students at the time when they enroll.[23]

All these moves are, at least rhetorically, driven by a concern with appropriate, effective use of public funds. Universities and their occupants must steward public investments by attending closely to the success of both projects and students. But the thing we are actually investing in when we put taxpayer money into research institutions is not the outcome for an individual or a grant. It is a set of organizations and networks that create and sustain capabilities that are found nowhere else and that contribute important things to our ability to foresee, create, and respond to our collective future.

The purpose of the university is knowledge. Its goals are collective rather than individual. Public support makes it able to identify and respond to problems our society does not yet know it has. In a political environment skeptical of hard-to-measure outcomes, public and private research universities, which both depend on extensive public investments, are very much at risk. Weakening them through inattention or through poorly devised policies that jeopardize their strengths in an effort to streamline their work will jeopardize our future.

I draw on economic sociology, organizational, and network theory to explain how research universities are unique components of our national and global system of innovation. Their distinctive features as sources, hubs, and anchors allow them to consistently innovate in response to new problems and opportunities. Put another way, universities help keep contemporary society able to develop and pursue knowledge that contribute dramatically to the health, wealth, and well-being of U.S. and global citizens. Public support, particularly federal research funding, is essential to these capabilities.

But where most efforts to explain the value of university research focus explicitly on publications or, more commonly, patenting and licensing, I choose instead to emphasize the work of people and networks. Research investments in our nation's campuses enable the complicated and uncertain work of discovery. That work yields immediate economic benefits as faculty investigators hire the people and buy the stuff necessary for research work. Economic stimulus is not the purpose of research, but it does contribute to the university's role as an anchor. More importantly, the work of research creates and sustains complex collaboration networks that are distinctive on different campuses. Those networks are the social grounds for discovery and training. They are the main thing that allows universities to be a continual source of knowledge and skills.

Intercampus variation in networks helps make sure that the academic research enterprise as a whole is capable of responding to new opportunities and needs that we may not be able to articulate. As discoveries and trained people leave the institution for destinations across the nation and the world, they make our universities into hubs: centrally positioned organizations in the large networks that constitute our society and economy.[24] These three interdependent features of the contemporary university account for both its immense success and the challenges we have faced in explaining it to skeptics outside (and sometimes inside) the academy.

While I strive to be clear-eyed, my view of the research university is essentially positive. This is not to say that I think research universities (or for that matter any higher-education institutions) are perfect. Indeed, their list of imperfections is long. They may not be as effective as they could be at the work of education;[25] they are not always the route to social mobility we imagine them to be; nor are they as safe, inclusive, and supportive as we might like.[26] The list of problems could go on, encompassing casualized academic labor, challenges of scientific replication, and the potential dangers and conflicts associated with commercialized research. When I say my view of research universities is essentially positive, I am not suggesting there is nothing to apologize for or improve. I am arguing that we too easily overlook (or undersee) the value unique to these institutions.

Despite all their problems and despite the skepticism they face, research universities remain the most impressive machine for developing, conserving, interpreting, teaching, and using knowledge ever to be found in human history. Current popular and scholarly languages for discussing universities miss the mark by conceptualizing them primarily as uncomfortable clusters of clashing activities and proposing trade-offs that emphasize one part of the mission at the expense of the others.

They are complicated and often contradictory. But treating these large institutions holistically, with the assumption that their prime and guiding purpose is to work with and develop knowledge for the collective good, comes closer to the truth. I hope to correct the prevailing, overwhelmingly negative, discourse around higher education and public support for research. Focusing specifically on research and considering all other aspects of university life to be in service to the knowledge mission clearly shows how academic work on a small but essential set of campuses consistently has broader social and economic effects.

Research universities are the only institutions in our society that do this set of things. Their publicly funded infrastructure for research, teaching, and service contributes dramatically to the general welfare of our society by creating and sustaining capabilities to create new possibilities and respond to currently unknown problems. That is why they are a central piece of our nation's infrastructure and why we should ask, and expect, coal miners and single moms as well as professors, well-to-do professionals, wealthy CEOs, and cash-rich corporations to support them. Understanding why that is requires that we rethink our view of the research university, beginning with our understanding of research itself.

1 A SYSTEM TO INSURE THE FUTURE

MOST FEDERALLY FUNDED FUNDAMENTAL research in the United States is conceptualized and conducted on university campuses.[1] In 2015, U.S. universities spent more than $214 for every man woman and child in the country to support academic research projects.[2] Most of that, about $0.55 of every $1, comes from the federal government. Our society makes that investment to increase human knowledge and improve the lives of those who ultimately pay the bills.

As pressure mounts to justify research in immediate practical terms, it has become clear that too little is known about how academic work generates economic and social returns to support wise decisions. Dangerous misconceptions thrive in the absence of rigorous, realistic analysis. As John Marburger, science advisor to President George W. Bush, said: "the social science of science policy needs to grow up, and quickly, to provide a basis for understanding the enormously complex dynamic of today's global, technology-based society."[3]

Explaining the public value of academic research requires a new framework for thinking about the contemporary research university. Public investments, such as grants, in university knowledge work yield short-term economic returns because the funds let investigators hire people and buy things.[4] Yet the true social and economic value of projects becomes clear only on a longer time scale as skills, techniques, and findings travel through multiple pathways from the campus into the larger world.

The discoveries that are made and the people that are trained with public funds thus shape technology, industry, the economy, and civil society. Activity in all those realms also influences work on campus. Entire academic fields including computer science, chemical engineering, and African American studies grew in response to developments outside the academy.[5]

This two-way flow of people and ideas allows investments in academe to contribute significantly to the general welfare. Understanding how this happens means shifting from a focus on what universities spend to an inquiry about what that spending lets them to do.

Let us both consider the text you are reading. The research that prepared me to write this book was supported by funds from seven external grants, direct investment by my university, and the time it allowed me to set aside for my research. The NSF awarded four of those grants to my institution across almost a decade. That money allowed me to hire some forty undergraduate research assistants who generally worked with me for a semester or a summer. I also hired ten doctoral students and postdocs whose work was longer and more intensive. Subcontracts and other arrangements supported work by six established collaborators on my campus and at four other organizations. We produced a substantial number of findings, papers, reports, presentations, dissertations, and undergraduate theses as well as code, data, documentation, and this book.

Other aspects of my research that are not germane to this book were supported by different grants, by institutional funds, or by no direct financial investments at all. The people who worked on those projects overlap, but only partially, with those who contributed to the studies that became this book. All my faculty colleagues also have other projects. Some of those are related to our joint work. Some are not. Regardless, the contributions my collaborators make to our research are informed by what they learn in other parts of their work, as are mine. My graduate students and postdoctoral fellows typically contribute to other projects as well. They also work to develop their own. Students carry information, techniques, ideas, and painfully won lessons about what doesn't work back and forth across teams and projects.

This book has my name on it and I alone stand behind its contents. In the strictest sense, though, it was produced in a complicated, far-reaching network of collaborators and students that spanned many grants, projects, and years. The doctoral students made their own discoveries and went on to work in other places—including universities, technology firms, nonprofit organizations, and government agencies—on new topics with different people where (I hope) the skills and knowledge they learned on my team served them well. The undergraduates dispersed to, well, everywhere. They are working and attending school nationally and internationally in fields such as politics, law, data science, and finance. A few went on to doctoral training, but most carried what they took from my research projects into nonacademic pursuits.

If you multiply my projects a few thousand times and expand them to include nearly every conceivable topic of research, the resulting web of relationships approximates the collaboration network at one large research university. If you imagine somewhere between one and two hundred such networks spanning the nation's most research-intensive universities and allow them to take on different characteristics in each new location, you will gain a sense of the scale and complexity of the academic research enterprise. If you begin to ask how people and ideas move across campuses and back and forth between universities and other settings, you will glimpse the national and global system that academic research and training feeds. Relationships at all of these levels allow universities to produce, absorb and translate new knowledge. Those networks are the social infrastructure that makes research investments into insurance against an uncertain future. They are the things public investments should cultivate and sustain.

Universities and Networks: Sources, Anchors, and Hubs

Universities contribute to our quality of life because they are *sources* of key inputs for the many other sectors. They use public investments to support work that generates knowledge and people who know how to use it. The ability to do this varies from campus to campus. That variation is due to differences in the structure, composition, and capabilities arrayed in distinctive collaboration networks.

Put simply, public investments such as federal grants and state appropriations enable work to happen on campus. That work spawns networks as faculty, staff, and students build teams that span individual projects. Those networks underpin a unique social system that creates knowledge and skilled people. People's movements back and forth between the academy and other parts of society allow for the application of knowledge, which generates many of the benefits that are the promise of our federally funded research system.

Research universities thus play significant roles in larger interorganizational networks. Their engagement with partners in many industries and sectors can be an important source of new problems and innovations that influence research. In the short term, universities contribute to society by serving as *anchors*[6] that add resilience and responsiveness to the regions, communities, polities, and industries with which they interact. In the longer term, universities create and sustain possibilities for innovation and growth because they are *hubs*[7] whose connections span all the major parts of our society.

Because universities are hubs, problems and opportunities flow to them from all over. Because they are sources, the knowledge and people necessary to recognize and respond to almost any sort of problem or opportunity reside in their networks. Because they are anchors, they represent a more or less permanent endowment that is at least somewhat independent of the immediate pressures of markets. These three features make research universities into unique machines to transform public investment into hedges against a risky and complicated future.

But if this is true, how will we know our system of universities is working?

Network Sources

Discovery and education are both the work of many hands. The social system that supports them is the proper target for public investment.

We can tell that the system works as a form of insurance and opportunity because important problems are routinely solved more or less independently by multiple individuals or teams.[8]

Multiple discoveries happen often. That fact suggests that our research enterprise is robust.[9] It affords many opportunities for different people and groups to pursue similar research topics. Those projects often use distinct approaches enabled by the particular capabilities and networks at play in their locations. While brilliant individuals and exceptional teams are essential to discovery, multiples suggest that the system is responding to opportunities and problems even when they might not have been foreseen. What, though, are the social conditions that we might expect to yield important multiples?

Let's begin at the turn of the twentieth century when two great geniuses, Albert Einstein—then a struggling, obscure German physicist working in the Bern Patent Office—and Henri Poincaré—then a celebrated French mathematician and philosopher who was also president of the Paris Bureau of Longitude—were both working to answer a fundamental question about the nature of time. They independently reached nearly identical conclusions, but Einstein's answer became a key part of the revolutionary theory of special relativity. Poincaré's discovery was all but forgotten.

Popular imagination and their own writings treat Einstein and Poincaré as abstract geniuses whose conceptual work was based on thought experiments divorced from the concerns of everyday life.[10] But Peter Galison, a prominent historian of science, has painstakingly demonstrated that this idealistic view is wrong.[11] The similar discoveries and their different impact resulted from the complicated social, political, and technical worlds each man inhabited.

The practical challenge of synchronizing distant clocks was an important technical problem facing European society in the early years of the last century. Philosophical, political, scientific, and economic forces aligned to make this problem at once an abstract concern of conventionalist philosophy and theoretical physics and an immensely pragmatic worry of engineers, navigators, and colonial powers bent on controlling far-flung empires. All these threads of concern aligned to produce a moment where whatever abstract or practical question one wished to address pertaining to time led back to coordinated clocks.

The threads of coordinated time converged in the patent office, where Einstein evaluated new inventions, and the Bureau of Longitude, where Poincaré struggled with methods to establish a ship's position at sea. The fact that these two brilliant men stood at such organizational "exchanges" made them "witnesses, spokesmen, competitors, and coordinators of the cross-flows of coordinated time."[12]

The places where Einstein and Poincaré worked, the problems they faced, and the people they interacted with made their multiple discovery possible. Their social positions also help explain why Einstein's solution to the problem of coordinated time revolutionized science while Poincaré's did not. The two solutions differed in just one particular. Poincaré, the established, elite scholar, tried to preserve the day's scientific consensus by integrating the now discredited concept of the ether in his theory. Einstein, the newcomer bent on rethinking physics, jettisoned this legacy of nineteenth-century mechanics with radical results.[13]

To be sure, neither the Bureau of Longitude nor the Bern Patent Office bear much resemblance to a major American research university. Nevertheless, the story of Einstein and Poincaré helps us clearly understand the conditions that allow today's universities to routinely serve as sources that produce multiple answers to pressing problems. This retelling of coordinated time suggests important ideas about the social conditions necessary for important multiple discoveries to occur.

People with necessary skills and capacities must be present and working in settings where many different problems that span practical and conceptual concerns are active. At least some of those people must be willing and able to discard conventional wisdom in order to pursue new answers. This points to a key tension for research universities. Academic training and discovery take place in a context where existing theories and knowledge hold strong sway. Established organizations can produce new things, but they must be configured to allow and support challenges to the status quo their own work helps create and sustain.

This means that failure is likely to be commonplace and should not be considered a disaster or a waste. It also suggests that established scholars must have the capacity to educate and mentor newcomers whose work may challenge the knowledge their advisors invested careers to build. Moreover, it implies that the system as a whole should be insulated from larger social pressures to conform to conventional beliefs. Such insulation should not come at the cost of separation from the concerns that animate contemporary social and economic life.

Radical discoveries like the theory of special relativity are exceptionally rare, but the conditions that gave rise to them should also enable less radical insights. Imagining universities as organizational scaffolds for complex collaboration networks and focal points where flows of ideas, people, and problems come together offers a systematic way to assess the potential for innovation and novelty as well as for multiple discoveries.

Unlike the story of Einstein and Poincaré, much of today's frontier research is the province of teams.[14] Even fields such as philosophy, sociology, and the arts that seem more individualistic are collaborative, shot through with relationships and networks.[15] Individual careers, knowledge, and the trajectories of fields are shaped by the structure and composition of groups even, as is the case with this book, when just one person is the author or inventor of record. In fields where research is costly, one of the key activities of a contemporary principal investigator (PI) is to define an intellectual agenda and marshal the resources necessary to pursue it. On a day-to-day basis, large-scale science, engineering, biomedical, and social research is a process fueled by increasingly cutthroat competition for grants, which PIs must bundle to sustain a career-long trajectory.[16]

One result of teamwork is collaboration networks. These structures evolve on and across campuses, creating many possibilities for ideas and techniques to be combined in new ways. Innovation results from such "recombinations."[17] Historical accidents, organizational differences, the physical arrangement of campuses,[18] the strategic decisions of funders or administrators, and even personality conflicts among researchers can lead otherwise similar networks to evolve in distinct directions at different universities. These diverse network configurations create conditions that allow the academic research system to produce and integrate unexpected discoveries.[19]

When a new problem arises, the size and diversity of the research system means it is likely to be identified quickly. More importantly, multiple approaches to its solution will be the rule. Public investments should be made to sustain the scale and diversity of the system rather than to identify the one efficient route to solving a known problem.

Understanding when campus collaboration networks are poised for creative innovation requires attention to the composition of the teams that actually do research work, to the structure of connections among people and teams, and to the capabilities that are arrayed in those structures. In the terms I developed earlier, the composition of research teams suggests the range of different intellectual and conceptual tools that can easily be brought to bear on a project and the possibility for risky approaches that challenge the current status quo.

The structure of networks is important because the relationships among people on campus determine how easy it is for individuals to search for, find, and integrate necessary techniques and information into their work. Finally, the content of projects pursued in these networks indexes the range of knowledge capabilities available for researchers to access and combine.

Community Anchors

At their best, universities also act as "contributing institutional citizens"[20] of their regions and the nation. In pursuing their own interests and attending to their locations, research universities add robustness and resilience of our society by being political, cultural, social, and economic *anchors*.

The metaphor has several related implications. In commonsense terms, an anchor holds an object in place. Being anchored yields a measure of stability, safety, and even permanence in the face of unexpected, changeable, or dangerous circumstances. Anchors are stabilizing points of contact. It makes sense to think of universities in these terms for several reasons. First, they are more geographically fixed than many other types of organizations and, at least until recently, their reliance on stable public funding of various sorts made them less prone bankruptcy than other types of organizations.

There are lots of things one could say about my institution, the University of Michigan, but two stand out in this regard. The first is that it is very unlikely to go out of business. The second is that it won't move to Tennessee or Alabama. Equivalently large and regionally important businesses routinely die or change locations, with predictable consequences.

The stability and fixity of universities helps explain why much of their activity generates local benefits. Even though federally funded research represents only part of the total work done on most campuses, it is important and instructive. When a new grant is awarded to an institution, the investigators whose project it funds tool up by hiring people and buying necessary goods and services. In a recent paper, my colleagues and I examined the characteristics of the workforce and vendor purchases supported by federal grants made to eight campuses that are members of the Big Ten Academic Alliance. We found that these grants paid wages to some fifty thousand people in fiscal 2012. Nearly three quarters of those individuals were students, postdoctoral fellows, or staff. Such hiring adds to the economy of regions that are home to universities because good jobs allow people to spend their earnings in local housing markets, restaurants, and shops.

We also tracked nearly $1 billion in vendor spending. Nearly $1 of every $3 used to purchase goods and services for research was spent within the state where a university was located. In the simplest terms, universities are anchors because they can usually be counted on to stay in one place and to consistently hire people and pursue activities—such as research, teaching, culture and arts production, and health care—that contribute directly and indirectly to that place. These near-term economic benefits are a happy by-product of core university missions, not their purpose or justification.

There are two other, more specialized ways to think about university anchors. The first is adapted from studies of retail marketing, which call the large department stores typically found at the ends of shopping malls "anchor tenants."[21] The big stores in malls are important because they draw shoppers to the mall and thus help create demand for products sold by smaller stores. But this means that anchor tenants also help define what kinds of specialized stores can thrive. Think about the differences between malls that are anchored by luxury department stores such as Saks Fifth Avenue and those that are anchored by less expensive brands such as Sears. In the former, shoppers are more likely to find a luxury jeweler. In the latter, a discount shoe store.

Universities too are anchor tenants because they draw lots of people to them. Research institutions also attract other organizations that seek to serve demand created by their people or to access the products of their work. It is a simple thing to note, but universities serve as anchors by attracting people who expand local markets for some types of goods and services more than others in the same way that some department stores increase traffic to high-end jewelers and others expand demand for discount shoes. In so doing university anchor tenants help set the tone for their regions.

They also serve as anchors for the networks of interorganizational relationships that characterize robust industrial districts.[22] When major universities like UC San Diego or MIT collaborate with corporations in their regions to develop and share information, they can play a distinctive matchmaking role because they do not directly compete with or seek to control the activities of their partners. As sociologist Walter Powell and colleagues put it in a study of the emergence of biotechnology clusters in the United States: "We think of an anchor . . . as a well-connected organization . . . which mobilizes others and fosters collective growth."[23] The most abstract sense of what it means for universities to be anchors focuses on how they occupy their positions in the broader world.

Connecting Hubs

The movement of people and ideas to, through, and from universities positions them in unique locations in national and global economic and social systems. Universities create and sustain possibilities for growth and for responses to unexpected challenges or opportunities because they are *hubs*. A hub is a common passage point and a focus of attention because it connects a system. Think about airports.

Hubs like Chicago's O'Hare have lots of flights on lots of carriers to lots of places. They are one hop from almost any destination in the world. Many people go to Chicago, but vast numbers of travelers pass through O'Hare on the way to somewhere else. In the global network of airports, hubs shorten the distance between any random pair of cities. Layovers notwithstanding, hubs are shortcuts. When they fail or close, the system grinds to a halt.

University campuses are hubs in a few of these senses. They are passage points for many people. This is obvious to professors, who face the same lecture halls filled with fresh new faces each year and who enjoy homecoming for the chance to hear where past students have taken themselves. Universities are also hubs in the sense that they are, metaphorically, one step from everywhere.

As sociologists Mitchell Stevens, Elizabeth Armstrong, and Richard Arum put it: "higher education is a hub connecting some of the most prominent institutional sectors of modern societies," and as such, universities are "sites where institutions intersect."[24] We would not be surprised to see travelers from many nations or to hear many languages spoken in the world's airport hubs. In much the same way, university campuses are places where it is not surprising to come across politicians, businesspeople, sports stars, humanitarians, scientists, entertainers, physicians, artists, diplomats, actors, military officers, entrepreneurs, musicians, journalists, lawyers . . .

The list could go on, but the point is an important one. A large university with a diverse portfolio of research and teaching is a shortcut between many parts of our world. Like airline hubs, if campuses close themselves off, knowledge and people have a harder time traveling where they need to go.

The movement of people and ideas from campus to other settings creates network connections that shorten the distance between different industries and sectors. For that reason campuses have a unique capability to be organizational "exchanges" where multiple "threads of concern" converge in the way that Galison described Einstein's patent office and Poincare's bureau.

An entire university is too large and diverse to provide an easy illustration of this idea, but consider one small part of a campus as a stand-in for the whole. Andrew Nelson, a business professor and musician, has spent the last fifteen years studying a research institute affiliated with the Stanford University Department of Music whose work nicely illustrates this concept. The Center for Computer Research on Music and Acoustics (CCRMA—pronounced "karma") brings together people from fields as diverse as music, computer science, drama, engineering, art, physics, and psychology to use computers in music performance and research on sound.

CCRMA is a study in contrasts. It is oriented toward avant-garde performances of electronic music and open-source approaches to scholarship and research, but it is also the source of one of Stanford's most valuable portfolios of patents.[25] CCRMA's faculty and staff interact with nonprofit organizations, large and small companies, user communities, and researchers in many different fields. Their connections allow them to quite successfully be a bit of all things to all people. In a telling example, Nelson cites a project on digital signal processing that was funded as a performance by the National Endowment for the Arts, as an advance in fundamental science by the NSF, and as new sonar application by the U.S. Navy. This "multivocality" is a source of CCRMA's success and a reflection of its hub-ness.[26]

Many threads of concern can come together on university campuses. When those campuses act as anchors and maintain the kinds of networks that can make them sources, they become utterly unique hubs in the global innovation system. Universities are typically stable institutions; after all, the University of Bologna was founded in 1088, and several U.S. universities are older than our nation. But the collaborative networks and research capabilities public investments have helped to create on campus since the end of World War II are fragile and difficult to engineer.

This is important because what makes universities into hubs is their fertility as sources. The productivity, the stability, and the reach of universities is the basis of their public value. Andrew Nelson's appraisal of the sources of CCRMA's success holds true for universities as well: "the success of an individual or group engaged in this system may depend, in fact, upon this diversity of perspectives, participants, and goals."[27]

Public support helps research universities create and sustain this precise type of environment. That happens when source networks are fed by stable research investments distributed across many fields. It happens when university anchors mobilize various types of partners for the collective good. It happens when they enable the free flow of people and ideas through campus to become hubs. The configuration and reconfiguration of these social and interorganizational networks drives both the outcomes and the impact of research and research training.

Consider a familiar example that illustrates many of the ways universities and their networks help to turn grants into knowledge into social and economic returns.

Google and Page Rank

While writing this in my local library, I rely heavily on a search engine, Google, to locate references, check facts, and procrastinate. The corporation whose website I visit, Google, Inc.,[28] is currently valued at nearly $662 billion. It employs more than fifty thousand people and completes about 12.7 billion searches per month from U.S. users alone. In addition to bringing me these facts, *Google* has entered the English lexicon as a verb. My elementary school children sagely suggest "Googling" questions I can't readily answer. Yet less than twenty years ago the search engine, the corporation, and the verb did not exist.[29]

It is not a cure for cancer or Alzheimer's disease, a solution for climate change, or a fix for persistent inequality, but Google is a spectacularly successful company that has driven economic growth, created jobs, and (mostly) improved the quality of life of the people who use its services. Google is just the sort of outcome that those concerned with the economic returns to science funding most hope to replicate.

The company's story is well known. As its investor relations page explains, "our founders, Larry Page and Sergey Brin, working out of a

Stanford University dorm room, developed a new approach to online search that quickly spread to information seekers around the globe."[30] Like many other visible technology companies, Google emerged from entrepreneurial efforts that began on a research university campus.

A 2004 NSF web page[31] explains that Google's core technology, an algorithm called PageRank, was developed and implemented under a grant to two computer science professors at Stanford. Those researchers were Hector Garcia-Molina and Terry Winograd, who was Larry Page's advisor. Funding from that grant spanned five years (1994–1999) and totaled more than $4.5 million. The project it supported, named the Stanford Integrated Digital Library Initiative (DLI), sought "to develop the enabling technologies for a single, integrated and 'universal' library, providing uniform access to the large number of emerging networked information sources and collections." As the project progressed, researchers recognized that an important "emerging networked information source" was the World Wide Web.

The DLI employed Larry Page as a graduate assistant and also involved Sergey Brin, who was supported by an NSF graduate research fellowship.[32] In 1995 Page and Brin began to work on PageRank. Stanford University filed a provisional patent in 1997.[33] Page and Brin presented a conference paper in 1998.[34] The utility patent that was filed in 1998 was issued in 2001. It acknowledged government support in the form of the NSF grant to Garcia-Molina and Winograd. Under the terms of the 1980 Bayh-Dole Act, that patent, which listed Larry Page as the sole inventor, was owned by Stanford University. Google was incorporated in 1999 with initial funding from an angel investor named Andy Bechtolsheim, who has a PhD in electrical engineering from Stanford and is a cofounder of Sun Microsystems. More investments followed from two high-profile Silicon Valley venture capital firms (Kleiner, Perkins, Caufield & Byers and Sequoia Capital). Those investors too have strong ties to Stanford.

Stanford signed an exclusive license granting sole right to use the PageRank algorithm to Google in 2001, a deal that was renegotiated to expand the term of exclusivity in 2003. In 2004, as Google approached its initial public offering (IPO), the prospectus it filed with the Securities and Exchange Commission (SEC) revealed that six of its fourteen officers and directors had affiliations with Stanford. The most prominent Stanford-affiliated board member was John Hennessy, then the university's president and a successful entrepreneur in his own right.

The DLI grant to Stanford seems like just the kind of obvious, high-impact research priority that a policy maker concerned with returns on individual investments would have federal science agencies pursue. Just four years after the grant was funded, Stanford filed for a patent on a new and important search technology. Ten years after funding, a new company went public. Two decades after funding, that company is worth nearly two thirds of a trillion dollars. With my tongue tucked tightly in cheek, I would say that those numbers suggest that the direct financial return on the U.S. government's initial $4.5 million investment is somewhere on the order of 147,000 percent.[35] At a time when entrepreneurial firms whose value exceeds $1 billion are so rare that investors call them "unicorns," that's a really big number. Big enough that it seems worth asking what we can do to direct public investments toward other such high-value targets.

Even this truncated and simplified story suggests that a complex web of relationships created by movements of ideas and people underpins both the invention of PageRank and its translation into a successful publicly traded company. But if we want to really understand how public investments catalyzed those developments, three questions need to be answered.

First, what did it take for Page and Brin to develop PageRank? Second, what enabled that clearly very good idea to become the core of an exceptionally successful company? Most importantly, what role did federal funding play?

The idea that funding the Stanford Digital Libraries project resulted directly in PageRank is appealing but wrong. Assuming direct impact of the DLI grant resembles a *New Yorker* cartoon where two scientists stand at a blackboard pondering chalked equations bracketing the phrase "and then a miracle happened." It is unlikely that even Larry Page could accurately and completely re-create the steps that led to his discovery.[36] Published descriptions of PageRank's invention highlight the dense web of talented and often entrepreneurial scientists that characterized the Stanford campus in the mid- to late 1990s.[37] Page's name is the only one on the patent. But relationships with collaborators and advisors and the social capacity encoded in Stanford's larger network help explain how a doctoral student's plan to archive the web transformed into a search algorithm that could be the basis of one of the world's most valuable companies.

Here too there are multiple discoveries. PageRank was one of three roughly contemporaneous inventions that used the link structure of the web as the basis for search. Another search algorithm, RankDex, was developed by Robin Li, an engineer working at a subsidiary of Dow Jones. RankDex later became the basis of Chinese search firm Baidu. That company now has a market capitalization of just under $66 billion and is an important global competitor in search.

A third approach, Hyperlink-Induced Topic Search (HITS), was developed by Jon Kleinberg, a Cornell computer science professor who was working as a visiting researcher at an IBM research lab. All three inventions were patented.[38] Two of the three algorithms supported the founding of a successful, publicly traded firm. In both those cases the inventors were founders of the company.

Stanford was not a unique source of relevant discoveries, but something about the environment created through its various relationships with individuals and organizations in Silicon Valley was key to Google's early success. The special sauce of vibrant regional technology clusters is hotly debated, but most scholars agree that some mix of social network ties among individuals and strategic relationships linking organizations is essential. The important role universities play in forging and sustaining both kinds of networks is just beginning to be understood.[39]

Stanford's PageRank patent and the licensing deal with Google is also an important part of the story. But the majority of academic patents (and indeed patents generally) are not lucrative.[40] A similar patented technology, HITS, did not result in a successful corporation. Only a few venture-funded technology companies achieve the kind of spectacular success that Google has enjoyed.[41] The 1998 conference paper and the patent were the only published descriptions of the algorithm authored by Page and Brin, who left Stanford to found Google only after efforts to sell their technology to existing search firms failed. The economic value of PageRank was not clear enough to entice either Yahoo or Excite to purchase the rights to it for around $1 million.[42] Page and Brin's departure from Stanford is the primary form of technology transfer that enabled the company's success.

It is tempting to draw simple lessons from the Google case. Favor projects that address key concerns for recognizable emerging technologies. Fund research conducted by established faculty on elite campuses. Emphasize grants with clear potential for short-term economic returns. Encourage and reward entrepreneurship. Aggressively patent findings and license them exclusively to start-ups. Encourage talented students to leave the academy to pursue entrepreneurial dreams. I fear that these are the kinds of guidelines that an overly simple, "commonsense" effort to guide federal research investments toward national priorities might adopt. They are wrong and dangerous.

Treating a complex and interdependent social process that occurs across relatively long time scales as if it had certain needs, short time frames, and clear returns is not just incorrect, it's destructive. The kinds of simple rules I suggested earlier represent what organizational theorist James March called "superstitious learning."[43] They are akin to arguing that because many successful Silicon Valley firms were founded in garages, economic growth is a simple matter of building more garages.[44] Understanding how universities work as sources, anchors, and hubs suggests an almost diametrically opposed set of rules for putting public resources into academic research.

Consider the idea that we should prioritize projects with clear applications to emerging technologies. That thought underpins much of the political debate about how to address national interests in research funding. Whether we are talking about nanotechnology or neuroscience, many funding programs target specific problems that appear ripe for social and economic impact. The Google case may seem to be exhibit A in this regard. After all, even the NSF draws a direct line from the Digital Library Project to PageRank and Google. But while it is easy to see that the World Wide Web was important and growing in retrospect, the Stanford DLI proposal did not mention it. In 1993 when the grant was probably written, the Mosaic browser had just been introduced and the World Wide Web as we know it was very much in its infancy. One of the PIs, Hector Garcia-Molina, noted in an interview with Steven Levy that "the theme of that project was interoperability" and went on to suggest that the interests of graduate students such as Page and Brin drove the project toward questions pertaining to the emerging World Wide Web.[45] Clearly the challenge of identifying projects with direct relevance to emerging technologies is more complicated than the standard story of PageRank suggests.

The defining role played by graduate students demonstrates how connections among people who might never appear on lists of PIs or authors are essential. Indeed, one such student, Scott Hassan, who was also a graduate assistant on the DLI project but not an author on the PageRank paper or an inventor on the PageRank patent, played an important role in implementing the algorithm.[46] An important, but relatively little understood role of federal funding on campus is to bring together talent while allowing younger scholars room to define their own projects, even, perhaps especially, when those topics aren't on the radar of their more seasoned professors.

Because they are also explicitly sites for education, university research teams can enable students to pursue approaches and topics that challenge or amend the status quo. Clearly the quality of faculty investigators and of the institutions where they work influences the horsepower and ambition of students, but focusing solely on established scientists and their campuses misses the point that discoveries depend on and use information drawn from local sources and from more distant locations.

The relatively short time from the DLI grant's funding (1994) to Google's incorporation (1999) and IPO (2004) might also be taken to support an effort to prioritize projects that promise relatively quick returns.[47] But consider a broader view of the knowledge that Page drew together in conceptualizing his algorithm. If we examine the PageRank patent closely, paying particular attention to what intellectual property geeks call prior art, we see that the DLI project was far from alone among federally funded contributions to the origins of PageRank.[48] Some of the key precursors were unlikely-seeming projects in fields far removed from information and computer science.

The PageRank patent application[49] cited sixteen academic papers and one prior patent. The latter was assigned to Carnegie Mellon University, which also had a prominent computer science department. The papers that Page apparently relied on report work by twenty-seven authors affiliated with nineteen different organizations. Reading the acknowledgments of those papers reveals that this work was supported by fifteen grants or contracts from NSF, the National Institutes of Health (NIH), the Office of Naval Research, the National Library of Medicine, two foundations, and two corporations.

If we include the DLI grant and an NSF contract to a bibliometric start-up firm, a plurality (six) of those investments came from NSF. They represent an interesting mix of disciplines spanning the social sciences, computer science, citation analysis, and computational field theory. The earliest grant was an $81,000 NSF award made to a sociology professor at SUNY Stony Brook for "Mathematical Analysis of Corporate Networks" in 1974. The 1974 grant was acknowledged in a 1986 paper whose lead author had worked on the project as a graduate student. The 1986 paper, which presented a new disaggregated measure of prominence in a social network, was cited in the 1998 PageRank patent application.[50] This project aimed to use network techniques to explore the power structure of American business.

In light of these connections, understanding the NSF's contributions to Google requires that we mentally add at least twenty years to the five-year lag between the DLI grant and Google's incorporation. The first NSF grant that we can easily identify that plausibly helped enable Page's discovery was made around the time he was born, on the other side of country, in a discipline far removed from computer science, at a time when the possible applications of mathematical network theory to the link structure of a massive online corpus of websites would have seemed like science fiction.

Moreover, the 1974 grant was to study the interlocking board of director memberships of large U.S. corporations in order to examine the possibility that our society was dominated by a cohesive power elite. That's a topic of interest to social scientists but one that not even the most prescient policy maker might associate with dramatic economic returns.[51] Yet this Marxist-themed analysis also resulted in methodological innovations that later contributed to another much larger network, the World Wide Web.

Between 1970 and 1997, the NSF made tens of thousands of research investments totaling more than $52 billion.[52] Of those, six grants and contracts[53] (for $10.5 million, 0.02 percent of the total) were awarded to investigators across two decades, four campuses, and multiple disciplines. They represent one very small needle in the haystack of the NSF's portfolio. Together those grants helped support the students and the discoveries that were important to the development of PageRank and, by extension, to the success of Google.

This retelling of the Google story dramatically changes the lessons we might take from the case. Instead of obvious investments in work directly relevant to a known problem that is solvable on a short time frame, we have a series of seemingly unrelated investments in projects far removed from the topic of interest over several decades. Instead of an easy and obvious problem, we are confronted by the possibility that the topic it was valuable to address was discovered only after, in some cases long after, the work was selected for funding.

Indeed, even after the key discovery was made, its value was far from apparent. Contemporary corporations that were the leaders in search decided not to purchase rights to the patent from Stanford, even though the price was pretty cheap. The problem wasn't clear. The solution wasn't obvious. Even if it had been, the relevant grant was not directed toward it. The inputs to the solution that emerged were far-flung in time, space, and field but nevertheless represented a vanishingly small portion of public investments in scientific research.

For goodness' sake, a relatively small grant in sociology plausibly contributed to the development of exactly the kind of corporate power elite they were trying to study. All of these points leave us with the distinctly uncomfortable realization that a case that should be exhibit A for a more priority-driven approach to public investments in research presents us instead with the possibility that we are making investments in today's knowledge when we probably know about as little about our longer-term needs as a sociology program officer working at NSF in 1974 knew about the World Wide Web.

Explaining how such public investments in research and training result in public value requires that we broaden our view beyond returns on investment to single grants, lone geniuses, flashes of inspiration, patents, publications, and the entrepreneurial culture of single campuses to focus on bodies of knowledge, complex networks, and the movements of people and ideas back and forth between universities and the larger environment.

That shift requires us to consider several things. First, we must think about the social and organizational context for academic research. This means examining the system of funding and the organization of universities. Second, we must examine how these key settings shape the strategic efforts of people and teams who work to accomplish difficult goals under challenging and often very competitive conditions. Third, we must attend to the content and structure of networks on and across campuses. Those networks of relationships are the social matrix where the knowledge work of discovery and learning happen. Fourth, despite the image of academe as an ivory tower, we must not lose sight of the fact that universities and their people are far from isolated. Instead we must attend to the distinctive positions that universities occupy in national and global networks that emerge to connect all parts of society as ideas and people move back and forth between their campuses and the world.

Many locations might have allowed smart computer scientists to develop technologies similar to PageRank. A faculty member from Cornell invented HITS while on leave at IBM. RankDex was invented by a corporate engineer. Universities are not the sole sources of good ideas. But they are the primary performers of publicly supported fundamental research, and many good ideas come from that work.

Good ideas alone are insufficient to yield economic returns. Stanford's position in the network of Silicon Valley was necessary to turn PageRank into Google. Google's success no doubt redounds to reinforce

Stanford's centrality in the valley, to attract a new generation of smart graduate students, and to more or less subtly reconfigure collaboration networks around engineering and computer science.

Sometimes public investments help universities become the rare and special social settings where activities taking place in multiple social registers align to make truly radical discoveries and their valuable applications possible. In the terms used by sociologist Walter Powell and his collaborators John Padgett[54] and Victoria Johnson,[55] federal research funding helps universities become sites where the entire innovation system is poised to both generate and integrate new discoveries and ideas. That view puts universities and their networks front and center and requires that we examine how public investments create and sustain their capacity to be sources, anchors, and hubs.

2 THE ORGANIZATION OF RESEARCH UNIVERSITIES

AT A TIME WHEN THE MOST IMPORTANT inputs for advanced economies are knowledge and creativity,[1] we entrust universities with some of the most pressing missions that a society concerned with its future can have. But universities are constantly under attack for being out of touch with "real world" concerns.[2] In some ways, they are. Many of their programs and at least some parts of their missions have very little to do with the immediate, practical concerns of the day. These are deeply conservative organizations that bear the obvious hallmark of their medieval origins and their many purposes. But they are also prolific sources of new discoveries that remain dedicated to the transmission of knowledge through education and its application through public service.[3]

Understanding why universities are important and why we are making it much harder for them to fulfill their promise requires that we grapple with three things that make these institutions difficult to explain, evaluate, and manage. First, they are defined by a fundamental tension between stable, conservative organizational arrangements and dynamic, risky work. Universities are both exceptionally difficult to change and the source of an amazing flow of ideas, technologies, and discoveries. As we will see, the features that make them slow-moving are essential to their ability to be effective sources of new knowledge.

Second, their work encompasses complex competing missions that can create important synergies. Their commitment to the work of discovery, learning, and application can often seem at odds. But all of these goals help them draw together the interests and needs of many different precincts of society. The benefits of their multiple, competing commitments are put at risk by calls to reduce their complexity by unbundling and streamlining individual activities.[4]

Finally, they are dedicated to maintaining comprehensive research and teaching portfolios. Supporting work that spans the whole range of human knowledge without privileging particular fields or approaches is an incredibly taxing remit. But that very portfolio creates the conditions for ongoing innovation. It also ensures that ideas and people from many walks of life flow to and from campus. Here too, calls to identify and reduce funding for fields that lack immediate and obvious economic prospects run counter to the generative possibilities inherent in maintaining deep, wide reservoirs of knowledge.[5]

The challenge that universities face now is a result of pressure to streamline their work and their organization in order to increase the efficiency of some parts of their missions at the expense of others. However, much of their social and economic value results precisely from their pluralism, commitment to both tradition and innovation, and engagement with the broadest range of topics and approaches to knowledge. In a time when narrowly economic, individualistic, and short-term assessments of value dominate public and political discourse, universities are both challenged and challenging. The very things that make them valuable sources, anchors, and hubs are among the hardest to explain and maintain.

Distinctive Organizations

In 1963, Clark Kerr—then the president of the University of California—predicted that the United States would soon be home to a distinctive type of university, "an institution not looking to other models, but serving, itself, as a model . . . for other parts of the globe." The "invisible product" of that institution is knowledge, "the most powerful single element in our culture . . . affecting the rise and fall of professions . . . of social classes . . . of regions and even of nations."[6]

Today, American research universities set the global standard and continue to attract students, researchers, and faculty from around the world.[7] Universities have become more central than even Kerr envisioned, adding new activities and expanding old endeavors as economic and political tides have turned. As a recent National Academy of Sciences report notes, "While Bell Labs and their counterparts have given way to Silicon Valley and their counterparts, American universities continue to provide the heartbeat that keeps major innovation alive."[8] Unlike either the nearly mythic corporate labs or the churning network of rivals in Silicon Valley, major research universities are relatively stable features of our world. They are conglomerate organizations that jointly produce knowledge and the skilled people whose ability to apply it improves our society as a whole.

Many types of organizations, including technology firms, entrepreneurial incubators, and national laboratories, seek to discover or apply knowledge. Others, including two- and four-year colleges and less research-intensive universities, emphasize teaching and the transmission of knowledge and skills. Only research universities do both things at a very high level across nearly every field of knowledge with a mandate to apply what they produce for the good of all.

After seeing research universities in this light, you might quickly look about for other institutions that serve as sources, anchors, and hubs. But even the federal government, national and corporate laboratories, industries such as software and biotechnology, and locales like Silicon Valley fall short on serving as all three. The federal government is stable, certainly, but it does not teach and is not dedicated to openness. Silicon Valley (and to a large extent high-tech industry) is also grounded in place and characterized by significant movement of individuals across organizational boundaries, but firms and clusters tend to focus on a small group of topics and to be driven by proprietary concerns.[9] Google's famous "moonshot laboratory" may approximate what I am describing, but its "extremely secretive" work makes it less of a source.[10]

The great corporate labs of the postwar era came very close to the model I am describing, though without an explicit education mission and across a narrower range of fields than a comprehensive research university. Even so, they have been gone from the scene for decades. The very fact of their demise raises questions about whether any corporate endeavor has the potential to serve as an anchor or hub in the same fashion as a publicly funded institution. Moreover, the workings of the most famous, AT&T's Bell Labs, was deeply shaped by its parent company's monopoly and consequent dependence on the federal government's willingness to allow it to continue. Indeed, "AT&T maintained its monopoly at the government's pleasure and with the understanding that its scientific work was in the public interest."[11] Some of the more "academic" features of these labs depended on a complicated, sometimes fraught relationship with the state.

The Accidents That Set the Stage

Today's research universities were not designed to be sources, anchors, and hubs. They weren't really designed at all. The U.S. research university we know today is a beautiful accident. It grew to its current form in fits and starts under political and economic conditions that no longer obtain.[12] If the political will and public resources necessary to create a major university from whole cloth existed today, I doubt the result would be either as muddled or as valuable as what we've got. While far from perfect, research universities are effective. That efficacy is a legacy of their long and conflicted history.

I cannot do anything like full justice to that history here. Many excellent books and articles trace the growth of U.S. universities from their origins in colonial colleges modeled on Oxford and Cambridge to the first graduate schools based on German research institutions[13] and the singularly American synthesis of practical and liberal arts articulated when Abraham Lincoln signed the Morrill Act of 1862 creating land-grant universities in the midst of the Civil War.[14]

For our purposes, the most important period in that history starts with the end of World War II. The size and scope of higher education exploded in the following decades. The year 1944 saw the passage of the G.I. Bill, and 1945 saw the appearance of Vannevar Bush's manifesto *Science: The Endless Frontier*, which set forth the basic rationale for today's system of peer-reviewed federal science funding. Dramatic growth in enrollments, the passage of key laws that drove huge influxes of public support for research and education, and the founding of federal science agencies such as the NSF led to a golden age of academia that roughly tracks with the Cold War.[15]

A brief few decades cemented the distinctive features of the American research university in a more or less stable system. While the structural and organizational features of the system remain in place, the language used to describe and evaluate them has changed dramatically. Both the sources of current arrangements and the shifting rhetoric of public support are important to our story. Indeed, while universities rely on substantial public support, a key outcome of this time period is the extent to which it is fragmented and framed in relatively narrow terms.

Historian of education David Larabee tells a somewhat similar story with a different emphasis.[16] In his view the early conditions of U.S. higher education gave rise to a loose system of institutions that, lacking the central organizing hand of either the state or the church, was perfectly messy, internally contradictory, deeply competitive, and directly responsive to the desires of its key consumers, students, and benefactors, philanthropically minded alumni. The weaknesses of this system became substantial strengths when Cold War policy battles resulted in an enormous influx of resources for research and education unaccompanied by clear central authority or a well-defined mission.

As a result, the American system of higher education was driven by a small coterie of high-profile, largely private, research-intensive campuses. Those universities reacted to federal largesse with characteristic entrepreneurialism. The outcomes of postwar policy debates, Cold War exigencies, and these peculiar historical endowments created the conditions that made it possible for the nation's universities to solve a long string of problems for the federal government, for industry, and for a growing number of other constituencies. The research universities that are our focus grew to their current shape through a piecemeal, iterative, and at least locally purposeful process whose contours were set by key policy debates that could have gone otherwise.

The first twenty years of the Cold War were an interesting time in America's political development. The challenges of bilateralism created a vested national interest in the direction and outcomes of both education and research conducted on university campuses. But both the history of higher education and the U.S. Constitution weighed against centralized federal intervention. American higher education began as a patchwork of private and religious institutions augmented by land-grant campuses that were enabled by federal action but oriented to their home states.[17] While some founding documents, such as the 1787 Northwest Ordinance, made explicit reference to education,[18] the U.S. Constitution did not, and the Tenth Amendment reserved for the states powers not explicitly delegated to the federal government.

Both tradition and law thus militated against the very kind of federal interventions that have come to define the contemporary research university. Indeed, skepticism about the ways in which federal funding might lead to national control persisted well beyond the immediate postwar years. Kerr himself expressed concerns about the dangers of federal support: "the better and more individual the university, the greater its chances of succumbing to the federal embrace. Washington did not waste its money on the second rate."[19] Hinted at in this snippet is a very real worry that substantial federal funding would flatten out distinctive features of individual universities. Despite all these concerns, the university became ever more central to the project of U.S. state building even as the federal government had to diffuse its control.[20]

Historian Margaret O'Mara points to this key challenge and an unexpected outcome important to our conversation: "The Cold War required a strong state, but American political traditions demanded a weak one. The solution was to empower universities and scientific industries to become agents and partners with the federal government, a choice that gave these local actors new influence over local economies and politics. It also created fiercely competitive dynamics among these partners, which in turn made institutions and industries more entrepreneurial and creative."[21] In terms of research, the results of Cold War politics regarding funding helped create a system in which rivalries among campuses were intense and relationships between universities, their states, and the federal government were complicated.

Matters were no less intricate in the realm of teaching and learning, where an equally strong Cold War mandate was apparent in fields as diverse as creative writing and the hard sciences.[22] Despite compelling national interests and the determinative effect of federal investments in higher education and research, we find ourselves with an academic system where, to quote historian Christopher Loss, "the role of the federal government has been unclear and uncoordinated."[23]

The tension between conceptualizing research universities in terms of federal support and the general welfare of the nation and imagining them as private or state projects more closely aligned with local interests and needs remains today. Its particular Cold War resolution helped create the conditions that allowed these institutions to be understood to serve the concrete needs of individual students, of national defense, and of particular industries.

Much has been lost from these early debates: a conception of the knowledge mission and its results as a public good; a sense of the need to unify all aspects of that mission; and a compelling argument for federal and state partnerships to support robust investment. All of these are things it is important for us to reclaim.

This is true despite the fact that today's universities emerged from particular circumstances that lasted a relatively short time, and may now be beyond easy recall. "Conceived of and nurtured into maturity as a private good, the American system of higher education remains a market-based organism. It took the threat of nuclear war to turn it—briefly—into a public good."[24] The Cold War years may have been a historical anomaly, but that is no reason to shy away from efforts to sustain and even expand the benefits that resulted. As market fundamentalism has grown more extreme in all precincts of American society, maintaining some of the key strengths of the academic research enterprise requires a return to some of the justifications and language of that exceptional time.[25]

"Higher Education for American Democracy"

In 1946 a huge influx of veterans enrolled in colleges and universities under the G.I. Bill, creating a "period of trial" for institutions of higher education. In response, President Harry Truman convened a committee of twenty-eight academic and civic leaders with a mandate to "reexamine our system of higher education in terms of its objectives, methods and facilities and in light of the social role it has to play."[26] A year later, in 1947, the Truman Commission released a six-volume report that represented "the U.S. government's first effort to set national goals for higher education."[27]

While the report did not result directly in legislation, it sparked significant public discussion about the role of the federal government.[28] The commission identified three overarching goals for higher education. The first was "education for a fuller realization of democracy in every phase of living."[29] Full realization of democracy drives the committee's manifest concern with equal access, and with education that emphasizes individual development: "to liberate and perfect the intrinsic powers of every citizen is the central purpose of democracy."[30]

This focus on education for the purpose of supporting a distinctive national culture eventually gave way to languages of individual excellence, identity, and efficiency.[31] Today, these more individualistic and market-based rhetorics fit uncomfortably with organizations that grew to their current shape and status under more collective assumptions. Continued justification for broad public support is difficult when key benefits are conceptualized primarily as private goods.

The commission's focus on democracy as an overriding goal of education also brought with it a set of corollaries for how higher education should be organized and funded. The committee often expressed concern that an overwhelming emphasis on natural science research would limit the ability of education to address fundamental issues for democratic society. As a result, they emphasize the need for both research and teaching in the "social sciences and technology."[32]

This recognition was part and parcel of the commission's claims for the national importance of the graduate schools within major research universities, which the committee believed had three major tasks: "basic research and the training of research personnel," "training "experts for . . . government, industry, commerce, agriculture, and public welfare," and "training teachers for all levels of higher education."[33] The work of the graduate schools along with that of the traditional professional schools thus made the newly emerging research universities a key part of the larger national ecology of higher education envisioned by the committee.

Perhaps recognizing the challenges our federalist system of government posed for a national plan, committee members emphasized the need for a diverse[34] set of institutions in a loosely coordinated confederation that relied on both state and federal support. The commission suggested a now-familiar model of financial aid in which grants and loans to those with financial need follow individual students who choose where to enroll.[35] They also recommended substantial direct investment from the federal government into institutions of higher education. The committee's most controversial recommendation (with two members strongly dissenting) proposed that direct federal support be limited to public universities and colleges.[36]

The sizable funds proposed would be allocated to the states, which would administer them on an "equalization basis" to ensure "an acceptable minimum program in the poorer states."[37] Those allocations would include significant support for graduate students in the form of multiyear fellowships, general operating support for public universities, and substantial funds for capital investment in facilities that would require two-for-one matching by the states.

The explicit rationale for this proposal placed universities and the products of their broadly conceptualized knowledge mission squarely at the interface between national and state interests. It thus emphasized a language of federal-state partnership that has essentially been lost. "The role of the federal government should be that of a partner with the states in their joint concerns for outcomes of education vital to the national interests and the rights of all American citizens under the Constitution."[38] All told, the committee recommended federal investment (above and beyond appropriations for financial aid that would flow directly to students) of $2.8 billion (in 2016 dollars) for 1948, growing quickly to $4.8 billion (in 2016 dollars) in 1952.[39]

More simply, the Truman Commission recommended a yearly federal investment in graduate training, operations, and capital projects at public institutions of higher education that was about 28 percent of the total amount the U.S. federal government spent on research and development in 1952.[40] If similar federal investment were made now, it would amount to about $38 billion, just slightly less than the combined 2016 appropriations for the NSF ($7.46 billion) and the NIH ($31.31 billion). Such an investment would also, like the 2009 American Recovery and Reinvestment Act (ARRA), include "maintenance of effort" provisions that make federal support contingent on states maintaining adequate levels of investment.[41]

Today this seems like an impossible direct federal investment in public higher education. And yet the report describes the need for federal funding without direct federal control. That offers one useful template for future investments that resonates with American higher education models that stretch back to at least the Morrill Act of 1862.

Also revolutionary was the proposal to integrate teaching at all levels with graduate and professional training—making both key pieces of a knowledge mission intended to meet both local and national needs. The call for instruction and research at high levels in all fields, including the social and human sciences, was bold too. It highlighted the need for academia to be able to address problems arising in multiple spheres of economy and society. Finally, the committee situated the entire growth of higher education within a mandate to equalize access—a call that sounds all too contemporary.[42]

Even though the report proved influential over time, these particular recommendations did not quickly come to pass. Contemporary commentators and historians of education highlight several reasons why. First, and most tellingly, the policy program this report outlined was "all dressed up with no place to go" as committee members lacked the access to Congress and the political clout necessary to push their agenda forward.[43] Lack of access coupled with split government and conflict between the Truman White House and the original "do nothing" 80th Congress led to gridlock.

Perhaps equally important was vocal public controversy sparked by the commission's recommendations. In the report's wake, critics expressed strong concerns about the benefits of dramatically expanding access to education, the "equalization" of funding across all states, the committee's particular view of both democracy and education, and especially the proposal to limit direct federal investment to publicly controlled organizations.[44] Resistance from representatives of private universities was swift and scathing.

This resistance is important because, as historians Julie Reuben and Linda Perkins argue, it "helped defeat proposals for federal aid to expand public systems of higher education . . . Instead of the program for institutional aid recommended by the committee, most federal monies for higher education . . . were linked to the nation's military agenda."[45] Many of the Truman Commission's recommendations were fulfilled in later legislation including the National Defense Education Act (NDEA) of 1958, which President Dwight Eisenhower signed in response to the Soviet Union's launch of Sputnik. Where the G.I. Bill made higher education available to a particular class of citizens, veterans, the NDEA expanded federal support to students in fields related to national security. In other words, the commission's language set the stage for the long and sometimes contested process of development that resulted in the particular system we have today.

Emphasizing defense and military applications further concentrated resources in a small number of (mostly private) institutions and an even smaller number of geographic locations, amplifying competition for position in highly stratified status order that still holds today.[46] Focusing on defense also privileged particular fields within those universities, associating federal support for advanced training, institutional, and research support with only one portion of the university.

In later years, the center of scientific gravity would shift from the physical sciences and engineering to biomedicine,[47] but the committee's vision of support across fields, like its emphasis on geographic equality, fell by the wayside. That loss took with it a holistic conception of the public value of the entire institution that animated the commission's concern with democracy. Research in the social sciences and humanities, as well as in natural science fields more distant from defense, came to be, at least rhetorically, divorced from national priorities. That cleavage set the stage for today's arguments about the need to reduce or eliminate funding for fields without apparent and immediate national security or economic implications.

Thus, the Truman Commission report represented a moment when articulating a collective purpose for higher education and associated national support could have resulted in a very different system. Instead, we ended up with a more decentralized system, focused on a limited number of fields, and a rhetoric that aligned the collective national purpose of universities with defense and national security. Thus, the report's aftermath cemented the status order that had been created by wartime contracts.

Absolutely critical for our purposes is the fact that the status order created through World War II research contracting also relates to a hierarchy of student selectivity.[48] In other words, the university landscape that we confront today—a highly stratified, decentralized, exceptionally competitive system that includes both learning and discovery but lacks a unified federal investment or a well-articulated federal-state partnership—is at least partially a result of failure: the failure of an early effort to articulate a clear, centrally coordinated system of higher education founded on a broad conception of national priorities.

The National Science Foundation

There's a similar turnkey moment when we look at the history of federal research funding. A multiyear legislative battle led to the 1950 founding of the National Science Foundation (NSF). These conflicts pitted a prominent New Deal senator, Harley Kilgore, against supporters of the vision proposed by Vannevar Bush.[49] Kilgore envisioned a federal science policy centralized in a single government agency directed by a broad set of constituencies with coordinating power to set substantive agendas and integrate them with industry.

Bush advocated for a decentralized system administered by scientists that emphasized fundamental research conducted in universities and had very little coordinating or agenda-setting power. Noting that Bush's report emerged from an ongoing political conflict about whether and how the federal government should support research in peacetime, historian Daniel Kevles sums up the difference quite nicely: "Kilgore wanted a foundation responsive to lay control and prepared to support research for the advancement of the general welfare. Bush and his colleagues wanted an agency run by scientists mainly for the purpose of advancing science."[50]

Battle lines were drawn between Kilgore and Bush in the form of competing 1945 bills to found and fund a National Science Foundation. They agreed on much, most notably the need to maintain the freedom of the "individual working scientist" from "political control."[51] They also differed on several key dimensions. The proposals varied in terms of how the foundation would be governed, whether it would support basic science alone or contribute to the translation and application of discoveries, whether the social sciences should have a role and be eligible for funding, how explicit a mandate should exist for spreading the wealth geographically and across different types of institutions, who should own inventions deriving from federally funded research, and whether the foundation should be charged with developing and pursuing a unified national research policy.

Sociologist Daniel Kleinman's book *Politics on the Endless Frontier* offers a detailed analysis of this debate and its outcome. The short version is Bush won and Kilgore lost. But that was as much a result of circumstance (Roosevelt's death, the election of a Republican Congress, Truman's veto of an early iteration of the bill, and the administrative decisions of the foundation's first director) as of a clean and clear policy mandate.[52] The time the debate took was equally important.

Kleinman notes that "the five year delay in establishing the National Science Foundation left the United States with a fragmented or pluralist

system for federal funding of research and the establishment of research priorities."[53] Instead of the single powerful agency envisioned by
Kilgore, many agencies with different missions were founded. We shall
see that the resulting decentralization of federal funding came to contribute to the power of today's system. But obscuring a unified national
interest also put universities at risk and contributed to the challenges we
face today.

Kleinman persuasively argues that Kilgore's vision of national science policy offers a reasonable counterfactual to the system we have
now. If just a few things had changed, the nation's entire infrastructure
for academic research might have been different—perhaps more un-
equivocally aligned with the kind of broad national interest articulated
in the Truman report.

We cannot know whether a more centralized federal research infrastructure would have been as successful as the system we have now.
Perhaps. However, the long history of decentralized American higher
education, the hold of markets on the national imagination, and the fed-
eralism of our political system suggest that reversing course now will be
at best problematic. The dangers are especially great if such a reversal
were accompanied by a more limited view, targeted narrowly toward
productive efficiency and obvious near-term returns on investment.

In discovery, in education, and, at their intersection, the warrant for
public investment in our universities has shifted dramatically even as
the system that resulted from early cold war politicking and the competitive ferment that followed has remained. Today's research universities are no less dependent on public support, but the general welfare
they serve and the investments they receive are harder to see and more
challenging to evaluate because of the conditions of their origins.

Collective National Purpose

I am not arguing for a return to the Truman years. Nor do I suggest that
we should disregard the outcomes of individual students or the needs of
national security and the economy. Nevertheless, the language that was
used to describe the public value of academia in these early debates is

worth resurrecting. Emphasizing joint pursuit of collective and individual outcomes is important. Understanding that such outcomes extend beyond the development of technology, jobs, and economic returns is even more essential.

A better language and logic might build on the current structure of academe by emphasizing not only the human but also the social capital created by universities and federal research funding. Networks, along with the knowledge they develop and sustain, are important not just because they make us more secure and spur economic growth but also because they render an uncertain future more tractable. That is why the system bequeathed to us in all its contingent messiness remains worth maintaining, even expanding. Our ability to do that depends on the uncomfortable bundle of activities, missions, and topics we have inherited.

But confusing organizations that persistently challenge the status quo—as research universities do—are unsettling. They can make easy targets in social and political conflicts over scarce public resources. Consider one high-profile example that exemplifies these distinctions. In early 2015, Wisconsin governor Scott Walker unveiled a budget that cut $300 million from the University of Wisconsin System. The same budget proposed a dramatic revision to the system's mission statement, which is colloquially known as the "Wisconsin Idea." After forceful protests around the state and the nation, Walker's office backtracked on the proposed revision, though not on the substantial budget cut.

The two alternative mission statements quoted here thus represent a useful thought experiment. Imagine the University of Wisconsin, and particularly its flagship research campus in Madison, which is one of the oldest and largest land-grant universities, under each of these two different missions.[54]

First, the actual mission of the University of Wisconsin System:[55]

The mission of the system is to develop human resources, to discover and disseminate knowledge, to extend knowledge and its application beyond the boundaries of its campuses and to serve and stimulate society by developing in students heightened intellectual, cultural, and human sensitivities, scientific, professional, and technological expertise, and a sense of purpose. Inherent in this broad mission are methods of instruction, research, extended training and public service designed to educate people and improve the human condition. Basic to every purpose of the system is the search for truth.

Next the proposed, and later retracted revision:

The mission of the system is to develop human resources to meet the state's workforce needs, to discover and disseminate knowledge, and to develop in students heightened intellectual, cultural, and human sensitivities, scientific, professional, and technological expertise, and a sense of purpose.

The second mission has the benefit of brevity. But that comes at the cost of dramatically pruning both the university's reach and its aspirations. I can imagine that the clarity of focus in the shorter mission might seem admirable in that it lends itself to easier evaluation. Is the university working? Under the revised mission the answer is yes if (a) students get jobs in the state and (b) local employers feel they have a sufficient pool of workers to choose from. That clarity, though, comes at the expense of the very features of universities that make them essential and unique.

The proposed revision is destructive for several reasons. It strips out the productive complications created by multiple missions, calculates value largely in individual terms across relatively short time frames, and implicitly limits the range of fields and topics that a university should prioritize. Perhaps most importantly, this vision of the university errs by making the institution's pole star currently known needs rather than a search for truth that might reach beyond today's sureties.

American-style universities don't appear around the globe because they are uniquely able to adapt to local workforce needs. Instead, this type of university is prevalent because, at its core, societies and economies that are based on knowledge are "built around the university, its abstracted and universalized understandings and its all important degree certification."[56] Contra Governor Walker, the value of the university is found not in its ability to respond to immediate needs but in an expectation that joining systematic inquiry and education will result in people and ideas that reach beyond local, sometimes parochial, concerns.

If we view universities in this holistic fashion, we change both the grounds of evaluation and the possible scope of their contributions. They prove essential precisely because they create and sustain networks founded on and responsive to knowledge. The networks are bedrock because the patterns of interaction among people are what make it possible for universities to identify and address problems of scientific or practical concern.

Centralized planning and top-down management work about as well on a university campus as they do in the economy as a whole. Instead individuals and teams pursue their interests through interaction and collaboration. People committed to different missions and approaches to knowledge compete for the resources and attention necessary to support their work. The inevitable miscues that accompany risky work can be absorbed and learned from because they happen within the vessel of a stable, conservative institution that is committed to no particular orthodoxy or status quo. Academic life can require a bit of hustle, but universities themselves are slow-moving.

When budgetary or political pressures narrow the institution's focus to emphasize easily documented returns, campuses will tighten their boundaries in an effort to more fully monitor, control, and profit from the products of their work. When a concern with the immediate and the practical reduces the number and diversity of programs, the university's reach into society will diminish and its capacity to bridge many needs will shrink. As that happens, the rationales for public support become less clear and the dangers of divestment more distant. Market discipline replaces the general welfare, and efficient responses to current needs become the watchword.[57]

The result of both trends will be to narrow the reach and aspirations of the academic mission in a fashion very similar to Governor Walker's proposed revision to Wisconsin's orienting ideals. This is why both the commercialization of academic knowledge and efforts to vocationalize the curriculum can be pernicious. By making it harder for universities to be anchors and by decreasing their ability to be hubs, we limit their potential to be stable and effective sources of knowledge and dramatically decrease their public value. If we take steps that have these consequences in an effort to document the clear, immediate, and direct returns to public investments in universities, we stand to dry the proverbial well in an effort to assure ourselves that it remains full.

But What About the Students?

This book is largely about the research and advanced training components of the university knowledge mission. The contributions of research are too little understood. But the institutions that are my focus also educate the plurality of our nation's undergraduates. Addressing the totality of higher education as such is beyond the scope of what can be accomplished here. But it is important to say a few words about students for several reasons. Teaching and learning too are essential components of the university knowledge mission. Tuition is the dominant form of revenue on most campuses. Education and the presence of undergraduates also helps explain many of the features of research universities that are our focus.

Viewed in terms of the contribution to general welfare that universities make, undergraduate students are important because they help universities stay stable, open, and connected across society. In other words, teaching undergraduates in a research environment is good for the development of knowledge because students help make our campuses better anchors and better hubs. Undergraduates and alumni create and support many of the traditions associated with higher education. They lead universities to project themselves and their aspirations both backward and forward in time. By doing so, they "institutionalize" higher education in the sense offered by sociologist Philip Selznick: "to institutionalize is to infuse with value beyond the technical requirements of the task at hand."[58] All these features help universities be effective anchors.

Students should be well served because higher education is the established path to social mobility and a remunerative career, because they pay to be on campus, and because they are one of the most essential vectors for the transmission and application of knowledge. Serving students well also benefits universities because it means they will be better positioned as hubs when their graduates prosper in many fields and feel enough affinity for their alma mater to return.

Education in a research environment also has larger benefits for society. We do not often acknowledge it, but the primary means of "technology transfer" from universities to the world is graduation. When undergraduates and alumni move back and forth across the boundaries of campus, they make our universities more of a hub. Accessible, high-quality universities help ensure productivity and equal opportunity in our society.

If talent is distributed evenly across the population, and if developing talent strengthens our society both morally and practically, then ensuring the quality and availability of education is essential. But that syllogism provides no justification for wedding education and discovery. Even in the aggregate, individual returns to education, social mobility, and contributions to the workforce we think we need now are not the right measures to justify and evaluate research universities.[59] Lincoln and the politicians who passed the Morrill Act of 1862, the Truman Commission, the architects of the National Science Foundation, and the authors of the Wisconsin Idea recognized the essential collective benefits of placing education together with the development and application of knowledge.

I know this represents a fundamental challenge to the way we commonly think and talk about higher education today. It may seem heretical (or perhaps just naïve) to suggest that the value individual undergraduates gain from their education is a secondary benefit of the larger public mission of the institution. Most people, even most academics, completely and fundamentally take for granted the idea that the highest purpose of the university is the development and success of each student.

Such strong and unquestioned assumptions exert an inexorable pull on organizations, and they are difficult to challenge.[60] If you close your eyes and think about what a university does, you probably imagine undergraduate teaching, football or basketball, and little else. You might go even further and imagine that when undergraduate instruction is done well, it enables students to secure good jobs in the careers they desire.[61] The way we think and talk about the value of the university is shaped by the nearly unquestioned assumption that the correct measure for evaluating success or failure is the value individual students receive. But certainty about our beliefs doesn't always mean they are right.

We all habitually treat teaching and learning as the primary role of research universities for several reasons. First, and most simply, teaching and learning *are* the primary missions of most of the higher education institutions in our society. More than 95 percent of colleges and universities are primarily dedicated to undergraduate and professional education, but that should not obscure the vital importance of those that are not.

Second, the public interacts with research universities by attending school, paying for school, and maybe celebrating the school that they graduated from. Jonathan Cole, former provost of Columbia University, recalls that even the most sophisticated and engaged alumni he encounters rarely ask what new and important discoveries have emerged from their alma mater.[62] We think that the main thing universities do is undergraduate education because that is the main thing universities do with most of us.

Third, undergraduate tuition was initially and has become an ever more necessary source of revenue for universities. As state investments have declined dramatically, tuition increases have been necessary to keep public research universities afloat. Tuition has always been a core revenue source for private institutions. Those dollars are particularly important because they are one of the sources of revenue that are fungible across missions and activities. Together with the overhead reimbursements that accompany federal research grants, some parts of endowment income, and, for public universities, state appropriations, tuition gives academic leaders the ability to make strategic investments in public goods for the campus and in initiatives to respond to new social demands or opportunities.

The paramount frame that governs most public, political, and academic discussion about the value of the university trades an individual student's or family's tuition payments for the opportunity for a better or more remunerative life. This is one reason why the dominant form of social scientific analysis of higher education today emphasizes status attainment. Beginning in the late 1960s with the publication of a book called *The American Occupational Structure*,[63] sociologists of education began to focus very closely on the role that social background plays in educational attainment and success. That link foregrounds the role education plays in social stratification by considering how students from different social origins have differential access to and outcomes from college.[64] Their laser focus on individuals dominates much of the language of analysis and evaluation for higher education today.[65]

A few studies by sociologists and economists explicitly consider the collective benefits of increasing education. For instance, Enrico Moretti finds that increasing the proportion of college-educated workers raises wages for everyone, including those who have only graduated from high school.[66] He also demonstrates that increasing education decreases crime rates.[67] Nevertheless, most of the literature on higher education and its effects treats universities as "sieves" that sort students into different outcomes.[68]

As sociologist Mike Hout noted in a recent review, the literature strongly suggests that "being educated is not only good in its own right; it also produces good outcomes for individuals, their communities and the nation as a whole."[69] Indeed, one careful study suggests that just one third of the value of a university education accrues to the individual being educated, with the rest appearing indirectly for the larger society.[70] While it is compelling, the research on collective social benefit is small relative to the giant literature that highlights the economic and other benefits of education for individuals.[71]

Nevertheless, current scholarship generally suggests that there is reason to remain bullish on the individual value of higher education *and* that too little has been said about collective returns to the general welfare. Attending to individual student outcomes is good and provides a route to social benefit. But understanding how the educational mission helps to make research universities unique and powerful homes for the cultivation of knowledge, the identification and solution of problems known and unknown is even better.

When the cost of an education is so great that debt precludes opportunity; when institutional indifference or the challenges of student life leave a degree out of reach; when the quality of an education is so poor that the investment is wasted; or when the gates of campus are closed to the talented, we correctly react with outrage and seek alternatives.[72] The persistent rhetoric about the impending student loan bubble, the furor over low-cost alternatives to residential education, the confident predictions that higher education is ripe for "disruption," and hand-wringing about the university's problematic business model all seem warranted in this overly skeptical view.[73] But tuition for individual opportunity is not the only contract.

Such an atomized approach undermines the very things that we should be investing in, the stability of the organization, the diversity of its activities, and the distinctive networks it creates and sustains as it does its work. Developing an alternative means asking how the research university's complicated features make sense.

How Are Universities Organized?

We need to step back from thinking about one university mission or another and instead try to imagine research universities as very complex organizations that encompass many missions and benefit from synergies among them. One common organizational response to the challenges of managing diverse activities is decentralization, which allows different parts of an organization relatively high degrees of autonomy.

Decentralization on campus is, at least in part, a function of both academic tradition and of the funding system that grew from the seeds of the Cold War. Those arguments demonstrate that the idea of decentralized and competitive institutions resonated with a characteristically American distrust of centralized planning. But a national, collective impulse is a harder sell today when individual returns and market rationales again predominate. The primary rhetorical challenge stems from the fact that understanding how university organization enables the kinds of collective benefits we have been discussing requires significant attention to and investment in public goods, resources that benefit everyone but that no one individual has an incentive to maintain. Universities both create and rely on such shared resources.

Imagine you are buying a car and have narrowed your choice down to three sport-utility vehicles; a Dodge, a Jeep, and a Chevy. Dodge and Jeep are both Chrysler brands. So when you are choosing your car, Chrysler is competing with itself and with General Motors for your business. Chrysler wants you to buy either the Dodge or the Jeep, but not the Chevy. The brand managers of Dodge and Jeep compete as both want you to buy their car. But their rivalry should not be destructive; both would rather you buy the other Chrysler brand before you settle on a Chevy.

Because Dodge and Jeep are both part of Chrysler, they share important resources in common. For instance, Chrysler Capital will happily make you a loan for either a Dodge or a Jeep, and that loan will likely be cheaper if Chrysler sells lots of cars across all its brands. In other words, both Dodge and Jeep benefit at least a little bit when you purchase the other's car. The brand you choose wins bigger, of course, but both stand to lose if you and others go with a different company entirely.

This mix of internal and external competition is common at universities too. Professors do many different things. As a result, we typically compete in some areas and collaborate in others with colleagues both near and far. On any given campus, common resources developed and maintained by the university make multiple types of work more effective. For instance, I routinely use the university's suite of online collaboration tools for teaching, for research, and for activities that blur the line between the two, as when I communicate with students who receive independent-study credit for participating in my ongoing research projects.

Like the library, these tools are a public good for the university. Everyone on campus can use them. No individual pays directly to do so. My use of them does not make it impossible for anyone else to use them. In the terms economists typically use, public goods are nonrivalrous and nonexcludable. The knowledge that universities produce has long been understood to be a public good in this sense.[74] Unlike, for instance, a pair of shoes, a generative idea is something you and I can both use at the same time, and its value often increases as more people use and improve it. That is why public funding to support research is necessary. No individual or company has a private incentive to create a public good.[75] If we leave the creation and maintenance of collective goods to the market, failures result and no one gets what they need.

By the same token, the public goods that universities maintain internally are necessary to create synergies across its various missions and to keep competition among its parts from becoming zero-sum. But no individual program or unit has a particular incentive to support them if internal competition driven by market responsiveness rather than joint pursuit of a collective mission becomes the standard.[76] Consider that many of the things students need to learn—such as how to reason and make decisions from numeric evidence, or how to write effectively from that reasoning—aren't actually taught in individual departments or by specific faculty. Many of the tools that students need to pursue the projects professors assign, a single department or college doesn't provide. In other words, the units that make up a university's teaching infrastructure are interdependent, and their benefits can't be pinned down so specifically as to locate them in one place on campus.

Under an increasingly prevalent model for decentralized university financing, called Responsibility Center Management (RCM), intracampus competition for students and research grants is the motor of resource allocation. In broad terms,[77] tuition funds follow students. The portion of grants dedicated to reimbursing the costs of facilities and administration, called overheads or indirects, follows researchers.[78] Units—generally, but not always, colleges such as arts and sciences or engineering—receive tuition and overhead funds based on enrollments in the classes their faculty teach and the research grants their faculty win. Those funds are "taxed" by the university's central administration for the maintenance of shared services such as enterprise-wide IT capacity, libraries, and heat, which is very important in my part of the world.[79]

The deans of the colleges use their "after-tax" revenues to support the work of the departments and programs that report to them. Where tuition revenue is fungible, indirect costs can only be used to address costs directly related to federally funded research. In principle the system works much like our national economy, in which taxes on individuals and businesses support investments in public goods like roads, police, education, and, yes, research. If classes in arts and sciences draw more students and the business school's classes draw fewer students, marginally more money goes to the arts and sciences dean than otherwise would. Thus, when departments that teach more students need something from their colleges, they have better grounds to argue for it. But that competition only works because everyone shares access to common resources and because cross-subsidies enable the university to maintain a broader portfolio than strict adherence to current market needs might otherwise allow.

Unlike Chrysler Capital, which must turn a profit on the loans it makes,[80] the central services provided by a university—for instance, information technology and library systems—are generally cost centers. They are expensive.[81] They contribute to both teaching and research, but they have little capacity to make money. The good they do depends on their being accessible to all students and faculty. When shared infrastructure is directly supported by public investments such as yearly allocations of funds from states to their public universities, the pressure to cover costs with tuition and grants declines, and competition among units can give way to greater synergies.

State investments in public universities have declined dramatically since 2001. National investments are generally pegged to individual students or particular projects. At the same time, a greater percentage of the costs of shared resources for research have been shifted from federal grants to the institution itself, a trend that affects public and private institutions alike. Other potential funders have not rushed to fill the gap. Thus more and more of the burden of covering the costs of on-campus public goods falls on students. Greater reliance on tuition revenue makes it more sensible to frame investments in universities in terms of individual returns on individual investments. But the shell game of pushing the costs of capacity that creates national public goods off onto individual students and families is distasteful and untenable. Laundering the costs of public goods in this fashion is only possible because university organization makes both the benefits of public investments and the detriments of their declines hard to see.

The Good and the Bad About Decentralization

Decentralized systems make drawing a line directly from, for instance, a state allocation or federal indirect-cost charge to a library's purchase and on to an outcome the public cares about very difficult. Even in the somewhat simpler case of private universities, the traces of common investments are hard to draw. How much of the PageRank invention I described in the last chapter can be attributed to Larry Page's access to the Stanford Libraries? Some, certainly, but determining exactly how much is a quixotic effort.

This is why efforts to evaluate university productivity can be so fraught with challenges. Organizational theorists Michael Cohen and James March help explain why that is the case by demonstrating that decentralization in service to multiple, competing missions makes universities into "organized anarchies" characterized by "problematic goals, unclear technologies and fluid participation."[82]

More plainly, universities have difficulty clearly describing their aspirations because they have so many of them and because they sometimes conflict. They are unsure about what, precisely, needs to be done to reach those goals because the work they do is uncertain and the materials they work with (people and ideas, mostly) are highly variable. They can't even be certain who will do the work and for how long. These uncertainties necessitate a style of decision making that fits few commonsense ideas about productivity and planning. They fly in the face of market discipline, and they should. Like the research enterprise that they anchor, universities pose substantial challenges for those who seek evidence of clear, direct returns on straightforward investments.

One response to this frustrating portrait is to simplify the view of the university and prioritize some aspects of the work done on campus. Because public investments are generally made in universities or even systems of universities, this tendency is particularly common among the regents, legislators, and governors who allocate state funds to public institutions. Pressures from outside (and sometimes from inside) campus often seek to solve the "problems" that result from all these uncertainties by unbundling the university's parts in search of greater efficiency and certainty. This is a grave mistake.

Instead, we should ask how contemporary universities can conduct themselves to allow sometimes discordant missions to help keep society poised to develop valuable new things and respond to complex and unexpected problems. The answer to that question lies in the organization of academic work, the formal and informal "rules of the game" that shape how that work is done, and the networks that work creates and sustains.

Universities are special places that deserve both the protections and the substantial investments our society makes in them. But they are also messy, complicated places that make clear accounts elusive. That lack of clarity can be a source of creativity,[83] but it is also a challenge in political debates about appropriate public investments in the academic mission. As a result of this ambiguity, pressure to emphasize clear and immediate returns and the greatest productive efficiency possible in each endeavor is becoming the norm. Thus, the emphasis in both public and academic discourse focuses on trade-offs and inefficiencies rather than articulating points of convergence.

This is a shame because seeking simplicity in an effort to enable clear cost-benefit analyses makes universities less likely to effectively fulfill their promise to society. The dissonance created by the intersection of many missions and fields can spark ingenuity because the clamor of multiple, coequal concerns makes it more difficult for a single orthodoxy to prevail.[84] Universities are defined by conflicts large and small, by the daily abrasion of different approaches to knowledge, and by distinct scales for weighing the value of their work.[85]

As Clark Kerr noted, the basis of a university's ability to be "a generating force for new ideas and critical commentary on the status quo" is precisely productive conflict in the interaction of different cultures of knowledge.[86] At their best, research universities transform both public and private investments into networks that draw complex intellectual capabilities together across fields and missions. Sometimes irreconcilable mandates loosen the grip of the status quo and create new possibilities for discovery.

Why are universities consistently able to act as sources of new things? Because their conservative nature makes them stable enough to keep the internal competitions and multiple means of assessing worth from tearing them apart. This creates precisely the kind of environment that is poised to yield new knowledge and solutions to unexpected problems.

Why should they maintain multiple missions, at the cost of confusion and potentially inefficiencies in the pursuit of any single activity? Because their commitment to different needs, constituencies, and purposes makes them more resilient while ensuring that no single definition of worth dominates their work.

Why should they continue to span the fullest possible range of fields of teaching and research? Because their true social value lies in their ability to connect to and absorb information from as much of society as possible and because they are a storehouse for knowledge and skills we do not know we need yet.

The public value of universities stems from the very things that make them hard to explain and justify in terms of clear, short-term private returns. Our universities emerged from the crucible of postwar politics to serve broadly public missions with substantial public investments. In the last thirty years the rhetoric justifying public investment has shifted back toward individual returns and productive efficiency. Public support is flat or declining. This renders internal competition more destructive and makes institutions more reliant on tuition, at least somewhat justifying a shift toward evaluation in terms of student outcomes.

As literary critic Jeffrey Williams describes the situation, universities are "no longer . . . a prime institution of the welfare state, providing a public service to the citizenry for a minimal fee but [have] become a prime institution of the neoliberal state, a pay-as-you-go consumer enterprise."[87] The seeds of this shift were present early on, as the process of defining both the education and research missions played out politically in the late 1940s. But while public rhetoric and public support made campus-level investments in common goods tenable, the tensions were productive, not pernicious. As both have changed, we run a grave risk of destroying the very features of the academic research system that have come to create so much benefit. Avoiding that fate starts with thinking and talking about the ways in which our research-intensive universities manage to be consistent sources.

3 SOURCES OF DISCOVERY

Networks on Campus

DISCOVERY IS THE ORIGINAL SOURCE of the good things that come from our research universities. Knowledge work is a spring. But the stream's uncertain course also powers enduring frustrations both on and off campus. Fully appreciating the research university and its work requires a toolkit that can explain how discovery is the consistent outcome of an organization that balances stability and novelty by creating and sustaining public goods.

Common resources help keep the competition and conflicts bred by diverse missions, disparate approaches to discovery, and widely varied fields of knowledge from tearing our universities apart. But shared capacities for research and learning do not defuse the resulting tensions. Instead, the university's resistance to change allows the clash of different views to be sustained and to generate unexpected things.

Discovery is the application of existing knowledge in the search for something new. In order for it to happen, there must be a mechanism to remember and transmit what is known as well as to challenge or revise the status quo. This is why research universities need museums and labs, archives and engineering facilities, libraries and high-capacity computing. It is also why open access to knowledge and data are both essential. Both conservation and novelty result from work. Students, staff, alumni, and especially faculty pursue their interests, goals, and duties on campus and as they move back and forth across its boundaries.

Their efforts never happen in complete isolation. The day-to-day job of research creates networks of relationships that enable large and small discoveries, the development of individual skills, and the growth of collective capabilities. Research-trained people carry knowledge out into society and turn it toward purposes that might never have been envisioned in the original work. For lack of a better term, I will call the new things that are discovered, the new skills that are developed, and the new purposes to which both are put *innovations*.[1]

That choice deliberately blurs the lines between research (usually associated with discovery), teaching (associated with learning and skill development), and service (associated with the application of knowledge and skills for the benefit of the public). All those activities are part of the knowledge mission of the research university and the jobs of its faculty. People learn things through all these processes.

The competition and collaboration enabled by decentralized organization, the pluralism and tension created when missions and fields collide, and the complex networks that emerge from knowledge work make universities sources by enabling them to produce new things on an ongoing basis. Their institutional and physical stability prevents them from succumbing to either internal strife or the kinds of "creative destruction" that economist Joseph Schumpeter took to be a fundamental result of innovation under capitalism.[2] One of the things that makes a research university a good source of knowledge is the fact that it is also an anchor. This is true in part because public support helps it avoid the fate Schumpeter predicted even while whole fields of knowledge inside it emerge, fade, or change dramatically.[3]

What Is Innovation?

Academic fields have their own scriptures. The study of innovation is no exception. Consider some scraps of original text and a commentary. First, Schumpeter notes that entrepreneurship, which he takes to be the distinctive force behind capitalist growth, is "the doing of new things, or the doing of things that have already been done in a new way."[4] The work of innovation, what Schumpeter earlier called the "creative response" to new situations, depends on the current state of knowledge.[5] Discovery and the social or economic goods that can stem from it result not from the creation of completely fresh things but instead from the repurposing of existing things to accomplish new goals. As was the case for Solomon, for many innovation scholars, "there is no new thing under the sun."[6] The same sentiment is implicit in the phrase commonly attributed to Isaac Newton: "If I have seen further, it is by standing on the shoulders of giants."[7]

What this all means for us is that understanding how universities create novelty requires that we think through the conditions that make it possible to effectively "recombine" elements from what we already know in order to do a new thing or to do an old thing in a new way. As economists Richard Nelson and Sidney Winter put it:

> the creation of any sort of novelty in art, science, or practical life consists to a substantial extent of the recombination of conceptual and physical materials that were previously in existence . . . each new achievement is not merely the answer to a particular problem but also a new item in the vast storehouse of components that are available for use . . . [in] the solution of other problems in the future.[8]

Implicit in this argument is the idea that research that may seem to have little use or even to have failed can increase the store of potentially useful knowledge. Moreover, the uses to which knowledge may eventually be put are often far removed from the intentions of their discoverers or funders.[9]

But saying there's nothing truly and completely new is a long way from implying there's nothing to discover. It is also a long way from saying that such discoveries are trivial. Consider a familiar example, the smartphone. One way to understand smartphones as innovations that combine existing technologies to do old things in new ways is by thinking about functions. The idea is highlighted in a 2014 blog post that compared the technologies in a 1991 Radio Shack newspaper ad to the functions of today's iPhone.[10] Viewed in these terms, smartphones might be best understood as the combination of music players, phones, audio recorders, computers, video cameras, calculators, and on and on and on. This also highlights how innovations can be a source of "creative destruction." Wide adoption of smartphones made the business model of companies such as Radio Shack much less tenable.

It's also easy to imagine smartphones as a combination of physical components: a touchscreen, a processor, memory, a miniaturized camera, speakers. Many of those component parts were developed for purposes other than smartphones. Most of them can trace their origins to earlier, publicly funded academic research.[11] Consider just one defining feature of smartphones, the touchscreen, which Steve Jobs modestly described as the "most revolutionary user interface since the mouse."[12]

A basic technology underlying the touchscreen was invented by Samuel Hurst, an engineer at the University of Kentucky, which applied for a patent in mid-1970.[13] The multi-touch functionality that allows us all to sweep and scroll and zoom resulted in part from work done by Michael Elias and Wayne Westerman at the University of Delaware, which applied for a patent in 1998. With Elias as chair, Westerman wrote a dissertation in 1999 that acknowledged support from the NSF in the form of a graduate fellowship.[14] Together they founded a small company called FingerWorks to develop the technology. Apple Computer purchased FingerWorks in 2005. Both Elias and Westerman took engineering jobs at Apple and continued to patent discoveries related to multi-touch technology.[15]

Solving the problem of how to control a phone with gestures required an immense amount of work at Apple, which first introduced the iPhone in early January 2007. That essential work too easily obscures the academic research and training that contributed to a technology many of us rely on every day. Companies such as Apple are the running backs who carry an innovation across the goal line to well-deserved cheers, but they run behind a massive front line of publicly supported academic research. The fact that public investments support many things we take to be the sole result of private industry offers another example of the ways in which hard-to-see benefits make the case for substantial public investments more difficult.[16] Stories like these also suggest that there may be a case for substantial private investments in the capacity represented by universities conceptualized as sources.

The University of Delaware, like the University of Kentucky before it, is an important though perhaps unexpected source for the iPhone. Westerman's research, like Sergey Brin's at Stanford a few years earlier, was supported by public funds in the form of an NSF graduate fellowship.[17] But the impossibility of assessing the return on investment that touchscreen technology created for a 1995 fellowship award suggests once again the dangers of direct efforts to measure the returns on particular investments.

In less than a decade, smartphones became a ubiquitous part of our world. Their uses and applications have expanded and they have helped to shift everything from social movements to romance, entertainment, and business. As Nelson and Winter might have predicted, the smartphone has itself quickly become a component part of the solution to many problems that were likely unforeseen at the time of its development. The various parts of the phone too have been repurposed for other uses. Consider all the places we now routinely find touchscreens.

Technologies like the smartphone clearly demonstrate how innovation results from recombination. This case also shows us how bringing together existing things in novel ways can result in fundamental, even radical change. As Schumpeter himself noted, the creative response that is the heart of innovation can change "social and economic systems for good."[18] If we seek to invest in academic research in a fashion that helps make this kind of change possible, we should attend very closely to university collaboration networks and the context in which they sit.

The Grounds of Discovery

Research is a process whereby people work to identify problems and their solutions. Both problems and solutions flow through organizations.[19] They are often discovered through interaction. One of the first things graduate students have to learn when starting research careers is how to identify a "good" problem. But what counts as a good problem varies across fields and across parts of the university. Economists and sociologists, for instance, differ in how they define a problem worth solving as well as in how they define what counts as a reasonable solution.

The way research happens can also vary dramatically from field to field. But, very generally, it requires some means for those doing it to search for information and problems. That can happen in a lab or archive, at a conference, or simply while sitting and reading. Such a search may proceed or follow a moment of insight. While the early glimmers of good ideas may start off inchoate, they can often offer guiding direction for the research process. At some point, the resources (be they people, reagents, computers, time, or something else entirely) must be marshaled to support the work of turning an idea into a finished piece of science or scholarship. In the natural sciences and parts of the social sciences, external grants, which necessitate lengthy bouts of proposal writing and pilot data collection, are the primary source of support.

Institutional differences in how fields define problems and solutions are matched by organizational differences. A sociologist employed in a medical school and one employed in the arts and sciences may also differ substantially in how they define problems and solutions. Universities that maintain high-quality research in a wide range of fields and that organize that research across differently focused units and missions contain the raw materials necessary to identify and solve many problems. But important problems rarely know what discipline or school they should be solved by. Mechanisms to allow information and skills to travel across the university are necessary as well.

If innovation is based on recombination, then three features of the research environment are essential to supporting it. First, there must be many problems in play. Pursuing multiple missions, drawing porous boundaries between campus and society, and supporting knowledge work in lots of different fields all increase access to problems by allowing universities to be more effective hubs.

This is also a reason why encouraging faculty to provide service to external entities in government or elsewhere can pay real dividends for discovery. Service work on panels convened by the National Academies or the American Academy of Arts and Sciences, agricultural extension efforts, or faculty work on the thousand or so advisory panels convened by the federal government can be a marvelous source of new problems.[20] These activities also exemplify the many kinds of pro bono work that universities and their faculties provide to society.

Second, the raw materials of innovative solutions are bits of existing knowledge and technology that may not have been successfully combined before. Rarer, atypical combinations are often the source of higher-impact discoveries.[21] Many of those bits come from outside a given organization or must traverse boundaries among separate units within it. Drawing on examples from areas such as manufacturing and high technology, management scholars Wesley Cohen and Daniel Levinthal argued that innovation encompasses both the discovery of new information and the ability to assimilate and make use of existing knowledge.[22] Cohen and Levinthal call this ability "absorptive capacity" and note that it depends on the "richness of the pre-existing knowledge structure."[23]

Learning is key to both research and development. New things are best and most easily learned when they relate to other things a person or organization knows well. For someone who already speaks French, Spanish or Italian is easier to learn than Finnish or Mandarin. In organizations, this means that for universities to be able to identify and respond to the kinds of problems that come their way because they are hubs requires a dense and diverse internal knowledge base. Richer knowledge inside the university increases the likelihood that it can absorb and respond to both new problems and new solutions. Being a good source of knowledge also makes universities more effective hubs in the larger society, and positive feedback across those two roles should be expanded.

The metaphor of absorption suggests that like a sponge, a knowledge-intensive organization works best when it is already damp with relevant internal know-how. Bone-dry sponges do a bad job of mopping up spills, and organizations without a rich knowledge base do a bad job of identifying and responding to problems. If one key goal of universities and the research enterprise they anchor is to be able to respond effectively to problems that have not yet been defined, then the more and more varied types of knowledge they encompass, the better.

Third, universities will be better able to develop new things when they maintain access to large amounts of existing, even seemingly out-of-date or currently useless knowledge. Another metaphor used by Cesar Hidalgo and Ricardo Hausmann to describe the sources of productivity of national economies is very useful in this regard. Hidalgo and Hausmann liken a national economy to a bucket of Lego bricks, noting that the complexity of what an economy can produce and the speed with which it can build something in response to new opportunities are dependent on the mix of bricks in their bucket.[24] But bricks that have been hoarded for private use or hidden away and forgotten cannot easily be turned to new building projects.[25]

Accessible results of prior knowledge work conducted on campus and beyond as well as the skills of the people working there represent essential sets of bricks. Networks that span many fields and units and an institutional bias toward conserving and sharing knowledge mean that few of those bricks are inaccessible when the time comes to find and use them.

Researchers must be able to identify problems and search through the possible components of potential solutions effectively. Because much federally funded university research is conducted for academic reasons that may have little to do with the solution to immediate practical problems, it is common for solutions to precede the challenges they might eventually help solve. Even in cases with obvious near-term applications, past innovations may offer future solutions to unforeseen problems. This may be one reason why federally funded research and research conducted in academic settings more consistently produces high-impact discoveries that run counter to current technological trajectories than do projects done in corporations.[26]

Once potential solutions are identified, organizations and their researchers must be able to draw together a complicated mix of tangible and intangible resources to make an innovative idea a reality or prove that it doesn't work. The creation of new things through recombination thus requires at least two stages. Initially, some person or group of people must have an "aha" moment when the seed of an idea becomes clear. For the sake of simplicity, I will call the "aha" an insight. Next some person or, more often, group of people must bring the necessary resources together and do the difficult, uncertain work of proving a new research concept. I will shorthand the result of such efforts a proof. Both insights and proofs emerge from work done in networks.

Insights and proofs are complicated by the fact that at the frontiers of knowledge, both problems and solutions are generally ill defined. As a result, researchers interested in developing new things often know they are searching for something but do not know precisely what it is. This is why blind alleys and failed experiments are commonplace on research frontiers. It is also why accidental discoveries can be such an important part of the progress of knowledge and its effects.

Serendipity can strike almost anywhere, but the ability to turn accident into insight and proof requires both a great degree of relevant knowledge and access to a wide array of resources. Absorptive capacity is also a means to capture the benefits of productive accidents. Part of what universities do is create environments for knowledge work that can cultivate serendipity and teach people to recognize and capitalize on unexpected opportunities. The ability to actively search through networks for things one knows one needs is fundamental to innovation, but so is the ability to use the unexpected things your network sometimes brings to you.

How Networks Work

What does it mean to ask how networks work? Two things. First, we must clarify exactly how the networks that exist on particular campuses create possibilities for serendipity, for search,[27] and for the familiarity, trust, and forbearance that are often essential to the coordination of risky, complicated work.[28]

Second, we need to understand networks as social systems that grow from and shape possibilities for individual action even though people have little capacity to see or map the full extent of their connections. The primary lever funding and policy decisions have to alter research outcomes, and their social or economic effects are not direct. Instead, they must proceed by changing the character of the networks that are the real source of discovery. Funding enables work. Work creates and sustains networks. Networks are the source of innovation and learning on campus.

Seeking to influence the growth of networks requires that we consider how they form in order to intervene. But we must do so with full knowledge that the kinds of outcomes we seek are nearly impossible to accurately foresee and thus equally hard to plan. As with the benefits of universities, we must think in terms of collective effects because individual incentives are insufficient to shape a network that "evolve[s] from individuals interacting but produce[s] extended structures that they had not imagined and in fact cannot see."[29]

Features of Innovative Research Networks

Three features of university networks are essential to understanding how academic research is a source of social and economic benefits. These are also the features we should strive to create and sustain through public investments and administrative efforts on our campuses.

Diversity

First, the networks that produce new and innovative things must be *diverse*. The people they connect should come from varied backgrounds and career stages. A mix of backgrounds is essential because, as complexity researcher Scott Page has shown, varied intellectual orientations carry with them different approaches to problems. Teams with assorted "cognitive toolboxes" come to better decisions and may even be able to identify better problems.[30]

Think back to the idea that a person's, group's, or organization's ability to absorb and use new ideas is a function of the richness of the knowledge they hold individually and collectively. In universities, a key source of such diversity is the institutional variation captured by different disciplinary approaches to problems. This doesn't mean, however, that every team should be diverse or interdisciplinary. It just means that the whole network should draw together a wide range of skills and knowledge.

A mix of backgrounds helps by making it easier for researchers to uncover relevant information that may be known to one of them but not to others. Diversity also helps make sure that no single approach to a problem or particular disciplinary scripture will necessarily dominate the work of a university, making it more likely that unorthodox solutions will emerge.

To the extent that we want university networks to be able to identify and address emerging problems in society, we should also emphasize participation by people from many different economic and social backgrounds. Concerns with access to education have generally been framed in terms of ensuring equality opportunity. But this view suggests that there may be a strong "business case" for universities to pursue diversity and inclusivity in their research networks as well.[31]

Similarly, a mix of career stages helps make certain that at least some team members have incentives to challenge the current state of knowledge. The mark of successful doctoral education is both mastery of a given field of knowledge and the ability to make a new contribution to that field. Ideally, graduate school from matriculation to graduation with one's own hood offers a microcosm of the innovation process on campus. For this reason, it behooves us to think of investments in graduate training in terms of collective as well as individual benefit.

More importantly, involving early-career researchers means that at least some of the skills and know-how developed in projects will move beyond the team or the university and into application in other parts of society. Students transmit knowledge out of universities. They also bring problems and potential solutions back to it when they return. This is one reason why it is critically important to combine the education and research missions.

Consider a recently published piece led by economists Julia Lane and Bruce Weinberg that makes just this point.[32] A group of nine researchers at four universities, a think tank, and the U.S. Census Bureau worked with information derived from human resources and sponsored-projects information from eight Big Ten campuses. We used these data in concert with federally protected information from the U.S. Census Bureau and information on completed doctorates drawn from a database maintained by a company called ProQuest to identify new PhDs who worked on federal and other sponsored research projects. We then asked where recent, research-trained PhDs took their next jobs.

The results offer some sense of what it means to call a university a source. The findings from this set of about 3,200 recent PhDs who were paid at least some of their wages by research grants also opens a small window on the ways that success in generating knowledge helps make campuses into anchors and hubs.[33] PhD students working in areas as diverse as humanities, social sciences, biology, computer science, and engineering left their campuses for jobs in industry (40 percent), academia (53 percent), and government (7 percent). Because the least is known about the role new PhDs play in industry, we focused most of our attention there. The private-sector establishments[34] that hired new PhDs were larger, paid higher wages, and grew faster than either the average establishment in the country or, a better comparison, than other employers that undertook internal R&D.

We also looked at the geography of jobs and the industries where new PhDs were overrepresented. Nearly 17 percent of the recent doctoral recipients we studied who got jobs with R&D-performing companies stayed in the state where they did their graduate work. Just over 10 percent took jobs within fifty miles of their university. In other words, research-trained doctoral students contribute to the anchoring effects universities have on their states as well as to national industrial capacity for R&D. These same graduates disproportionately got jobs in knowledge-intensive settings like pharmaceuticals, semiconductors, computer systems design, software, engineering services, and hospitals. In other words, diverse networks of researchers on campus are sources of both new discoveries and people who carry their skills far and wide in the knowledge economy, making the university more of a hub.

Complexity

Second, networks that produce new things must be complex in the sense offered by Hidalgo and Hausmann's "Lego bricks" metaphor. Contacts among people that encompass and connect a wide array of various types of knowledge enable researchers to accidentally bump into or actively look for important components of innovation that might otherwise remain unknown or difficult to access. One reason the team of authors on the paper I just described was so large and distributed across so many places is that the research required us to combine many types of data and skills.

Both search and serendipity depend on a social form of proximity that allows people to encounter one another and share information. Some of the most productive of those interactions are unplanned. I might not know that a problem I'm trying to solve would be simple for a good algebraic topologist, but if someone I talk with is (or works with) a mathematician, then they can help point me in the right direction. When, as is quite frequently the case, I don't have the skills I need to solve a given problem, the networks I've developed as a faculty member can help me find them, even if I don't know exactly what I'm looking for when I begin my search.

We must learn how extended networks of collaborators draw different types of knowledge closer together. The more and more varied Lego bricks a given campus's networks contain, the more complex, interesting, and potentially valuable the things its researchers can conceptualize and build will be. The collaboration networks that emerge from research on different campuses put topics together in disparate ways because networks grow in and are shaped by their contexts.[35]

If every campus had the same knowledge arrayed in the same way, the system as a whole would be less resilient and effective. But this is not an argument for specialization. The more specialized a knowledge base is, the more difficult it will be to generate radically new things through recombination, and the more challenging it will be to absorb and react to unexpected problems that arise. A specialized or fragmented knowledge base makes it hard for an organization to recognize, absorb, and respond to problems that are outside its current sphere.[36] Those are exactly the kinds of problems that we need our universities to address effectively.

Balance

Finally, the networks that make universities sources must be *balanced*. They must mix open space where people have access to widely different knowledge and pockets of tightly knit collaborators who can work in concert to prove a novel insight. This same kind of structure leaves room for challenges to existing knowledge that come from inside the university itself. This is a complicated idea that we should spend a little time thinking through together.

First, it is necessary to realize that the magic of large networks has more to do with the relationships any given individual doesn't have than it does with the friends and collaborators they do have. On its face, that sounds a bit crazy. How can relationships I don't have improve my ability to solve problems? The answer has to do with what network researchers call *indirect ties*. These friend-of-a-friend connections are what can make search and serendipity powerful outcomes of complex networks.

A Network Interlude The idea is an obvious one if you put it in the context of social media. If you maintain a LinkedIn profile, you've seen indirect connections in action. When you search for someone you don't know, the system will tell you how many introductions away from them you are and who among your friends can start you down the chain. When I type in the name of someone I am acquainted with but with whom I am not connected online, LinkedIn provides me with an indication of the online social distance between us.

Chains of indirect connections like these are essential to understanding networks because they are the pipes through which information— be it gossip, scientific ideas, or both—and more tangible resources flow among people.[37] They are also a basis for the formation of new relationships. A network sociologist, Mark Granovetter, highlighted this idea in 1973 when he noted that if a person has two good friends, it is extremely unlikely that they are not at least acquainted with one another. This was such an uncommon pattern that a psychologist writing in 1946 had dubbed a network configuration where one person knew two others who didn't also know each other the "forbidden triad."[38] In other words, long chains of network connections tend to bring strangers who share friends or collaborators into contact.

Those same indirect ties give networks their structure, which in turn creates different opportunities and challenges for people and groups who occupy them. In classical sociological terms, networks are the backbone of *social capital*.[39] Like more traditional views of financial capital, the idea behind social capital is that the structure of one's relationships is a thing of value in itself that can be invested to yield returns. As is the case with financial resources, everyone's social capital is not equal. By virtue of their networks, some people and groups are more likely to succeed at and be recognized for the tasks they undertake than others. Often, the tasks one has the opportunity to undertake also result from social capital. Networks are the context in which human capital is developed and its potential realized.[40]

When I say the collaboration networks that are the wellspring of university innovation must be balanced, what I mean is that their effectiveness depends on a particular structure that allows them to sustain both phases of the innovation process, insight and proof. So let us double back to the idea that effective university collaboration networks should allow researchers to actively prospect for the necessary components of innovation, remain open to productive accidents, and be able to do the complicated, collective work of proving or disproving their insights.

Thinking About Network Balance: Brokerage and Cohesion We should begin with the moment of insight. How do networks help make it possible for people and groups to have good ideas? According to sociologist Ron Burt, the answer has to do once again with the connections that are missing from an overall structure. Burt argues that people have greater social capital when their connections span "structural holes," places in a network where no or few ties exist to connect groups.[41] Put more simply, if you are the only person who has friends or colleagues in two groups that otherwise have no connections linking them, you are in a powerful structural position.

Whether you exercise that power by passing on useful information, holding it for your own purposes, or making introductions that bring the groups together,[42] being in a position that lets you bridge otherwise unconnected portions of a network creates a particular sort of social capital called *brokerage*. Networks that are indirectly connected but more open, that have more structural holes, have more people who are in positions to broker and thus can generate more novel insights.[43]

Brokerage increases insight for three reasons. First, new ideas come from the combination of existing knowledge. Second, the less often that bits of knowledge have been combined in the past, the more likely their synthesis is to generate something new. Third, people who are in the same groups share more similar knowledge, opinions, and behavior than people who are in different groups.

Brokerage increases the likelihood of good ideas, but having good ideas doesn't mean they will be implemented. Burt studied the relationship between structural holes and good ideas among managers in a large electronics firm. He found that those who had opportunities for brokerage communicated more ideas, had their ideas listened to more often, and had ideas that were more likely to be considered valuable. However, when he returned to the company ten months later to see which managers had begun the work to mobilize support for the ideas that had been rated most valuable, he discovered that most (84 percent) had not taken steps to make their ideas a reality.[44] In other words, the kind of social capital that helped people generate useful insights did not help them move from concept to proof.

A different type of social capital is helpful there. Brokerage is primarily about the ability to access and combine disparate bits of information. Being able to do the hard and uncertain work that is necessary to move from insight to proof has more to do with the call one has on the attention, resources, and skills of actual and potential collaborators.[45]

At the frontiers of knowledge, researchers are often feeling their way along. This means that new techniques, new materials, and new ways of thinking need to be developed in order to prove an insight. In today's competitive academy, that uncertain work often has to take place with others breathing down one's neck.[46] The work of proving an insight is difficult and risky. It can also require that researchers coordinate their efforts while pursuing many different tasks. In interdisciplinary research, it is often essential to rely on the work of collaborators when one cannot fully grasp the details of what they have done.[47] Moreover, new work is often based on knowledge whose details are difficult to formally articulate. Tacit knowledge is often the characteristic feature of new discoveries.[48]

All these aspects of the discovery process mean that moving from insight to proof often requires an ensemble of researchers who trust one another, are sympathetic when faced with failure, share a sense of commitment to their projects, are able to coordinate their work even when they cannot fully describe it, and can move relatively fast under pressure.

The powerful position held by brokers does not convey these benefits. Instead, networks in which every participant is connected to many others are essential. Cohesive networks increase trust and forbearance. They also help coordinate complicated work and enforce norms of behavior that can make groups more effective.[49] All the features of cohesive groups that make them bad for the generation of insights make them good for facilitating the work needed for proof.

Universities and other knowledge-intensive workplaces are thus caught in a bind. Innovation requires both insight and proof. But the types of social capital that facilitate one make the other more difficult. Researchers who seek to move from insight to proof often face the same challenge. For universities, the answer to this conundrum is to seek networks that are balanced in the sense that they contain a mix of open spaces where brokers can thrive and cohesive pockets where repeated connections can make the work of research a little easier.

Balanced networks that are populated by diverse individuals and that draw a complex mix of knowledge closer together through chains of indirect ties offer the most effective grounds for innovation and discovery. They work better when the people in them are actively pursuing research. For this reason, universities around the country and around the world seek to "gather the most research productive faculty [and] the brightest students" in order to create "the highest-quality academic and cultural environment achievable."[50]

In order to be effective sources of knowledge, universities need particular kinds of research networks that connect engaged faculty and students to create a distinctive social space for the work of insight and proof. But how can administrators or funders seed and sustain such networks? As is true with many things about the university, complex networks are tough to manipulate directly. Instead, they must be cultivated through indirect means. But doing so requires that we attend to how they grow.

How Networks Grow

Big research networks change and grow as individuals enter and leave universities and as those that stay form and break collaborations. In order to understand how networks grow, we have to return to the organization of the university and its researchers. The closer you are to someone, the more likely you are to connect with them.[51] But as you might have guessed, proximity is complicated. There are lots of different ways to be "close." I've already mentioned one. People are close to one another in a social space defined by relationships when the chain of indirect connections linking them is shorter. When people are directly connected, for instance as collaborators, they are as close as they can possibly be in this network space.

The forbidden triad implies that people connected at distance two (collaborators of collaborators) are themselves likely to become connected provided that the ties that already exist are friendly.[52] In our context this means that researchers who have collaborated successfully in the past are more likely to do so again in the future. It also means that those who share collaborators in common are likely to undertake projects together at some point.[53]

The networks that grow on campus as researchers pursue their work enable one type of proximity. The complicated and decentralized organization of the university suggests another type of closeness. In the last chapter I said that making sociological sense of the university and its work requires that we think in three different but related registers: the organizational, the institutional, and the network. We've dispensed with the last of these. But consider the first two.

In organizational terms, the university is a decentralized set of units (schools, departments, programs) that map loosely onto the various missions and problems it addresses. Engineering schools generally take on different classes of problems than public policy schools. In most universities, their budgets and procedures are different. Departments generally subdivide schools. Engineering might be broken up into a department of mechanical engineering, a department of electrical engineering, and so on. People are closer to each other when they occupy the same organizational units. Two researchers, whether engineers or not, are nearer to one another in organizational terms when both are employed by the engineering school. Two people who share the same department are nearer still.

Organizational proximity is important because it increases the likelihood of regular interaction if only because of attendance at faculty meetings, colloquia, and other events. Shared mentoring of graduate students provides another type of proximity and suggests another reason to combine research and teaching. The size of the organizational unit also matters. My department is located in the college of Literature, Science, and the Arts (LSA), which is home to more than one thousand faculty members. Presuming that I talk with another professor because we share an LSA affiliation is naïve.

All other things being equal, though, I am probably more likely to have unplanned interactions with someone in my college than with someone working in another college. For this reason, I'm also likely to be closer to other arts and sciences professors in network terms. Those unplanned interactions are one way to keep up to date with discoveries outside my specialty. They are also a way for me to search through my networks and a mechanism for serendipitous discovery.

The university is also shot through with institutional distinctions. These are more abstract divisions, but they are nevertheless very real differences that matter in the lives of faculty and students. One key institutional difference results from disciplinary training.

Sometimes disciplinary differences map on to organizational ones, as when a chemist is employed in a department of chemistry. Quite often they do not. For instance, a microbiologist might be employed in a department of environmental engineering. If that organizational affiliation led her to interact primarily with engineers rather than other microbiologists, social influence would lead us to expect that she would become more like the engineers than like her disciplinary colleagues.

Nevertheless, some differences based on field of training are likely to persist because institutions are very sticky things.

Disciplinary differences carry with them (among other things) assumptions about what counts as a good problem, ideas about how best to proceed with research, expectations about whether and how to seek grant support, beliefs about how collaborations should work and how credit should be shared, norms for collegial behavior and skepticism, and standard technologies for doing research. These differences can make interdisciplinary work very difficult as even small issues can stymie conversation.

Here too, proximity matters. People who share the same disciplinary affiliation are more likely to interact and to find the interactions easier than people who do not. But organizational affiliations and existing network connections matter too.

Consider a famous example. World War II led to a huge ramp-up in interdisciplinary work, including the Manhattan Project, which produced the first nuclear bomb at Los Alamos, New Mexico, and MIT's famous Radiation Lab (Rad Lab), which was tasked with developing usable radar systems for land, sea, and air. At its height, the Rad Lab managed $1.5 billion[54] in contracts and employed some four thousand people working in fields such as physics, engineering, weapons design, metallurgy, and manufacturing. At the core of this project was a group of physicists who were characterized by a distinctive disciplinary subculture.

Historian of science Peter Galison reports that interdisciplinary collaborations in the Rad Lab faced early difficulties because engineers and physicists had different norms for calculating key equations. In some instances, the differences were small. Each group used different Greek letters to represent the same constant, which caused some confusion. In other cases, the problems were larger. Physicists tended toward detailed calculations that were difficult and not strictly necessary for the task at hand. Engineers adopted a more pragmatic approach that the physicists initially disdained.

These relatively small differences in disciplinary expectations created challenges that the collaboration had to overcome. In this case there is also evidence of the power of organizational proximity as the theoretical physicists employed in the Rad Lab eventually came around to the approach favored by the "instrument makers." Adopting that style of work shifted both later expectations for collaboration and the approach that at least some physicists took to subsequent projects. Galison reports that Julian Schwinger, a prominent physicist of the day, led the effort to develop shared practical rules for calculating Maxwell's equations. That work in the Rad Lab in turn "reconfigured the strategy by which Schwinger approached physical problems."[55]

Let's turn briefly to other "spaces" in which researchers can be proximate or distant. The first is a space defined by relevant knowledge. This too overlaps at least partially with organizational and institutional divisions in universities, but not completely.

Researchers seek out some points of intellectual overlap in potential collaborators. But too much proximity in knowledge space decreases the likelihood of collaboration, as does too much distance. Instead, researchers generally adopt a Goldilocks strategy because "too much overlap in researchers' ideas" means "there is little novelty to be gained, while if there is too little overlap, researchers will have difficulty assimilating each other's ideas."[56] Here too, balancing closeness and distance is essential to understanding how research networks grow and how they produce new and interesting innovations.

Finally, let's think about the most obvious way that people can be near to or far from one another, physically. Large research universities build and maintain millions of square feet of facilities devoted to knowledge work. These substantial and specialized fixed costs help explain why research can be such an expensive proposition. But the relative position of buildings and their architecture also shape how people move through their workdays and thus whom they will have contact with, how easily they can consult one another, and how likely they are to work together.

If you are like most people, you spend time in a very small portion of the building where you work or even the one where you live. The area you routinely move around in is what researchers going back to the 1950s have called a *functional zone*.[57] What researchers haven't been able to do is systematically measure and quantify the functional zones of lots of individuals.

We did just that for faculty working in two interdisciplinary life sciences buildings on a single campus. In order to define the functional zone of each person, we identified their office; their lab space; and the nearest relevant bathroom, elevator, and staircase. We assumed that researchers basically moved among these spaces in a habitual fashion that minimized the amount they had to walk. In other words, we bet on the idea that people are a little lazy and that once they know where they are going they really don't think too much about how they get there.

Based on these assumptions, we identified the shortest walking paths that every researcher in the building could take between the lab, the office, the bathroom, and a point of egress. We hypothesized that two people who had never collaborated would be more likely to start working together if their walking paths had more overlap. Our insight was that they would be more likely to run into each other routinely, to become familiar with each other, and to start talking.

We also expected that more overlap in walking paths would increase the success of new collaborations by creating more chances for people to bump into each other during normal daily business. Those brief, unplanned, but relatively common encounters would make it easier for new collaborators to coordinate and to troubleshoot the problems that crop up in the early stages of laboratory research.

When we tested out this idea, we found that for every additional 100 feet of overlap in the walking paths of two scientists who have not collaborated before, there is about a 17 percent increase in the chance they will start a new project together. The same overlap increased by almost 20 percent the likelihood that a grant to support the new collaboration would be funded. We also found evidence that being in the same department and having lots of existing connections to others in the building increased the chances of new collaboration. Simply put, architecture and the assignment of space on campus shapes the likelihood that new network ties will form in pretty striking ways.[58]

These various dimensions of proximity help us understand some of the sources of new and innovative ideas. This is true in fields such as biomedicine where networks are easy to see. But it also holds in more artisanal fields such as the humanities where traces of intellectual influence and collaboration can be harder to register. The acknowledgments sections of books in fields where sole authorship is the norm suggest that humanists are no less collaborative than scientists. The ties they rely on are just harder to trace. But what's interesting is that there's no reason to believe that networks don't function about the same way in these fields.

Consider a prominent example where overlaps in physical and knowledge space brought eminent thinkers from many organizations and disciplines together in a network that helped spawn important research. The year 1990 witnessed the publication of a landmark book for feminist and gender theory, Judith Butler's *Gender Trouble: Feminism and the Subversion of Identity*.[59] By any measure, *Gender Trouble* represents an important piece of research. According to Google Scholar, the book has been cited somewhere north of forty-two thousand times. Commentators and reviewers credit it with helping to jump-start several fields of study;[60] providing fuel for activism,[61] the arts, popular culture,[62] and law;[63] and influencing psychological definitions of gender disorders.[64]

Clearly the idea that gender identity is a performance rather than the reflection of something essential about a person is not the same kind of thing as a touchscreen or an algorithm to search the web. But on many dimensions its reach and implications are comparable. Thus it represents just the kind of thing that emerges from academic research networks and travels beyond the university to influence the wider world.

In this case, the ability of universities and academic networks to support work that challenges existing orthodoxy is much in evidence in debates about the book's famously difficult language.[65] As Butler herself notes in a *New York Times* op-ed written in response to "winning" a bad-writing prize: "scholars in the humanities . . . are obliged to question common sense, interrogate its tacit presumptions and provoke new ways of looking at a familiar world. . . . Language that takes up this challenge can help point the way to a more socially just world."[66] The implications for the kinds of things university research can and should produce seem clear. But what's interesting for our purposes is that this book, which on its face seems precisely the kind of work that is not the product of a team, highlights some of the ways that intellectual networks work similarly across very different fields.

When *Gender Trouble* was published, Butler was a faculty member at Johns Hopkins University. She had drafted much of the manuscript a couple years earlier during a fellowship at Princeton University's Institute for Advanced Study (IAS). IAS brought together scholars from around the country and the world to spend a year exploring "meanings of male and female." Butler joined at the invitation of her friend Joan Scott, another noted feminist scholar.[67] The preface to the first edition of *Gender Trouble* acknowledges intellectual and personal debts Butler accrued in the course of writing to no fewer than twenty-nine people. This, then, is the trace of a social network that provided some of the ground from which *Gender Trouble* grew.

In addition to Scott, whom Butler called "an invaluable and incisive critic," the 1990 preface listed eight other participants in the IAS group. They represent a who's who of prominent feminist scholars[68] trained in fields including anthropology, biology, history, physics, and sociology. Butler's own PhD is in philosophy.

What do we have in this story? Evidence of intellectual connections that contributed to an important piece of scholarship? Surely. A hint of brokerage in the form of Scott's move to include Butler in the gathering? Yes. An indication of the importance of proximity in knowledge ("meanings of male and female") and physical (Princeton's IAS) space as a means to draw together scholars separated by institutional distance (at least six different disciplines) and organizational distance (only Scott appears to have been a faculty member at Princeton)? Indeed. Networks that grew in the social, physical, institutional, knowledge, and organizational spaces of academe are clearly in evidence here. But can we say that these networks mattered for *Gender Trouble*, which is after all the work of a single individual?

Butler herself certainly can, and does very clearly in a recently published interview.

It is true that when I started *Gender Trouble* I proposed to write a book on "the philosophical foundations of gender" so I was working within some established set of philosophical norms at that moment. But it is interesting how my engagement with scholars in anthropology, history of science, feminist history, and literary theory all turned my head, as it were, and I ended up writing, I think, an antifoundational treatise on gender. What a deviation that was! That turning of my head was also my departure from more traditional ways of "doing philosophy" and though that was a loss to me, I was also glad to be released into a broader world of interdisciplinary scholars. Every conversation with Donna Haraway blew my mind, and some of the feminists who were working in literary criticism challenged me in ways that took a long time to work through and understand (still not sure I am there!).[69]

While the style of academic work and the ways in which it exerts a larger influence may differ dramatically across books like *Gender Trouble* and technologies like touchscreens, this case suggests that networks are as important for the scholarly work and career trajectory of a prominent humanist as they are for scientists and engineers. Butler even suggests that the "deviation" that resulted in *Gender Trouble* might plausibly be taken to represent a recombination of ideas enabled by the diverse and complex network of researchers at IAS.

This case also suggests some important reasons why the diversity of university research and the range of their missions allow them to serve as hubs. Try to think of another institution where similar social conditions produced things as different as *Gender Trouble* and PageRank. Finally, note the importance of a broader, more social view of the role of universities in society. Butler herself notes that the target of her difficult language is not economic growth but justice.

How University Networks Get Their Shape

When we expand beyond a single anecdote to think about how campus networks as a whole come to have differing levels of diversity, complexity, and balance, it's easy to imagine the kinds of small differences that can lead to distinctive structures. The location of buildings and the proximity of departments within them can vary from campus to campus. The organization of departments and schools might bring people working in different fields into closer contact in some places than in others. Even decisions like whether to subsidize creation of a particular seminar series, or to support an institute like IAS, can have implications for the networks on a university's campus.

Small choices about shared resources and larger decisions about how to focus faculty searches or to allocate space can change the structure of networks and thus result in different possibilities for innovation. Even if we imagine that most large research campuses cover the same general intellectual terrain, the way they put knowledge together through differently structured and composed networks results in a diverse national research system.

The different contexts in which university collaboration networks emerge mean that while every campus has complex knowledge networks, they are each likely to be complex in different ways. This is one strength of our complicated, decentralized academic research system. It depends on public investments.

Why Are Public Investments Necessary?

First, the federal government is, and hopefully will remain, the largest supporter of academic research. According to data maintained by the NSF, U.S. universities spent more than $68.7 billion from all sources on research in all fields in 2015. Just over 55 percent of that money came from the federal government. About 24 percent came from the institutions themselves. State and local governments accounted for just under 6 percent. Businesses and nonprofits each funded between 5 percent and 6 percent.[70] Nearly two out of every three dollars spent to support research on our nation's campuses came directly from public sources.

The largest pot, federal funding, breaks down into direct expenditures (the money someone like me can spend to pursue grant-funded research) and indirect costs (the money that allows my institution to recover costs necessary to do things like keep the lights on and ensure appropriate protection of human subjects for my research projects). Direct costs are the money that PIs use to hire the people and buy the stuff necessary to get research work done. The people who are hired on these grants are the core of the networks that shape science, engineering, biomedical, and some types of social science research. Without both direct and indirect federal support those networks would be gutted.

As the case of *Gender Trouble* demonstrates, research in fields where federal funding is less important also depends on networks. Those fields are even more dependent on the shared resources created by universities and the time they leave for faculty to pursue research. Thus, it's reasonable to imagine that scholarship in fields without substantial grant revenue is even more susceptible to quiet damage done by rising concerns with efficiency in teaching and declining public investments. Regardless of the area of research, removing or seriously curtailing public funding would make academic research as we know it today impossible. Our universities would cease to be reliable sources of knowledge and skills.

A second important feature of federal funding support is the mechanism by which most of it is awarded. Consider the two largest federal funders of research, the NSF and the NIH. Both these organizations emphasize *investigator-initiated grants*. Generally speaking, units within the NIH or the NSF set more or less broad parameters on the topics of grants they will consider. Then, mostly, they wait for people working in research to send them proposals. Those proposals typically support specific projects of limited duration.[71] Grant proposals are peer-reviewed in a very competitive process. Any given proposal has a low probability of success. In my experience even strong proposals require substantial revision before they are eventually funded.

There are well-known problems with both the peer review process and with "hypercompetition" for grant funding.[72] Nevertheless, the system has many positive features. Focusing on investigator-initiated grants through a more or less open competitive process means that PIs from many locations who are situated in different networks can propose and sometimes pursue research they devise. Their proposals are evaluated by people who are experts in a given field with a primary focus on scientific merit and their potential for more general impact. All this means that the diversity of campus-level knowledge networks will generate lots of different insights and that those insights will have some chance to bubble up through the peer review process.

Finally, let's think about indirect costs. That money is spent by the university rather than by the investigators who win the grants. Administrators at various levels use indirect costs recovered through grants to help sustain the infrastructure and resources necessary for research work. This is one way that universities compete strategically.

On many campuses this money is allocated through the decentralized process of RCM. Contributions to the cost of buildings and utilities are a concrete use of indirect costs. Indirect-cost recovery is just one of the important means that universities have to sustain shared resources. They are largely invisible to many of the people on a campus, but their effects on collaboration and networks, on the university's ability to be a source, are substantial.

In order to see how, we need to look at an area of research where both direct and indirect costs from federal sources became visible and contested: human embryonic stem cell research.

Human Embryonic Stem Cells, Federal Funding, and Universities as Sources

Before diving deeply into this section, it is important to say a few things about what I will not be doing. I will not be offering a comprehensive overview of the science, ethics, and politics of pluripotent stem cell research. Several good books exist that can orient the interested reader.[73] Nor will I be articulating a specific policy proposal for this still somewhat controversial field. I am on record in that regard in several places.[74] In the same vein I will not be discussing the interesting and complicated intellectual property history and conflicts surrounding human embryonic stem cell lines. Finally, I do not seek to present a representative or comprehensive account of how working scientists in this field have understood and reacted to the regulations imposed by the federal government or their states.

Instead, I will use this interesting case to illuminate the ways that federal research funding, or more to the point, its lack, shapes collaboration, research, and careers in a field with significant implications for both fundamental understanding and therapeutic and commercial impact. This demonstration will rely heavily on work I have conducted with two important collaborators, Jennifer McCormick of the Pennsylvania State University and Christopher Thomas Scott of Stanford University. It will also rely heavily on the voices of working stem cell scientists whom we interviewed during 2009 and 2010. I follow common convention for qualitative research in the social sciences and identify the scientists we interviewed using pseudonyms and general descriptions that obscure their identities.

In 1998 two research teams led by James Thomson at the University of Wisconsin and John Gearhart at Johns Hopkins University published separate papers reporting the successful derivation of human embryonic stem cells (hESCs).[75]

Human embryonic stem cells are pluripotent, which means that, at least in theory, they can be stimulated to develop into any of the types of cells found in the human body. They are controversial because the most common method used to derive them requires the destruction of a two-to-four-day-old human embryo. Research using embryonic stem cells can contribute directly to our understanding of the process by which a single cell develops into a human body.

Pluripotence also created significant enthusiasm about new therapies that might treat some of our most devastating diseases and injuries. Research work with hESCs has shown some promise for treating central nervous system diseases such as Parkinson's disease and amyotrophic lateral sclerosis (ALS), cardiac diseases, some types of congenital blindness, diabetes, spinal cord injuries, and traumatic brain injury. Pluripotent cell lines are a cornerstone of what has come to be called *regenerative medicine*. More recent advances in induced pluripotent stem cells hold out the promise of truly personalized cell therapies.

Thomson's work with rhesus monkeys was funded by the NIH, but both his and Gearhart's research on humans was privately funded by the Geron Corporation, a biotechnology company. The shift from public to private funding took place because a 1996 rider to a federal appropriations bill, the Dickey-Wicker Amendment, prevents the Department of Health and Human Services (which houses the NIH) from using federal funds to support research that harms human embryos.

In 1998, the Clinton administration issued a legal opinion drawing a distinction between human embryos and embryonic stem cells, which allowed the NIH to issue calls for proposals to support hESC research but not the creation of cell lines. George W. Bush stopped review of those proposals upon taking office in 2000. Stem cell research was a topic of much political and public concern in the early months of his administration, which issued an executive order that struck a compromise by allowing federal funding for research using a small number of hESC lines derived before August 9, 2001. Research using other lines was not eligible for federal funding.

Stem cell research was a significant topic in both the 2004 and 2008 presidential races. In March 2009 President Barack Obama fulfilled a campaign promise by issuing an executive order relaxing restrictions on funding for hESC research. That executive order triggered a significant review process by the NIH to evaluate the ethical and legal conditions under which existing and new cell lines were created. Some of the lines that were eligible for federal funding under the Bush policy were ruled ineligible, while many new lines were added to the registry. Political and public controversy also continued at the state level, where some states relaxed federal regulations and provided public funds to support hESC research while others tightened rules and even imposed outright bans on this research area.

Over this entire time period, scientific work continued and expanded, though most of the work focused on a small number of cell lines derived at the University of Wisconsin that were eligible for funding under the Bush executive order.[76] The most elite researchers and universities were often able to develop nonfederal resources sufficient to allow them to derive and pursue research with cell lines that were not eligible for federal funding.[77] However, scientists working at less elite institutions or in states that enacted stronger regulations limiting HESC research were generally not so lucky.

Most researchers in this new area faced a difficult choice. Neither the direct-costs nor the indirect-costs portions of federal grants could be used to support research with cell lines that were not approved. Researchers who thought their scientific questions could be best addressed with newer cell lines had to either settle for approved lines that might be less appropriate or undertake the additional cost and effort of developing alternative funding sources.

The jury is still out on exactly what the long-term effects of federal policies on pluripotent stem cell research actually are. For our purposes, though, this fascinating case offers a useful window on the role federal funding plays in research collaboration, discovery, learning, and careers. It also puts some flesh on the abstract bones of this chapter's discussion of collaboration networks.

In what follows I draw selectively on the transcripts of interviews with thirty-eight first and last authors from papers reporting research using pluripotent human stem cells. The interviews were conducted by me, by my collaborators Jennifer McCormick and Christopher Thomas Scott, and by their students. They illustrate, in the words of a small number of working scientists, how federal funding plays an essential role in making universities sources.

Policy and Practice in Scientific Research

One of the first and most important things to note about hESC research is the passion with which these researchers approached their topics. Most of the scientists we interviewed described their interests in terms of new and exciting biological knowledge and in terms of the potential for improving life for real patients. This mix of attention to fundamental and practical outcomes of research is characteristic of what policy researcher Donald Stokes called "use-inspired" basic research.[78] Enthusiasm about potential treatments also explains the willingness of corporations, foundations, patient groups, and even the citizens of states such as California to fund hESC research that the federal government would not.

As Dave, an MD/PhD and assistant professor of medicine whose work uses hESCs to study the development of the human heart, reported:

The process of embryo genesis is just fascinating. How you go from one cell to a beating heart, to a living animal is just captivating to scientists and to laymen in general. It's just a remarkable phenomenon. But during my time as a medical student, you couldn't help but start thinking about the applications of the science. It was a specific day. I was in this surgical suite with pediatric cases that have a hypoplastic left heart, where the right side of the heart just hasn't developed and there's only one chamber to do all the work. That morning I was working with embryonic stem cells and how they form in the developing embryo to [make] a normal heart. It was very obvious on that day that if you had a cell you could deliver to this weak heart in this child, then this surgery might be more efficacious in the long term . . . now you can actually think about the possibility of using cells not only development in the embryo, but for repairing tissue in these children.

The line between curiosity-driven laboratory research and clinical application is particularly blurry for Dave, whose training and faculty appointment in a clinical department at a large medical school allow him to move regularly between the lab bench and the bedside. His insight sprang from interactions with different portions of the university knowledge network. Many other stem cell researchers tell similar stories. More importantly for our purposes, combining fundamental research on cells and human development with work to discover effective medical applications often requires collaboration that spans multiple types of expertise. Complex networks are generative.

Another stem cell researcher made just this point in talking about how the patchwork of support for hESC research created by shifting federal and state regulations limits possibilities for productive collaboration.[79] Mike, a senior professor at a private university, told us that regulatory challenges led "many people at many institutions" to "shy away" from hESC research entirely while "at the highest levels of an institution" hESC work "seemed a bit risky too." He went on to explain why this was a problem:

Stem cell biologists, we're pretty good at growing stem cells, but we're not experts in, let's say, heart cells or kidney cells, or pancreas cells.

What we need is the most open possibility [for] experts in various fields, to come together and participate. If we're ever going to succeed [in developing treatments], we need both kinds of people . . . [T]he basic process of science requires that the best and most interested people get together, and if you limit that because some states' legislation bans a certain kind of tool, well, that is going to exclude those very important investigators who just happen to live in that state.

Mike articulates concerns that we found were common among stem cell scientists. In particular, he worries that the restrictions and uncertainties that varied and shifting federal and state regulations impose on the key tools of his research, cell lines, will hamper exactly the kinds of collaborations that make universities sources.

But why would such regulations cause investigators and potentially entire universities to avoid stem cell research? Much of the capacity to do innovative work in this field relies on collaboration, sharing research tools such as reagents and cell lines, and expensive equipment such as confocal microscopes and cell-sorting machines. Restrictions on federal funding for some cell lines make accessing and sharing those resources much more difficult.

In our terms, bans on the use of direct and indirect costs make it impossible for researchers using nonapproved cell lines to access the shared resources, the public goods, that federal funding allows universities to create and sustain for their researchers. In doing so, these restrictions reshaped possibilities for collaboration by forcing researchers to balance scientific and resource concerns in a fashion that is uncommon in any other field. As a new assistant professor put it, "If you wanted to use [nonapproved] cell lines, you had to set up a different lab where all the equipment, all the reagents [and] all the cultures were purchased and supported entirely by non-federal money. I couldn't handle that. So I just totally forgot about [using nonapproved lines.]"

Another senior researcher offered a more detailed discussion of just what these restrictions mean for the day-to-day work of science and institutional requirements for research administration in a phone interview.

I've just turned my chair to look on the shelf where all these little "NP" stickers are all over the bottles—"NP" for Non-Presidential. All of that stuff is privately funded, including having to buy a new centrifuge. I'm looking at one on the bench on the right. It's almost identical to the one on the bench on left, but we had to buy a new one because the one on the left was bought with NIH money.

Such descriptions of sticker systems, duplicate equipment, and segregated workspaces ranging from "NIH-free" rooms to entire buildings constructed for research without federal support were common. At least they were common among scientists at institutions where significant nonfederal funds could be had. Even in such elite locations, the physical segregation of researchers and the additional costs imposed by working with nonapproved lines stand to change the way relevant networks grow and enable innovation.

People working in places without access to such resources simply found their choice of research materials, collaborators, and even careers severely truncated. At the university level, the cost of new facilities and specialized administrative arrangements can combine with the perceived risk of supporting controversial research to make getting new stem cell research programs off the ground a tricky proposition.

This may seem like a small and isolated case. After all, restrictions on cell lines in a single young field seem unlikely to spill out into the university as a whole. That may be true, but the concerns and decisions of hESC researchers demonstrate in microcosm both the tangible and the intangible ways that public support enables work and creates networks and shared resources that make universities a consistent source of new knowledge and skills. They thus provide a sense of what might happen to the networks that make universities sources if public funding were diminished, constrained, or removed.

How do the kinds of concerns that were raised by the mostly established researchers quoted in this chapter play out at the lab bench and in the career choices of young scientists? To answer that question, I turn to an interview I did with a woman named Caitlin.

When we spoke, Caitlin was an advanced graduate student at a university with significant resources to support work on nonapproved stem cell lines. As a neuroscientist she was fascinated by the process by which neurons develop and by the possibilities stem-cell-based therapies might open for treating spinal cord and traumatic brain injuries. She had just published a paper that demonstrated a new method for using embryonic stem cells to test the role certain genes play in the development of neurons.

Her future seemed bright and she was starting to think about the next stages of her career. In neuroscience, that most likely meant an extended period as a postdoc. Caitlin told me a little about her goals: "One of my aspirations is in working . . . for the military because what keeps me really excited about my work is the benefit. I think it would be great to use the skills that I have to benefit the military. . . I mean they're risking their lives every day to give me my freedom so I can do what I can do." Her prospects, though, were complicated by the cell line she chose to work with.

Caitlin and her advisor chose to use an embryonic stem cell line called HUES 9. That line is one of a large group derived with private funding in the Harvard University laboratories of a high-profile stem cell scientist named Douglas Melton. Because the lines were created after the Bush administration executive order, they were not eligible for federal funding. I asked Caitlin why she chose HUES 9.

> Well, we thought once Bush was gone it [federal funding for the HUES lines] was not going to be an issue anymore. We were drawn to the HUES series of lines for strictly scientific reasons. There are multiple HUES lines. They've been adapted to enzymatic passaging,[80] which makes it much easier to work with them. At the time, if [the cells] were not adapted to enzymatic passaging, you had to do manual passaging. That is very time consuming. Also, the experiment I was doing [required] that you get single cells. Without enzymatic passaging, that's nearly impossible. So, the ability to get single cells was something that really drew us to the HUES lines. We chose the HUES 9 line, specifically because [others] have looked at the different lines to see [what happens] if you just put them in some basic differentiation media without any morphogens to try and pattern them.[81] The HUES 9 line wants to become neurons.

This response is interesting because of its infusion of politics into what is otherwise a purely scientific rationale for Caitlin's choice of cell line. It also highlights a few key features of stem cell research that are characteristic of the kinds of difficult, uncertain work that leads to proof. Culturing, maintaining, and patterning stem cells can be a challenging and technically demanding process. Working with cell lines requires a lot of care and attention. Researchers we spoke to often attribute personalities to their lines, likening them to pets or, ironically, children. One feature of these personalities looms large in Caitlin's decision. For reasons that are not fully understood, different lines "want" to become different types of tissue. This means that the best cell line for a given job may not be one that is approved for funding.

Cell line idiosyncrasies also mean that laboratory protocols are rarely one-size-fits-all. Much experimentation is necessary to allow a particular line to be used for a specific purpose. In Caitlin's case, years of effort went into the "simple" task of learning to work with HUES 9 to prove her early insights.

That investment of time and energy may not transfer directly to another cell line, so she viewed the possibility of having to change cell lines with significant unease. This was exactly the challenge she faced after the NIH's implementation of Obama's 2009 executive order loosening restrictions on federal funding. Caitlin and her advisor bet that HUES 9, the line most scientifically suited to their chosen problem, would be made eligible for federal support. But that turned out to be only partially true. After an extensive review of the line's derivation, the NIH determined that the informed-consent documents associated with HUES 9 were written in a fashion that only gave consent for its use in studies pertaining to diabetes. As a result, research that used HUES 9 to create pancreas cells was ruled eligible for federal funding, but patterning the same line to make other types of cells was not.[82]

For Caitlin the excitement that accompanied Obama's executive order was followed by a "horrible time" after NIH review made it clear that her research using HUES 9 to study neurons would likely never be eligible for federal grants.

> When Obama won the election, I was very excited . . . because I thought, "Oh my gosh, my work's going to be so much easier." I have to be concerned about everything. I have to make sure the things I order are ordered with non-federal money. I have to make sure the equipment I'm using was purchased with non-federal money. I can only be paid with non-federal money. We have a microscopy facility, they have amazing microscopes but it's all federal money, so it was hands off. Then, all of a sudden, all these things were open to me, and then they were gone again.

This change in fortunes also led Caitlin to be concerned about her career prospects. Because she had invested a great deal of time and effort in developing a new tool using HUES 9, inability to use federal funds severely limited possibilities for her to continue her work in another location.

I do not know if she was ever offered the position she hoped for in the federal government. If she had been, she would have had to begin her work all over again with a different hESC line. The same would be true if she came to work in a university that had not invested in the parallel infrastructure necessary to support work without federal funding. If, as she reported telling her advisor, "I am not doing that again with another line," then the NIH's decision, while correct, truncated her job prospects. Caitlin is now working for a major corporation in a role that does not include hESC research.

The case of human embryonic stem cells can offer many lessons to students of science and science policy. For us, the shifting regulations and bans on funding highlight the complicated ways that direct and indirect costs from federal grants support the growth of networks on and across university campuses. The stem cell scientists we've heard from all emphasize different ways that removing or limiting federal funding stands to damage them. Limiting opportunities for collaboration, creating barriers for proof and the application of knowledge, imposing extra costs and frictions on laboratory work, and shifting the calculus of young researchers as they pick problems and pursue careers all stand to change the structure and composition of university knowledge networks.

Even in places where substantial nonfederal funds are available for research, the need to use them exclusively without allowing any commingling of direct or indirect costs subtly shifts the ways networks involving stem cell scientists grow. This suggests two immediate implications of reduced or restricted funding. First, hESC researchers who cannot use federal funds are often, like Caitlin, faced with limited access to shared resources such as those found in microscopy facilities. This can make their work harder and create significant waste. Common equipment creates opportunities for interactions that span relatively distant parts of knowledge, institutional, and organizational space. Thus, restrictions like these may also truncate networks that may be useful for developing new insights.

Second, because work with non-approved hESC lines is often sequestered in separate rooms or buildings, the integrating effects of overlapping physical space are also likely to be limited. This may not do much harm in the proof-of-concept stage of innovation, but it certainly has the potential to limit new collaborations and serendipitous discoveries. These dangers may be particularly acute to the extent that Mike is correct and the application of hESC-based discoveries requires significant input from non-stem-cell biologists whose participation in relevant networks increases the complexity of collaboration structures.

Moreover, existing collaboration networks are a scaffold that shapes future connections. As a result, short-term interruptions or restrictions on funding can have lasting effects if they remove key individuals from networks, or even if they limit possibilities for the kinds of bridging connections that underpin brokerage.

Federal—or, more accurately, public—support for research is essential to universities' ability to serve as a source. It allows work to be pursued with some stability at a scale that enables long chains of indirect ties to form, creating complex, diverse, and balanced networks. Facilities and administration funds are important because they help universities sustain common resources that make scientific work easier and more efficient. Shared resources also provide locations for key types of network connections to form.

4 COMMUNITY ANCHORS
Building Resilience and Connection

IN ADDITION TO BEING SOURCES, universities are anchors. The metaphor suggests three things. First, whether they attach a boat to the seafloor or a bookshelf to the wall, anchors help hold things in place. Well-anchored things can better weather storms or earthquakes. They are less likely to drift or fall. Thinking of universities in these terms suggests that they steady the things they are connected to. Scientific fields, industries, regions, communities, or other social and economic systems are more resilient when they include and rely on universities.

This is particularly apparent in terms of geography. Universities tend to stay put and to strongly associate themselves with their locations. Practically speaking, their massive and often specialized physical infrastructure holds them in place.[1] Tradition, history, and the legacy of state and local origins also result in strong associations between universities and their places. Think about how many institutions, both public and private, are named for their city or state. Universities make significant investments in their regions because their ability to draw students and faculty to their campuses depends on their environment as well as their own attractions. Their presence, their work, and their people shape the places where they are located.[2]

The effects universities exert on their regions are most obvious when they are the primary anchor. While they might be harder to see on the street, universities' influence on the larger and more diverse economies of cities are still empirically clear, though they are hardest to pinpoint in the largest metropolitan areas.[3] For instance, a recent Brookings Institution report found that on average, the hundred largest cities in the nation receive half a billion dollars in university research funds from the federal government. In some cities federal R&D investments can represent a significant portion of the metro area's gross domestic product.[4]

Second, universities are anchors in the sense used by marketing researchers. Think of a shopping mall. The anchor tenants of the mall are the large stores that typically can be found at the ends. Anchor tenants set the tone for the mall by drawing foot traffic. Their presence helps determine what other tenants occupy the mall, the rents mall owners can charge, and how well tenant businesses do. When an anchor tenant departs a mall, rental rates decline by about 25 percent and storefronts stay empty.[5]

Anchor tenants are so important to the profitability of malls that developers significantly discount their rent in order to attract them. "By generating mall traffic, anchors create external economies by indirectly increasing sales and/or reducing promotion and other costs of a host of smaller mall stores."[6] More simply, small stores in malls have to spend a lot less on advertising to attract customers if a larger store brings lots of people to the location who might be inclined to browse and buy their wares. The result is that they can sell more of their products while incurring fewer costs. But those benefits require some alignment between the kinds of customers anchors attract and those that other mall tenants need. In this fashion, the anchors also shape the kinds of goods and services offered in their malls.

Economists and others have imported the anchor tenant idea into the study of high-technology industries, demonstrating that universities and their research are strongly associated with nearby industrial research.[7] They also note that large firms can play the same role. Economic geographers have advanced the argument, emphasizing the particular types of externalities anchors create as they "attract skilled labor pools, specialized intermediate industries, and provide knowledge spillovers that benefit new technology-intensive firms in an industry."[8]

Universities play a particular role in the early stages of an industry's development. Their work helps to shape the technical character of the industries they support[9] while imprinting the collaborative and product development strategies of companies in their regions.[10]

Universities are anchors in this sense because of the positive externalities their work creates. That means thinking about the things universities produce, their work as sources. It also requires us to consider the things their work attracts to them. Finally, we need to examine how their institutional and organizational arrangements lead them to behave in unique ways.

Which brings us to the third and most abstract way to think about universities as anchors. University anchors do more than passively create externalities by acting in their own interests. Their public mission and commitment to openness also allow them to convene groups and organizations with multiple and sometimes competing interests. Their stability can allow them to take a long view of their missions and their regions. More importantly, their unique features mean they can bring together many constituencies without needing to control or hoard the results of collective work. Decentralization, concern for the general welfare, and at least some insulation from immediate market pressures allows universities to play distinct and important roles. They anchor larger networks.

Sociologist Walter Powell and his collaborators make this point explicitly in a recent study of the genesis of regional clusters in biotechnology. In addition to providing the kinds of externalities that help get new industries off the ground, universities are like trellises that help networks linking regional players to grow. This view of universities encompasses active matchmaking, but it depends on the distinct institutional features of universities that make them a commons. Their work as sources aids in both by creating shared benefits in the form of accessible knowledge and skilled people.

"The anchor tenant is not disinterested, in the sense of being neutral, but it neither directly competes with nor dictates to the other organizations that inhabit the community." Being interested in collective outcomes without being controlling is the key difference between academic and, for instance, corporate anchors. "When central organizations insist that others play by their rules and do not engage in collective problem solving they become '800 pound gorillas' rather than anchors."[11] When we widen our lens to think about the role universities play in national and global networks, we will see that many features that help them be anchors also help make them hubs.

The features of universities that are difficult to square with narrow conceptions of efficient production and near-term return on investment prove essential to anchoring. Universities are best suited to convene and contribute to collective work without needing to control it when they foreground their various academic missions rather than trying to adapt themselves to other modes of work. It is not too circular to say that universities contribute to the communities they participate in precisely by being and acting like universities.

Stable, Public Organizations

What does it mean to say universities should act like universities? First and foremost, understanding university anchors requires that we pay special attention to what it means to say that universities are stable and that they are public. Even private nonprofit universities, in this view, are public institutions because of their missions, their history, and their deep reliance on subsidies (such as those conferred by nonprofit status) and investments (such as those made through federal R&D support or student financial aid) from the public.

Stability implies more than simply being inured to change and hard to kill. It also suggests a kind of adaptability. The seeming contradiction between being conservative and being adaptable that animated Chapter 2 is one more place where puzzling features of university organization can result in good outcomes. More abstractly, stability suggests a strong connection to the past, in the form of tradition, coupled with persistent efforts to engage the needs of the present while imagining and working to shape the future.

Saying universities are public organizations has a few additional implications. Some can be extracted from the requirements for nonprofit

(501[c][3]) status in the United States.[12] First, a nonprofit must be organized and operated for a "charitable purpose." The advancement of education and science offers a justification for tax exemption for most universities. Second, the earnings of a nonprofit must not be used for private benefit. When nonprofit universities attract donations, or tuition, or research grants, or royalty payments, the money they bring in must be used to support their mission and not to enrich shareholders or other owners as would be the case with a for-profit.[13]

The investments that flow into universities can be more fully distributed across the economy and society than they might be in organizations seeking to expand their margins. This is one of the general roles nonprofits play in a mixed economy.[14] Finally, the assets of a nonprofit must be "permanently dedicated" to its charitable purpose.[15]

Think about what these formal requirements suggest about how universities should act. Their focus should be the public good. Money that flows into them is disbursed for that purpose. Absent a profit motive, any efficiencies they realize in operations simply allow more of their revenues to be turned to public benefit. Finally their assets, both financial endowments and the kinds of capital investments instantiated in buildings, grounds, collections, and large-scale equipment, permanently serve their public purpose.

What this all means is that when universities engage with other organizations and groups, when they invest in their campuses and their locations, when their leaders choose how to pursue their interests locally and globally, they do so with the goal of forwarding their knowledge mission for the general welfare. There are certainly private benefits too.

Students gain skills and knowledge they can parlay into more lucrative careers and better lives. Corporate partners gain access to discoveries and talent they develop in pursuit of profit. Individual researchers gain reputations and knowledge that make them more marketable and accelerate their careers. Particular universities become more competitive in their pursuit of the best students and faculty. But the fact that universities generate private returns does not mean we should lose sight of their public benefits. Their knowledge mission and institutional commitments are what allow them to serve as anchors.

Universities are not neutral. They have real interests and pursue them pragmatically and competitively. But their public nature means they should, or at least can, be open and responsive to the concerns of many types of partners. They are inclined to act in a fashion that does not require them to control the outcomes of collective efforts. Stable public institutions make a particularly valuable type of anchor. To see how, we should start with the simplest sense of the term, bearing in mind the more complicated and abstract notions. That simple view starts with the campus itself and emphasizes both longevity and fixity in place.

The Campus Itself

The land and buildings that make up a campus are a major university asset. The physical plant of a university is also one of the key means for the institution to acknowledge (or create) history and tradition. In *The American College Town*, geographer Blake Gumprecht cites then Princeton University president Woodrow Wilson to explain the University of Oklahoma's choice of Collegiate Gothic as a unifying architectural theme: "As Woodrow Wilson noted in making a similar decision at Princeton, Gothic forms 'added a thousand years' to the school's history."[16] In Princeton, New Jersey, or Norman, Oklahoma, architecture that evokes Greek antiquity and campus organization that points to great American and European institutions creates a sense of continuity with the past even as much of the work of campus is oriented toward the future.

Gumprecht uses the University of Oklahoma to answer key questions about the physical campuses of U.S. universities: "Why . . . should the campus be a public space, a meeting ground, and a cultural center for the college town?"[17] The answer speaks directly to some of the ways that universities serve as anchors. One response to the question is competition. A beautiful campus with programs (such as athletics, performances, and museum exhibits) that serve the public and alumni as well as current students helps to sell the campus to its publics and aids in increasingly cutthroat competition for students and faculty.[18]

Campuses maintain classrooms and performance spaces, football teams, and FMRI machines not just because their missions encompass teaching and research, but also because the public-facing aspects of their physical plants and endeavors make them more of a commons for their communities. Lovely physical settings with plenty to attract the people who will do the university's knowledge work as well as the public helps make these institutions the defining feature of the towns they occupy.

Unlike the University of Oklahoma and Norman, the campuses of urban universities like Columbia or NYU are only a small part of the pastiche that is New York City. Nevertheless, urban campuses can serve important purposes, as Jane Jacobs notes in her classic *The Death and Life of Great American Cities*. Jacobs distinguishes metaphorically between boundaries, such as the edges of campuses, that serve as barriers and those that function as "seams"—"lines of exchange along which two areas are sewn together." She goes on to note that universities could serve important roles for their cities by mindfully making their campuses more seamlike. This would, she thought, require placing "their uses intended for the public at strategic points on their perimeters," and opening up "as scenes their elements congenial to public view and public interest." The challenge of this, for Jacobs, is for urban universities to give "thought or imagination to the unique establishments they are" and stop pretending to be cloisters or office buildings.[19] In other words, taking the physical manifestations of their anchor role seriously. Urban campus anchors may do less to define their locales than they do to integrate them.

Understood purely as teaching facilities, universities could be arranged like large suburban high schools. Conceived as research organizations, they might reasonably be arranged like office parks.[20] But college buildings need to look like college buildings. The visual signals draw on and reference long-standing academic traditions. They also create and sustain communities of students and alumni connected to the institution by links of affinity and nostalgia. As Dan Chambliss notes in a study of selective colleges, present-day instantiations of very old institutions often have little in common with their historical incarnations except their locations and well-preserved physical plants: "Old buildings and nostalgically beloved settings make colleges locationally conservative in a way that very few businesses are anymore."[21] Like colleges, universities are fixed in place, bound to their locations by investments that simultaneously enable specialized work, engage their neighbors and communities, and align both with long traditions.

The result of all this is an institution whose mission and livelihood depends very strongly on its association with a place. The financial costs of picking up and moving a major university would be extraordinary. In reputational terms they might be simply unfathomable. Try, for instance, imagining a Yale University somewhere other than New Haven, or a University of Alabama relocated to Wyoming. Being fixed in place is the first condition for serving as an anchor. Now try to imagine a New Haven no longer home to Yale or a Tuscaloosa without its university. That thought suggests how research universities shape their places.

The investments universities make in their locations can be large, sustained, and multidimensional. They can also meet with resistance from local communities.[22] Town-and-gown relationships are often far from smooth. Regardless, university interactions with their cities, towns, and states can represent an important part of what makes them anchors.

Yale, New Haven, and Biotechnology

In the late 1980s and early 1990s, New Haven, Connecticut, and its most well-known organization, Yale University, had serious image problems. Poverty, crime, and associated social problems were on the rise, contributing to a sense of crisis that led some to characterize the city as a "war zone"[23] while others suggested that "the wheels were coming off" at Yale.[24]

The challenges facing the city and those facing the institution were intertwined. Economic geographer Shiri Bresnitz highlights just how in an analysis of Yale's role in the development of a cluster of biotechnology firms in the city and its environs.[25] New Haven is home to one of the nation's oldest and most highly regarded research universities as well as six other institutions of higher education. But both the city and the state of Connecticut lagged far behind their neighbors in high-technology economic development.

In 1993, New Haven had just 6 biotechnology companies, far fewer than nearby Boston's 129. By 2013 the region was home to 70 firms in the industry, growth that Bresnitz attributes to changes in the university's "policy, organization, and culture."[26] Yale also played a "pivotal role of leadership and organization" in a coalition that included municipal and state government as well as local industry.[27] This is an example of how a major research university acts as an anchor in all three of the senses we are considering. Think about how Yale's fortunes, its constituents, and its region depended on its reliance on and contribution to its location.[28]

Much of the work Bresnitz describes happened under the leadership of Richard Levin, who took over the presidency of Yale in 1993. In a 2013 interview Levin elaborated the problems and some of the reasons Yale needed to respond. He noted that his speech accepting the presidency "enunciated the importance of local development" as a means to emphasize that problems in the university's home city were problems for Yale "in the sense that our position in attracting faculty and students had begun to drop, with people citing the environment as a reason for declining offers of jobs or admission."[29] Attending to its location was straightforwardly in Yale's interests.

Some of the changes Yale made, such as fundamentally reorganizing its technology transfer efforts, were designed to help its world-class biomedical researchers feed local and national industry. They aimed at improving Yale's ability to be a particular type of source. Other shifts may seem more surprising until we view the university as an anchor.

Despite an operating deficit of nearly $15 million in 1993, the university invested $2 million in a project to add streetlights and other safety features to its campus. Some initiatives focused on the university's role as a landlord, where investments in its downtown properties helped create "a mix of local and national businesses and national chains" that "transformed the area into a vibrant shopping area and late-night gathering spot."[30] Still other initiatives in partnership with the city were designed to increase rates of homeownership by providing support to employees looking to purchase houses in New Haven and contributing to local public schools.[31] This kind of local investment is not without challenges, as recent conflicts over Yale's tax-exempt status in New Haven and concerns about the effects of gentrification and rising prices on the local community demonstrate.[32]

In a 2003 speech, Levin presented a comprehensive summary of the joint work done by New Haven and Yale. The speech describes the importance of open dialogue and taking a long view of productive partnerships. He talked about encouraging and supporting student volunteerism and baking community outreach into the jobs of faculty and staff administrators, as well as programs designed to strengthen neighborhoods, improve the city's image, foster economic development, and increase the safety and vitality of the city's downtown.

Levin concluded on a valedictory note:

> Universities are uniquely poised to strengthen urban America. As large employers seeking to attract students and faculty from afar, we have compelling practical reasons to do so. But our efforts also flow naturally from our mission and purpose. On our campuses we are devoted to the full development of human potential, and we provide extraordinary resources to facilitate such development in our students and faculty. Outside our walls, many of our neighbors lack the opportunity to flourish. To the extent that we can help those without privilege access such opportunity, we will help to insure the health of our democracy. Our responsibility transcends pragmatism. We must help our cities become what we aspire to be on our campuses—a place where human potential can be fully realized.[33]

Note the quick transition from the university's immediate practical interests in recruiting students and faculty to the institution's larger mission and purpose. That mission is framed in the kind of collective terms that were characteristic of early statements about the role that higher-education institutions play in democracy. Here too, a prominent university effort that reaches beyond the classroom and the laboratory is framed in terms of creating and sustaining public goods for the general welfare.[34]

The fact that this effort unfolded on multiple dimensions over a relatively long time period emphasizes the importance of stability. Moreover, the language Levin used wedded university work to the development of human potential not just for the people that pass through its campuses but also for the communities it serves. Finally, the case of Yale and New Haven suggests ways that universities can add directly to regional resilience and capacity.

Setting the Tone

Academic knowledge work produces externalities that help define the character of the areas where universities are located. Research universities draw people and resources to them as they pursue their knowledge mission. One obvious example is the seasonal influx of undergraduates. Another is the national and international recruitment of graduate students, trainees, and faculty. The work these people do and the lives they lead while doing it create indirect effects that can positively influence outcomes for others in the community.

I opened this chapter by likening universities to the large stores in shopping malls. The analogy is a good one, though imperfect. It is imperfect because large department stores create a pretty simple set of externalities that benefit other stores in the mall. They draw shoppers. The tastes and budgets of shoppers that come to a mall's department stores bear heavily on smaller occupants' possibilities for success. In this way anchor tenants set the tone. The students that come to university towns are, for many of the businesses in those towns, a direct analogue to the customers drawn to malls by anchor tenants.

Unlike retailers, universities do lots of different types of work with and for lots of different constituencies. As a result, understanding their role as anchor tenants requires that we think hard about the externalities their work creates. Consider research grants. Those grants allow faculty to hire the people and buy the stuff necessary to do research. Indirect costs on those grants allow universities to support part of the facilities and administrative needs that research work entails. The goods and services that university researchers purchase and the salaries their grants pay both contribute to local and national economies as vendors see increases in revenue that support their own growth and as employees go about their lives, buying houses, raising children, and participating in their communities.

To the extent that research and education draw people to a campus who wouldn't otherwise come to its location, universities are acting precisely like the anchor tenants of shopping malls. Unlike shopping, undergraduate and graduate education improve the skills and capabilities of students, making them better contributors to society and better hires for potential employees. When these students stay and work in the areas where they are were trained, the result is a deep pool of human potential. A skilled workforce is one of the key externalities that economists and economic geographers identify as a factor in regional growth.[35] This is why so many universities partner with their cities and states to develop programs designed to keep more of their graduates close.[36]

By extension, when the work of universities draws revenue to the campus, the fact that those monies flow directly into mission-related work means that these investments too can contribute to the local economy. New research provides some evidence that the stable research work of large universities can draw suppliers to locate near them, bolstering regions.[37] University research expenditures pump significant revenue into businesses in the institutions' home counties and states.[38] A substantial portion of even the most scientifically trained doctoral students get their first jobs near the universities that trained them.[39] "Stimulus" spending for R&D under the American Recovery and Reinvestment Act was much more likely to go to counties with a major university, where every $1 million of investment created as many as twenty-seven jobs.[40] These effects happen with and help expand the well-known "knowledge spillovers" of university research.[41]

If we knit these threads together, we see several ways that universities help set the tone for their regions. Beyond the direct investments they can make in their locations, universities create greater certainty for businesses that supply them and depend on people they draw to the area. This is another function of stability. Greater certainty about funding helps attract and support businesses whose livelihoods depend less on the patronage of students than on the specialized purchasing needs of researchers, hospitals, and other parts of a major research campus. Procurement relationships can even increase the ability of vendors to pursue their own innovations.[42]

This is all fine and good to say. But many types of public and private investments can have anchoring effects. Large corporations do some of the same things universities do (though usually without the teaching component). Casinos, professional sporting venues, and hunting and fishing opportunities draw people to regions and those flows have some of the same effects on local businesses as flows of students to universities. Public prisons reside in fairly stable and specialized facilities, depend on more or less certain sources of public funds, and thus might add similar sorts of resilience to their regions.

It is unreasonable to argue that universities do good things by serving as anchors relative to fallow fields or burning piles of cash. If public funds weren't invested in university research, the money wouldn't disappear. Instead it would be repurposed. Even large public investments in, just for instance, building giant walls in relatively isolated places would have some of the kinds of economic stimulus effects I have described here. Thus, capturing the tone-setting nature of university-generated regional externalities requires a new approach to research and data that emphasizes not just the work done on campus but also the kinds of local communities, businesses, and activities that work enables. It's beyond the scope of what we can do here, but any such effort should make use of information that allows comparison to other types of anchors.

Such an effort must also account for the distinctive missions of universities, which create many different avenues for them to serve as anchors. New evidence about the community and economic benefits of arts and education and production at universities and colleges suggests that this kind of thinking should be sensitive to the many different ways—social, political, cultural, and economic—that universities anchor their communities.[43] Such a view also points out that beneficial flows of people and ideas run in both directions.

Major research universities are, in the words of economic geographer Richard Florida, "a key—if not the key—to the Creative Economy."

But "a university cannot do it alone." "The surrounding community must also have the capacity to exploit the innovation and technologies that the university produces, and the will to put in place the broader lifestyle amenities and qualities of place" that highly trained and creative people seek.[44] In order to better understand how universities in places like Boston, San Francisco, New York, and even New Haven help make this work more likely, we have to shift our attention to the third way in which universities are anchors.

Convening and Connecting

The simple fact that a major university exists in a place that has the ability to absorb and expand on its products is not enough to guarantee the next Silicon Valley. Recent work suggests that how a university behaves is essential.[45] A campus's ability and willingness to act as a network anchor by pursuing its interests collaboratively and helping partners develop independent capabilities is essential. Universities contribute to their communities by serving as anchors that help local networks grow among many other types of organizations.

Some of these kinds of work are on display in the contributions that extension services make to state and regional agriculture[46] or that universities make to the general zeitgeist of their regions.[47] A recent analysis of one interesting case provides a compelling example that brings science, agriculture, and the cultural characteristics of a location together. Cracking into it, though, requires that we step back to 1976 and across the Atlantic to Paris.

UC Davis and Napa Valley

On a sunny day in late May 1976,[48] nine French wine experts gathered in the Paris InterContinental hotel for a blind wine tasting. The competition pitted some of the most well-known French labels against "upstart" wines made with the same grapes in California. Two flights of wines, one Chardonnay, the other Cabernet Sauvignon, were tasted in what journalist George Taber called a "non-event" because "clearly France would win."[49] As it turned out, to the glee of the American press and of California winemakers and to the shock of their French competitors, bottles from the Napa Valley took the laurels in both categories.

The result was dramatic for California and Napa. The victories helped spark dramatic growth in the region's wineries, production, and prices.[50] Warren Winiarski, the winemaker behind the Stags Leap Wine Cellars Cabernet that won the red wine tasting, characterized it as "a Copernican moment. Nothing was the same after that. We looked at what we could do with different eyes."[51] Speaking of different eyes, how did we get to a Parisian wine tasting? The story of Napa Valley up to and after the Paris tasting is inextricably linked with that of the University of California, Davis.[52]

As historian James Lapsley and economist Daniel Sumner tell the tale, UC Davis and Napa are symbiotic. Their interdependence highlights how universities contribute to their regions and how regions shape their anchors.[53] The latter is as important to us as the former because it demonstrates that being a well-connected anchor enables universities to expand their work by being clearinghouses for knowledge and for problems.

Of course the university did not create the possibility for great wine to be grown in its region. Soil, geography, and climate did that, along with the famously entrepreneurial and experimental spirit of winemakers who sought elusive quality above narrow economic returns.[54] But as Richard Florida suggested earlier, those features may not have been sufficient without the addition of UC Davis, a campus that boasts one of the best research, graduate, and undergraduate programs in viticulture and enology in the world.

It's also difficult to imagine a truly world-class program of grape and wine research and teaching someplace where few grapes grow and little wine is made. Napa Valley is clearly a generative home for an institution that, among other things, pursues the development, transmission, and application of knowledge about wine. About 98 percent of the region's half-a-billion-dollars-a-year agricultural revenue was derived from wine grape sales in 2011. In the same year sales of Napa wine topped $4.4 billion and wine tourism brought another billion or so dollars to the region.[55]

The University of California was chartered as a land-grant institution that now includes ten campuses. The Davis campus alone invested nearly three quarters of a billion dollars in research in 2015. Most of the knowledge work that it does and the research networks it sustains with that money are not directly relevant to winemaking. Public data don't allow us to zoom in to the level of a particular program or department, but Davis researchers pursued sponsored projects from all sources in agricultural fields to the tune of just over $137 million while maintaining substantial teaching and research interests across a broad range of fields.[56]

The amount of money a university invests in research is less important than the work it does with that money and the ways that work sustains relationships on and off campus. What is often most important is the sometimes surprising mix of disciplines and fields that researchers on a campus can bring to bear to identify and solve problems both academic and practical.

An article in *Nature* by Davis authors suggests the many domains of research implicated in the business of wine. Marketing, engineering and operations, social and behavioral science, the genetics of taste and smell, biochemistry, sustainable agriculture, medical and nutritional research, and more directly relevant questions about budwood, rootstock, pest and virus reduction, grape cultivation, fermentation, and a host of other topics pertinent to the making of fine (and even not so fine) wines are at play.[57]

Lapsley and Sumner identify four essential ways that Davis contributes to Napa's growth and regional character. Research is just one. The other three are teaching, vinicultural extension, and professional continuing education.[58] In other words, the relationships and activities that allowed Napa and Davis to co-evolve into wine powerhouses engage all the aspects of the knowledge mission, many different fields of study and teaching, and a set of ongoing relationships that reach beyond the campus to engage with local, national, and international partners.[59]

The story stretches back at least to Prohibition. So I'll stick to some highlights. First, Davis is a source. The fact that Napa Valley growers emphasize Cabernet Sauvignon and Chardonnay at all comes down to its 1950s-era research and extension work. Just ten years before the Paris tasting, the varieties that put Napa wines in the competition were "rarities." Cabernet was the fourth most important red variety grown in Napa in 1966. Chardonnay was the sixth most common white grape.[60]

Lapsley and Sumner make a compelling direct connection between Davis and Winiarski's award-winning Stag's Leap Wine Cellars Cabernet. The advice of a Napa Farm Advisor and Davis viticulture graduate whose brother was a professor in the program led to Winiarski's decision to plant Cabernet. Even more telling, the budwood he used was a virus-free variant developed through Davis research. He obtained it from Martha's Vineyard, which had originally sourced it from the university's Oakville Research Station.[61]

Both the raw materials (grapes) and the processes that transformed them into beautiful wine bear the indelible mark of Davis research, extension, and teaching. A scion of one of the region's most well-known wine families, Peter Mondavi, described the early years of Napa winemaking as "taming the wild west." He said that Napa pioneers were "learning and self taught. Europe had generations of tradition, but we were just beginning. We needed an institution like Davis to aggregate information."[62] Note the subtle distinction here between understanding the university as a knowledge producer and thinking of it as an aggregator of information shared across a network of cooperating rivals.[63]

One way that happened was through teaching. Another was faculty and student participation in routine gatherings of winemakers such as the Napa Valley Wine Technical Group, where "ideas that once would have been considered 'trade secrets' were openly shared, as winemakers and owners realized that everyone benefited from the enhanced regional reputation associated with higher-quality wines."[64]

Like the networks on campus that allow both research findings and dead ends to be broadly shared, gatherings such as these enabled both problems and solutions to flow from vineyards and wineries to the university and back again. Finally, experimental vineyards maintained by Davis, short continuing-education courses for professionals and novices alike, and the extension work of the Oakville Research Station provide further examples of UC Davis's multifaceted role as a convener and channel for relevant knowledge, people, skills, and materials.

The larger lesson for us is that many aspects of the university's knowledge mission made it a network anchor for this thriving regional industry, and they cannot be untangled. The Napa-Davis example is not unique. In a very different industry, human therapeutic and diagnostic biotechnology, university anchors play many of the same roles and imprint the networks they help anchor with similar commitments to openness and cooperation. When networks among titular competitors flow through universities, they serve more as open channels than as closed conduits.[65]

In Napa, in biotechnology and elsewhere, the university supplies knowledge and well-educated people while partners help identify problems and, in some cases, provide funding and other support to help get them solved. As John Hennessy, the past president of Stanford, told me in an interview many years ago, such collaborations are valuable for the university because of just these kinds of information flows:

> More important than diverse sources of funding are the various kinds of industrial support you couldn't buy for any amount of money that you could afford to pay. . . for us that has meant getting companies in the region to contribute various types of expertise and to give us information about things which help us build a research program we otherwise couldn't build.

University anchors serve their own interests while their work can come to bear the imprint of key partnerships. Much like Yale's engagement with New Haven, UC Davis's role in Napa shapes the university too. That happens in much the fashion that Hennessey describes as Napa winemakers contribute funds, expertise, materials, and even labor to relevant knowledge work at the university.

These connections also contribute to the diversity of the U.S. research enterprise and its ability to generate robust, multiple responses to problems. Different institutions exist in disparate places and engage with varied mixes of communities and partners. There is a real risk that industrial and other partnerships will capture our universities. Moves to narrow their focus, streamline their missions, and emphasize the research and the teaching we know are relevant now only exacerbate that danger.

Napa also illustrates how broad education that reaches beyond the narrow technical needs of local industry is important. The ongoing relationship between wineries and UC Davis wine programs improves teaching and learning and tunes students' skills to current industrial needs. That's good for students in that it makes them more saleable and increases their ability to get the kinds of jobs they might want in the industry. Indeed, "UC Davis graduates dominate wine production in the Napa Valley and have for at least a generation."[66]

But to simply imagine that specific technical skills harmonized to current human resource needs are what employers in this industry really want misses the point. John Williams, the founder of Napa's Frog's Leap winery and a graduate of Davis's master's program, explains that the kinds of education provided by Davis go much further. "It is the role of the university not just to train people to be competent technicians—and, after all, when stripped of its romance, winemaking is really a branch of food processing—but to be critical thinkers."[67]

Other prominent winemakers expand on the sentiment. Tim Mondavi notes that "the most important thing that Davis brought to the California industry was instilling curiosity in its students."[68] Still more Napa luminaries highlighted the way that a broad education that reaches beyond current technical needs fosters the ability to take creative risks and push the edge of their field. Williams again noted that a Davis education taught his employees to "communicate and advance knowledge."[69]

Davis made many contributions to Napa and arguably received as much or more in return. But note a few key features of the story that pertain to a university's anchor role. Davis has been an important presence in the valley since at least Prohibition, so long in fact that its students represent several generations of industry leadership. Some of the results of its research have been part of the taken-for-granted endowments of Napa. When problems, such as the devastating phylloxera[70] outbreak of the 1980s, arise, the university can be part of the solution.[71]

Many talented winemakers and potential winemakers would come to the Napa Valley were Davis not located there, but the draw of the university is a powerful addition. Its long role in the region and the industry did much to help set the valley's tone. Some of the most important ways that happened are evidenced in the third sense of the anchor metaphor. By serving as a convener and an aggregator of knowledge developed outside its borders, the university helped to foster and sustain the particular experimental and collaborative form of information sharing that helps to make Napa Valley and its wine distinctive.

This work is no doubt helped by the agricultural extension component that is a traditional part of the land-grant university mission. UC Davis was a better anchor for the Napa Valley by virtue of its world-class role as a relevant source. But the symbiosis between the region, the industry, and the university was expanded by the fact that part of the university's mission was to give away the products of its knowledge, essentially for free, to relevant producers in its state.

The university's multiple missions, range of research and teaching, commitment to place, and openness were all essential. The fact that its work engaged directly with immediate and practical needs of partners while not losing sight of larger educational concerns or limiting the horizons of its research all contributed to its ability to serve as an anchor. And Davis is not unique. Other U.S. universities are constructive institutional citizens of their regions too. I don't know of others that play this kind of role in winemaking. But we wouldn't expect many to.

Universities act as anchors for many different sectors and industries. That is part of the strength of the academic research enterprise that they also anchor. Indeed, when we broaden our lens to think beyond single industries and particular places, it becomes clear that many of the same things that make universities generative sources and stable anchors also make them hubs that knit together national and international communities spanning places and concerns.

5 HUBS LINKING COMMUNITIES
Generating Solutions for Known and Unknown Problems

ALL THIS WORK BRINGS US to our last metaphor for understanding what research universities do. Universities are hubs that draw far-flung parts of the world closer together, facilitating the movement of ideas and people. In so doing they become central locations that can serve as a clearinghouse and aggregator for knowledge, problems, and skills from all over.

When university hubs are also good sources, they will have the absorptive capacity to allow them not only to warehouse information but also to combine it with existing knowledge to create new things that support social benefit and economic growth.[1] The key to research universities' ability to serve as a consistent, robust source of responses to as yet unknown problems is the access to information that their "hubness" enables coupled with the generative possibilities inherent in their organization, institutions, and, especially, networks.

The word *hub* evokes two things: wheels and airports. The hub of a wheel is its center, the piece to which all other parts connect. It is also, quite critically, the point at which the wheel connects to a larger system. On a bike, a car, or a wagon the hub is the point of contact between the wheel and the frame or axle. It's also the piece whose particular connection enables the whole to move. Universities are a point of contact between many different parts of society that helps the whole to move forward.

The second sense of the metaphor aligns very nicely with the network sensibility that has infused the whole of this book. Universities are hubs in the same way that some airports, such as Atlanta's Hartsfield-Jackson International Airport, are hubs. Hubs are airports where one or more major airlines concentrate their business. The result of this concentration is that it is often necessary for a traveler to pass through a hub on the way to a final destination.

Hub airports are recognizable to many travelers even if they never stay in the hub city for business or pleasure. Hub airports connect lots of places. For instance, Atlanta, the largest U.S. hub, has flights that offer passenger service to more than 150 U.S. destinations and cities in fifty other countries. More than 275,000 people pass through the airport each day on some 2,500 flights.[2] While it's safe to assume that many travelers arrive to spend time in and around Atlanta, I suspect that most keep going right through to somewhere else without ever leaving the airport.

Universities are also hubs in that they attract large flows of people from locations around the nation and the world. For most they are a temporary stopping point rather than a final destination. The movements of people and knowledge to, through, and from universities connect them to a broad range of locations in the economy and civil society. As a result, universities, like hub airports, are central organizations that serve as network shortcuts between otherwise distant places.

The hub-and-spoke system of airports is intensely designed and competitive.[3] Like airports, universities help people and the knowledge they carry move between many origins and destinations. But, as we saw in Chapter 2, they are not really designed for efficiency. Instead, their decentralized organization and pluralist institutional arrangements make it difficult if not impossible for a single purpose, stakeholder, or approach to dominate. This is part of their strength, as it helps ensure both their reach and their openness by making it difficult for any one constituency or interest to turn them into a fortress.

Unlike airline hubs, universities have evolved to do many things and to facilitate many types of movement. The people and things that pass through universities are often improved by virtue of their time there. I spend a lot of time on the road and I cannot say the same thing of my days in airports. As a result we must expand the hub analogy to fit major research universities.

This is where the more abstract institutional and organizational features of universities become important again. Yes, connections forged by the movements of ideas and people link universities to many different partners, making them central players in a network involving organizations from multiple sectors and industries. But those connections are enabled by the university's institutional pluralism. Universities are places that can serve as a shortcut between, for instance, high-technology firms and arts organizations or K–12 schools and professional sports, to say nothing of fields of inquiry and areas of knowledge.

Put more simply, the campus of a major research university is only one step away from pretty much any other part of our economy and society.[4] This means that universities are uniquely suited to attract knowledge and problems, to facilitate or impede the movement of people and ideas, and to innovate as a result of both. When they work as hubs, universities can serve as brokers in the same sense, and with some of the same implications, as the researchers who span otherwise unconnected parts of networks.

Universities are obligatory passage points and credentialing machines for people seeking a middle-class life and for those who hope to practice in an established profession.[5] Whether you are talking about medicine, law, social work, education, public health, nursing, or architecture, universities are a necessary stop for aspiring professionals. As a result, the knowledge they produce and the degrees they certify make them key features of professions themselves.[6]

Universities share something else in common with large airports. When they shut down or close themselves off, information and people have a much harder time getting where they need to go. This means that changes or difficulties that strike campuses are likely to be felt more broadly and more quickly than those that strike other types of organizations. For this reason, we should be careful about how we propose to alter these institutions and about the ways we might implement changes.

Being a hub also means that the work of campuses and their constituent parts are more likely to be politicized or attacked, which can make taking care difficult. This is the case because being a hub means their work is visible to and touches on lots of competing interests. It's also true because there is much at stake for many different constituencies in how they do their work. Universities benefit from being hubs. We are all strengthened when they do it well. But the visibility and importance of university hubs makes them vulnerable too.

Seeing Hubs Clearly

The problem with this abstract way of thinking about universities is that it's hard to see clearly. In a little while I'll describe a single case that highlights some of what I mean when I say that universities are hubs. But that case doesn't do justice to the breadth of what I mean by the term. The problem, really, is that the data necessary to systematically document how universities are hubs do not yet exist.[7]

As was the case with understanding universities as sources, part of what's important is realizing that campuses differ in the types of partners they connect to and the ways they connect with them. These differences contribute to making the system as a whole more effective. It's not the case that all universities span all aspects of society. Instead, the system of research universities serves this purpose. It is more effective because of the variation apparent across specific campuses.

So, what would count as evidence that universities are hubs? Answering that question requires a little more work to specify the key characteristics of a hub. It's not enough to simply have lots of connections. Many types of organizations, including hub airports, do that. The key to how universities act as hubs is to emphasize not just connections but also the ways they are created and their implications for individual campuses and the system of universities.

The connections we are interested in are created by flows of people and ideas that result from universities' pursuit of their knowledge mission. The movement of both disembodied and tacit knowledge is the proximate source of application and impact. Those movements along with the diversity of sources and destinations, the tendency of people affiliated with universities to return, and the institutional openness that helps them be good anchors are what make a university into a hub.

This is not to say that universities are the only potential hubs in contemporary society. Some large firms, for instance, serve as a kind of crossroads for their industries.[8] For entrepreneurial and high-tech communities, incubators such as Y Combinator may play some of these roles. Law firms and venture capitalists also do some of this work.[9] Management and design consulting companies may be especially likely to be hubs, as they often have engagements with clients in many different industries.[10] But even a successful product design firm such as IDEO works across a small range of fields and industries relative to a major university.[11] Regardless, a large part of what makes these firms consistent innovators in product design is precisely their central, brokering location at the intersection of multiple industries.[12] The same is true on a larger scale with universities.

Much of what makes a university a unique hub is its educational work. Students—undergraduate, graduate, and professional—are a key path for knowledge to leave and return to the university. Their movements as they pursue careers make these institutions much more central players in larger interorganizational networks than even the more codified forms of knowledge research also produces. Universities are hubs because they produce knowledge and they produce people, together, in a huge range of fields. Even more important, they have significant incentives to let both go and to do what they can to facilitate their landing and success in other locales. By virtue of nonprofit status and public investments, they can pursue interests other than increasing their margins. It's absurd to imagine universities asking their students to sign noncompete agreements. The same cannot be said of businesses.

Networks, Institutions, and Hubs

Networks work the way they do because indirect connections link each node to many others. Expanding this logic to encompass a network sense of what it means to be a hub is pretty straightforward. Hubs are things that shorten the indirect paths between many different partners. They do this by being a broker that connects lots of otherwise unconnected or loosely connected organizations.

If we add to that the idea that organizations are particularly hublike when the partners they connect are different in character, we see the intersection between a purely network story and a more institutional approach. Of course, the way a hub organization acts and its internal organization is also essential. An organization that occupies the kind of network position and institutional location that could make it a hub will only actually be one if it acts as a network anchor to facilitate the movement of ideas and people among its partners. It might benefit individually and in the nearer term by acting like an eight-hundred-pound gorilla, but to do so would sacrifice many longer-term possibilities.

Finally, what makes universities very distinctive hubs is the range of their activities and missions. It's entirely possible for a research university to find itself on more than one side of the same problem or approaching the same topic from multiple angles. This is a strength because it minimizes the dominance of single approaches to problems on campus and because it positions universities to act as anchors and hubs. The components of the knowledge mission—improvement, discovery, transmission, and application—all contribute to the kinds of connections that make universities hubs. We'll return more explicitly to talking about students, the transmission of knowledge, and its application as people leave the institution, but for now consider one quadrant of university research (science and engineering) and one topic, collaboration.

Research Collaborations

Collaboration has become more prevalent across all fields of research, but the shift toward large, diverse teams is particularly pronounced in the science and engineering fields.[13] As sociologist Erin Leahey notes in a recent literature review: "The trend toward team science is robust and undisputed: it does not depend on the data source or measure."[14] Across all fields, research is becoming "bigger." For our purposes right now, two trends are interesting. Research teams increasingly span multiple universities,[15] and they more often involve researchers from many different types of organizations (government, industry, nonprofit, university).[16]

Let's look at some data presented in the 2016 issue of *Science and Engineering Indicators*, a report on the state of U.S. research produced every other year by the NSF. The data reported here are at a relatively high level of aggregation, but they provide some important insights into patterns of collaboration apparent in science and engineering (S&E) publications.[17]

The amount of published research coming out of U.S. organizations has grown pretty dramatically in the thirteen years (2000–2013) represented in these data. That time frame saw a more than 77 percent increase in total S&E publications, with the bulk of the growth coming from academic researchers. The challenges of inferring information about the research process from just one of its primary outputs means this is a bit of an ambivalent fact. It could mean that U.S. research is more productive; it could also suggest that the average publication is getting less rich in the sense that it covers less empirical or theoretical terrain. The latter could be a result, for instance, of increasing pressure to produce a high volume of publications. In practice, both things are probably happening and as a result, counting publications should be taken as just one indicator of what's going on in research.

With that disclaimer in place, academic authors produced the lion's share of papers in both 2000 (70.1 percent) and in 2013 (74.2 percent), a proportional difference that is statistically significant. Co-authorship became even more important in these fields. In 2000, about 63 percent of S&E publications were co-authored; by 2013, that number was north of 77 percent, more than three of every four articles. Collaborations that span multiple organizations and multiple sectors are also important and on the rise. Here we find telling evidence of one way that research universities, the primary sources of published discoveries, are also hubs.

Science and Engineering Indicators presents information on several different "sectors" that produce S&E research. In addition to academia, they include publications with authors employed in the federal government (for instance, intramural researchers at agencies such as the NIH, the Census Bureau, the Environmental Protection Agency [EPA], or the Department of Energy), industry (for instance, publications that come from researchers employed at companies like Genentech or Facebook), private nonprofits (such as freestanding research institutes like the Salk Foundation), and state or local governments. When we speak about the growth in multisector collaboration, what we are talking about is papers that report on research discoveries made by teams of researchers who work at more than one of these different kinds of institutions.

If we play out our metaphor, that means the ideas and resources necessary to successful (in this case published) research in many different sectors flows through research universities. It also means those universities have both the technical and the institutional resources necessary to understand, translate, and apply them. Thus, the work of academic researchers positions universities at the center of a network of collaborations that spans the many sectors involved in research. That's exactly what we see. In 2000, academic researchers produced about 52 percent of their co-authored publications with researchers in other U.S. sectors. By 2013, that number was 53.7 percent. If we look out from the university toward other research organizations, we see that about half of the discoveries that result in publications rely on people working in other kinds of organizations.

A tour of the view from those other sectors, though, demonstrates that universities are the essential partners for every other type of organization performing research.[18] Researchers in the federal government published about forty-eight thousand papers in 2013 (7.2 percent of the total). Just under 70 percent of those papers were co-authored with partners in another sector. More than 89 percent of those (about 60 percent of all federal government papers) involved a university co-author. That number is not out of line with the rates in other sectors. Industrial scientists who publish author about 87 percent of their multisector papers with academe. For private nonprofits, the number is 94 percent. Regardless of where a researcher is doing publishable science and engineering work, the likelihood of their collaborating with an academic partner is high.

It has also grown over time. Academic co-authors have become more important to the system and, on this measure at least, universities are becoming more important hubs. As a result, information and techniques developed pretty much anywhere in the U.S. research system have a good chance of flowing to universities and through them to other sectors. But, concretely, how does that look? One interesting case requires that we turn our attention to Utah.

The Race for BRCA1

In 1990, a geneticist at Berkeley named Mary-Claire King led a team that published a paper that identified the general area where a gene linked to breast cancer susceptibility, which she called BRCA1, was located.[19] The seven authors on this paper were affiliated with Berkeley. In the terms we used earlier, this would be a co-authored paper that involved a single organization and one sector, academia. The publication of that paper sparked a "fervid race" to be the first to identify and sequence BRCA1.[20]

The competition involved several international and intersector collaborations. In 1994, one of them won, publishing a paper in *Science* that isolated the gene.[21] That team was led by Mark Skolnick, at the time a professor of medical informatics at the University of Utah. Skolnick was also the founder of a biotechnology company named Myriad Genetics. The forty-five authors on that paper were affiliated with the University of Utah, Myriad, a North Carolina–based laboratory run by the NIH, and with Eli Lilly, a large pharmaceutical firm. In the terms we used earlier, this paper is a multisectoral collaboration that included government, academia, and industry.[22]

That's all fine and good, but what does it tell us about the idea that universities are hubs? Several things. Some are obvious in the author list and the paper itself. Others require a little more digging. Those point to the need to reach beyond bibliometric information to include the movements of people, business deals involving intellectual property, and even broader institutional features of research universities in our discussion.

There are many reasons why collaborations like this one get so large and span so many organizations. Collaborations grow like this because they require more resources (or more types of resources) than can be brought together under a single roof[23] and because the speed with which scientific knowledge expands increasingly requires teams of highly specialized researchers.[24] In some fields, such as gravity wave physics or global climate change, the scale of the phenomena themselves make it all but impossible to do effective research in a single location or organization.[25] In other fields, like bioinformatics, the range of resources and skills necessary requires a substantial team of specialized experts.

The work Skolnick and his colleagues did depends on the ability to collect, analyze, and integrate lots of different types of evidence. Establishing the potential location of a gene is most often accomplished by appeal to detailed genealogical and epidemiological information about large extended families. By looking at familial relationships and incidence of particular diseases (say breast cancer), researchers can infer things about the genetic sources of disease.[26] But taking the next step also requires access to biological samples from members of the families and the ability to use those samples to amplify and sequence particular strands of DNA.

Doing this kind of research requires, at a minimum, access to detailed genealogical data for large families with particular cancers; accurate epidemiological data about family members' illnesses; blood and tissue samples from family members; the computing capacity to analyze large-scale bioinformatic data; the "wet lab" capabilities and tools necessary to store, process, and work with those biological samples; and the skills to do all parts of the project and integrate them into a set of knowledge claims that will stand up to significant skepticism and efforts at replication. No one person can do all that. Indeed few single organizations have all the necessary capabilities. This is especially true because the necessary research infrastructure can take decades to develop. Universities are among the few, which may help account for their centrality in these kinds of collaboration networks.

The University of Utah[27] proved an important hub for this work for several reasons. Utah was the first university to found a department of biomedical informatics, in 1964.[28] Equally important, the University of Utah had access to an essential resource for this kind of study, the extensive genealogical database maintained by the Mormon church. Turning that trove of genealogical data on a "founder" population of great importance[29] into a research resource was part of the work Skolnick started upon his arrival at the University of Utah in the early 1970s.

Skolnick notes that BRCA1 was the culmination of nearly thirty years of his work. That work began when he was an undergraduate studying economic demography at Berkeley's Institute for Population and Urban Research and Department of Economics.[30] Undergraduate study led him to realize that "demographic research could be successfully merged with genetic research through the study of individuals in multi-generational families."[31] Here we see an instance where early education in a field a far removed from an investigator's eventual area of research exerts a significant and perhaps surprising influence on an important, controversial, valuable, and high-profile discovery.

During graduate training in genetics, Skolnick worked on techniques to collect, computerize, and analyze genealogical records. Grad school also brought him into contact with representatives from the Mormon church who were collecting genealogical records in Parma, Italy, where Skolnick was doing some of his dissertation research. That meeting led Skolnick to "put a check in the back of my mind that Utah was where my career was taking me."[32] He made good on the promise to himself by visiting in 1973. There he was excited to learn about the Church of Jesus Christ of Latter-Day Saints' genealogical database and about the state of Utah's extensive cancer registry, which collected information about almost every incidence of cancer in the state.

The Utah Cancer Registry was founded by a physician at the Latter-Day Saints Hospital in Salt Lake City in 1966. It is currently housed at the University of Utah.[33] Skolnick "made a proposal that was audacious at the time: reconstruct the entire Utah Mormon Genealogy . . . and link the genealogy to the Utah Cancer Registry, which had a record for every cancer statewide for the current generation."[34] The result of that early work still exists. It is called the Utah Population Database and is still housed at the University of Utah.[35] It was the source of some of the data that helped researchers identify and understand the "cancer families" that are so important to this kind of genetic research.

But even the amount of work necessary to bring together academic research with church genealogical records and state medical registry records wasn't enough. Recall that biological samples from members of the relevant families were necessary to go from insights about the hereditary aspects of particular cancers to knowledge about particular genes and mutations. As Donna Shattuck, one of the leaders of the Myriad Genetics part of the collaboration, notes: "one of the keys to . . . characterizing BRCA1 was the large, well documented, and highly informative collection of family pedigrees (Breast and Ovarian cancer kindreds) . . . and the numerous DNA samples obtained from many members of these kindreds."[36]

Collecting those DNA samples required an entirely different type of infrastructure, a clinic. The University of Utah founded a familial cancer screening clinic, which over the course of several decades and at the cost of more than "100 person years" collected tens of thousands of genetic samples from cancer "kindreds" in the Utah Population Database.[37] Using a major research university as a platform, Skolnick and his colleagues managed, over nearly thirty years, to assemble the "technological, informatics, and pedigree" innovations that set the stage for successful identification of BRCA1.[38] Doing this required the integration of multiple different fields (genetics, demography, medicine, informatics) and resources derived from the work of a major religious organization, a state medical registry, and thousands of individual Utahans across a long time period. This disparate set of requirements highlights just the kind of things that a research university, conceptualized as source, anchor, and particularly hub, can assemble.

When King's group announced the general location of BRCA1 in 1990, another essential piece of the puzzle was still missing in Utah. Skolnick's team at the university lacked the scale to be truly competitive in applying the complicated molecular and genetic "wet lab" techniques necessary to identify the gene. Facing a relative lack of NIH funding, at least in relation to one of his primary competitors, Francis Collins,[39] Skolnick took the then-still-unusual step of founding a company as a means to accelerate his group's efforts to discover BRCA1.

Skolnick partnered with Walter Gilbert, a Nobel laureate and founder of Biogen, one of the first generation of biotechnology firms, after starting Myriad Genetics in 1991. The company was founded with initial investments from a venture capital company and an established pharmaceutical firm, Eli Lilly. Myriad began in Salt Lake City, which Gilbert called "the place" to go after the most important genes. One outcome of all the work on bioinformatics in Utah was to make the university a network anchor for an important biomedical cluster.[40]

The move to found Myriad was important for our story because it allowed Skolnick's team to mobilize a large amount of money from private sources to support research and eventual commercialization of the resulting discoveries.[41] As Skolnick himself put it:

> All the technological, informatics, and pedigree innovations we had made were in danger of dying on the vine for lack of funding. Fortunately, I did not wait for NIH funding. I was acutely aware of the diagnostic importance of BRCA1. I was also aware that many other important discoveries had failed to benefit society due to the lack of an interested corporate party. I decided to create a company, Myriad Genetics, to allow our group to couple adequate molecular resources with our exceptional family data to permit us to discover BRCA1 and ensure the public would benefit from our discovery. I am most proud of this strategy, perhaps my most important innovation.[42]

Skolnick describes founding a corporation as an innovative strategy for winning a complicated and highly competitive academic race. The movement of people, ideas, and resources from the university to the firm and back (recall that Skolnick lists his affiliations as both Myriad and the University of Utah in the key 1994 paper) are framed as essential to both discovery and eventual public benefit.

Focusing in on Skolnick himself offers some insights into how research universities can act as hubs and how their faculty are the key employees that make much of their knowledge work possible. Skolnick is what sociologist Walter Powell has called an "amphibious" entrepreneur.[43] Powell and his co-author, Kurt Sandholtz, were interested in explaining how human therapeutic and diagnostic biotechnology firms came to have the characteristics they do.

Their answer hinges on the combination of different approaches to organizing science, business, and finance, drawn from academia, the corporate world, and private equity. The key organizational innovation of biotechnology, in this view, is the integration of what might have been uncomfortable bedfellows, a largely academic approach to science with the milestone-driven financial model of venture capital funding.

It is in this sense that early entrepreneurs needed to be "amphibious," in that they "occupied positions of influence in disparate social worlds." Thus they carried "practices and assumptions across domains."[44] Skolnick's argument that Myriad was a fundamental innovation points to this kind of thinking. This innovation too is a form of recombination that arises from the university while both depending on and deepening that institution's role as a hub. It is no surprise that people capable of working at a high level in different institutional domains emerge from universities. The fact that our campuses are hubs increases the likelihood that such movements and the associated transpositions of knowledge can happen.

I've cast Skolnick as the hero of this tale, but the larger point is that others can (and do) undertake the same type of work. In this case, we could tell a similar story about either Mary-Claire King at Berkeley, or Francis Collins, the second director of the Human Genome Project and current NIH director, who at the time was leading another team in pursuit of BRCA1. These are clearly the elite of the elite among geneticists. Most professors and researchers will never achieve the same kind of visibility and success. Though stories like these are rare, they are not anomalies. One thing that research universities do is support the kinds of careers that can help generate new discoveries and innovations.

Every field has equivalents to Collins, Skolnick, and King. But what it means to be at the top of a particular field, and the ways in which that requires leading researchers to become amphibious, can vary dramatically. A prominent academic novelist, playwright, or composer, for instance, must also work across and exert influence in multiple worlds, but the worlds are different and probably won't include biotechnology. The same is true of academic engineers, political scientists, social workers, and architects.

A too-little recognized part of the university knowledge mission is the transitions many successful researchers make across different fields of training and work as their education and careers progress. Those travels generally also cross many different institutions. Part of what universities do is provide platforms for varied kinds of careers, which increasingly span multiple sectors and organizations. Universities are good at that in part because they are hubs. At the same time those careers and their outcomes, individually and collectively, reinforce and expand the ability of the institution to be a source, an anchor, and especially a hub.

These kinds of collaborations and the movement of people back and forth across sectors and industries are one key way that we can understand the network view of universities as hubs. The University of Utah's capability to bring together not only industrial partners but also a religious institution, a federal research institute, state clinical resources, and ordinary citizens speaks to the more institutional view of the university as a hub.

Universities and High-Tech Industry—Movement of Ideas and People

Step back from the details of BRCA1, the University of Utah, and Mark Skolnick for a moment and think about the larger ways that the story of this collaboration could be taken to suggest network questions about how universities act as hubs that connect multiple industries. There are at least two key points here. First, universities collaborate with industrial partners in research. Second, they produce things (mostly knowledge and people but also resources such as cancer pedigrees and genetic data) that provide inputs to corporate efforts. Connections created by the movements of people and knowledge, as well as active collaborations, position universities in the center of high-technology industries.

One way to see how this happens draws on a project I began back in the early 2000s that was designed to understand just how networks connecting many different kinds of organizations drove the dynamics and success of research-intensive industries.[45] To do this work, a large group of students helped me extract data about the kinds of relationships that firms in five high-technology sectors build as they transition from private to public corporations via IPOs. The data I report on in this section come from SEC filings.[46]

We were particularly interested in two types of connections that linked research-intensive firms to each other and to other companies, universities, financiers, and other organizations. First we tracked what we called "formal ties," contractual relationships that governed the flows of both tangible and intangible resources among organizations. Of particular interest to me were agreements between universities and high-tech companies governing the use of intellectual property and joint research efforts. The licensing deal between Stanford and Google that transferred rights to PageRank that we considered in Chapter 1 is an example of the former. The contract that likely governed collaboration between Myriad Genetics and the University of Utah would be an example of the latter. In the terms we have been using, these are indications of the movement of knowledge between firms and universities that are important enough for the firms to formalize and report to shareholders and regulators.

In addition to formal connections, we tracked what we called "informal ties." These links connected organizations through the movements of people without contractually committing them to any kind of mutual work. While a formal tie connected Google and Stanford, an informal tie of this sort linked Google and the University of Michigan. Larry Page, one of Google's founders, is a Michigan alum who returned to the campus in 2009 to give the university's commencement address. In that speech, he highlighted some of the ways that his undergraduate education prepared him to pursue his graduate research at Stanford and eventually his work at Google.[47]

While the fact that someone is an alumnus of a particular university does not in any way obligate them or their current organization to the university, the presence of these "informal" connections suggests (1) how firms and other organizations depend on the educational work of universities and (2) how information and resources might flow between the organizations through the movements of people. More concretely, it's not unreasonable to think that Page might have spoken with Michigan's then president, Mary Sue Coleman, or with other administrators and researchers on campus about matters of mutual interest during his visit. That's why these network connections are informal. They capture some sense of the flows of tacit knowledge and the kinds of personal affinities that help make universities into hubs. In our terms, informal ties capture the movement of people back and forth between universities and the top of high-technology companies.[48]

What's interesting for us is the role that research universities play in these industries. Companies in every industry rely on the same set of campuses. In other words, research universities are network hubs for technology sectors because they contribute to and thus provide shortcuts between companies working in different fields. The kind of story that I told about the University of Utah and BRCA1 is confined neither to single areas of research, such as genetics, nor to a particular university.

How does that look in practice? We examined the formal and informal network connections linking IPO firms in these five industries to the 110 U.S. universities that had ever been among the top 100 recipients of federal R&D funding.[49] First, let's start with some generalities. In raw terms, 122 of the firms we studied (almost one in five, 18 percent) have a formal contract with a U.S. research university that governs access to intellectual property or the details of joint research. That number varies dramatically across sectors, ranging from just 3 percent of semiconductor and computer hardware firms to nearly 50 percent of drug development and analytic service firms. The research universities we were interested in represent 22 percent of the campuses that have ties to these firms, but they account for nearly 61 percent of the connections.

The fact that industries vary in their direct reliance on university research is nothing new.[50] Nor is the finding that biotech and drug development is among the most closely tied to academe while semiconductors are among the least.[51] What is interesting here is the fact that the most research-intensive universities are formally connected to the cutting edge of multiple industries. Those connections help make them hubs and overwhelmingly result from their work as relevant sources.

The data I'm presenting here represent one of the most restrictive views of the contribution universities make to various industries that it's possible to develop. In order for a connection to register, it must formally link a university to a company. That company must be successful enough to pursue a public offering of stock *and* the agreement must be of enough material importance to the company for it to be reported to a key federal regulator. These restrictions mean we are sure to dramatically underestimate how the university knowledge mission informs industrial work. Nevertheless, just under half (47.2 percent) of the U.S. research universities that we studied in this project have formal ties to firms in two or more industries.

Put more simply, these institutions serve as hubs linking some the highest-growth technology companies in multiple sectors. To be sure, other types of organizations, most notably law and venture capital firms, play a similar connecting role across multiple high-tech industries. The spanning connections created by investors and lawyers have been shown to help determine which geographic regions are home to successful multi-industry clusters.[52] But these small professional firms lack many of the features that make universities particularly impressive and important hubs.

Consider education. Our picture becomes even more clear when we think about connections created by the movements of people. Recall that we're defining informal ties strictly by looking at the reported affiliations of corporate executives and directors in these firms. Here too, the bar for finding a connection is high. But one of the most important channels for transfer of knowledge and information between universities and corporations is hiring.[53] Once again, attending to students and the learning dimension of the knowledge mission is essential to understanding how, precisely, universities are positioned to be hubs.

The 684 companies we studied reported biographical information about slightly fewer than four thousand executives and directors. Of those, 43 percent reported having at least one degree from a research university. Again that number varied from industry to industry. About

38 percent of executives and directors in software and information firms, which are famous routes to success for technically skilled entrepreneurs who may not have completed an advanced degree,[54] report affiliations with research universities. In drug development that number is 55 percent.

As you might expect, a much broader range of educational institutions from around the world "send" leaders to the successful high-technology firms we studied. For instance, the California State University System and Santa Clara University are both important players in the informal tie network but not in the formal tie network.[55] All of the 110 research universities that were part of this study have informal connections into these industries. Fully 75 percent of them are sources of both people and knowledge as evidenced by formal ties. They account for slightly more than 55 percent of all the affiliations reported by technology firm executives and directors despite the fact that they are only about 10 percent of the universities and colleges we observe. When viewed as sources of people, research universities appear much more hublike.

More than 96 percent (106) of these research universities have informal ties with high-tech firms in two or more of the sectors we studied. Sixty-five percent (72) of them have alumni at the highest echelons of newly public companies in all five sectors. This is precisely the kind of thing that I mean when I say that the movements of people to, from, and through the campuses of research universities make them hubs in a network sense of the term.

The Institutional Pluralism of Hubs

At this point you may be a bit uncomfortable that I'm talking solely about universities serving as hubs linking different industries. That's an important role, which helps these public institutions contribute in a variety of ways to the global innovation system, but it misses universities' connections to important parts of our society that are not as market driven. Data to support this view are a bit harder to come by, but consider a broader view of what it means to be a hub that takes a wider range of institutional domains into account. The best way to see this is to think about students and the educational aspects of the university knowledge mission.

Part of what makes U.S. research universities distinctive is the combination of research and education in a wide range of arts and sciences fields as well as in the "practical arts." In other words, the movements of students out of the university and into careers position these research institutions as hubs that connect not only different types of businesses but also many public, nonprofit, professional, and social organizations and domains. The range of fields that are the subject of research and teaching on the campus of a research university help ensure that an exceptionally broad range of these kinds of "informal" connections are possible. Think for a moment about two domains you might not immediately put together: the military and the judiciary.

How does the education component of a research university's knowledge mission put it "one step" away from the military? Simple. Most research university campuses are also home to a Reserve Officers' Training Corps (ROTC) program. ROTC is a major source of commissioned officers in all the branches of the U.S. military.

Consider the 115 universities with a Carnegie Classification that indicates the highest research intensity in 2015. According to IPEDS data, nearly 95 percent (109) of them have at least one ROTC program. More than half (51 percent, 59) of them are home to ROTC programs for every service branch.[56] While I cannot determine how many active-duty officers passed through these particular research universities, 37.1 percent of the 2015 officer corps received their commission through the ROTC.[57] In other words, college and university training programs outside the service academies account for a plurality of the commissioned officers in the active-duty military. Most research universities are home to at least one such program. It seems safe to say that one thing that these institutions do is help educate and prepare a significant number of military officers.

Another thing they do is train lawyers. Returning to IPEDS data, we find that 74 of the 115 most research-intensive universities (64.3 percent) report students enrolled in JD or LL.B. programs.[58] All told, 47,763 law students were enrolled on these campuses in the 2014–2015 school year. When these students graduate and move on to legal or related careers, they connect their campus to that profession in much the same way that ROTC alumni link their campuses to the military.

Presidents George W. Bush and Barack Obama successfully appointed 618 federal judges to the bench during their combined four terms in office.[59] Those 618 judges received their law degrees from 149 universities. About 47 percent of those (70) were among the 115 most research-intensive Carnegie institutions in IPEDS. Those 70 universities granted law degrees to nearly three quarters (73.6 percent, 455) of the federal judges appointed by Presidents Bush and Obama. In other words, a substantial majority of federal judges appointed by the last two presidents received their legal education on the campuses of research universities.

Pause for a moment to think about what these two small examples mean for how we should think and talk about these campuses. I am not suggesting that the fact that significant numbers of future military officers and future federal judges both attend school on research campuses means that they know each other. Universities are machines for creating and sustaining network connections among people. Those connections are driven at least partially by shared coursework and other activities.[60] But it would be absurd to argue that any particular pair of people who happened to share the campus of a major university for a few years might have a relationship.

While some certainly do, the larger point of this institutional view is not about concrete network ties but about the particular way that research universities create shortcuts between far-flung parts of society. That ability depends both on being able to "send" people and ideas to many different places and on being able to collect and work with information that returns through those connections. Put more concretely, it's difficult to imagine an organization other than a major research university that simultaneously spans multiple technology industries, the judiciary, and the military. Moreover, that's just a small part of the picture.

The benefit of being the center of a Venn diagram for many, if not all, of our society's most important institutional domains is that it creates the conditions necessary for universities to be fertile sources of knowledge as well as training grounds and homes to amphibious entrepreneurs. As we saw in Chapter 3, the conditions for consistent discovery include pluralistic institutional arrangements shot through with balanced networks populated by diverse people and lacking a clear commitment to a single orthodoxy or status quo. Being an institutional and network hub expands all the features that make universities effective sources.

Being this kind of hub is also what makes universities complicated organizations that are targets for many external interests. Sitting at the intersection of some of the most important arenas in economic and social life embroils them in conflicts that reach far beyond the narrow technical details of their missions. This kind of position also makes their shortcomings even more important. This is part of what it means to be a truly public institution, but it is also a reason why being conservative and stable is useful. The institutional pluralism that makes research universities into such important hubs also helps explain some of the complicated internal organization we addressed in Chapter 2.

As sociologists Matthew Kraatz and Emily Block note, pluralist organizations have multiple identities "conferred upon" them "by different segments of [their] . . . environment."[61] Interactions with the military, in other words, are likely to prime the university's identity as a producer of military officers, while interactions with the judiciary do the same for judges, and those with alums from industry highlight contributions to business. All of these things happen all of the time on a large university campus. The various identities are genuine, even and perhaps especially when they are in conflict. The result is, in Clark Kerr's words, an "institution that must, of necessity, be partially at war with itself."[62] It is at war with itself because it is a hub connecting many different interests and activities that are more or less at war with each other. Even in symbolic conflicts, control of the crossroads offers a strategic advantage.

The university's importance is even more vivid when we consider the entire architecture of social and extracurricular activities that characterize student life. I have been talking explicitly about the ways that knowledge work and education make universities into hubs. But think about all the other things that students do during their time on campus. Asking how student life in and out of the classroom makes universities an institutional hub simply expands the domains and the conflicts that have come to be part of a research university's necessary repertoire.

Students on university campuses do much more than simply sit in classes. In addition to developing skills and knowledge through coursework and co-curricular activities, students also gain and lose religious and political convictions, personal habits, career aspirations, friendships, sexual partners and mates, avocations, opportunities for economic mobility, social capital, and even sports allegiances.[63] Much as the fields of knowledge that universities exist to preserve and improve span pretty much every sphere of human existence, the (intentional and unintentional) things that students derive from their time on campus touch on and stand to alter pretty much every aspect of social life: the family, politics, sexuality, religion, and job markets. No wonder, then, that with all these potential issues in play, universities live with internal contradictions and with conflicting pressures from various constituencies. It should also come as no surprise that the process of determining who gains access to our campuses and what happens to them while they are there is often contested.

This is what I mean when I say that major research universities are, at least metaphorically, one step from everywhere. In both network and institutional terms they are a stable point where social and economic worlds overlap, allowing new possibilities for movement and with it for transposition and innovation. This truth is hard to see because it is so large and so diffuse. But it is an essential feature of the university, a key part of the explanation for why they are important, and a reason why they need to be protected. Protection is necessary despite—well, really because of—their contradictions and complications. While all colleges and universities have some of this character, research universities exemplify it precisely because of their combination of all the different aspects of the knowledge mission.

In order to fully nail down some of the features of being a hub that matter for research universities, it's necessary to indulge in a bit of synecdoche. As with any effort to allow a graspable part to stand in for a complicated whole, the choice of topic obscures some things. Most notably absent in the story that follows are the kinds of connections forged by undergraduate education and student life.

Language Acquisition, Retail Space, and "Social TV"

The MIT Media Lab was founded in 1980. It grew from and remains a part of the university's School of Architecture and Planning. The lab exists to "design technologies for people to create a better future."[64] Much has been written and said about the Media Lab; I will do justice to very little of it here.[65] What is of particular importance for us is the Media Lab's funding model, its mode of interacting with external constituents, and the ways in which those interactions reflect larger features of what it means to be a hub.

While I am not suggesting that either the business or the scholarly model of the Media Lab should be broadly adopted by universities, it offers some important insights. First, the funding model, which was developed by the Media Lab's founders Jerome Wiesner, MIT's president and a former presidential science advisor, and Nicholas Negroponte, who was also the group's first director. According to Frank Moss, a past director of the lab, the group's unorthodox business model was to "convince a number of large companies . . . to enter into an unprecedented financial and intellectual collaboration. The companies would fund the operations of the Media Lab in return for an equal, but non-exclusive share in the resulting intellectual property the researchers generated."[66] In other words, companies in a variety of fields bought memberships in the lab in return for rights to use the discoveries it produced. While this kind of setup might reasonably raise questions about the independence of research done in the lab, it points to the fact that what the group produces is valued by a wide range of organizations outside the university *and* to the idea that such partnerships can be a mechanism for problems and ideas from outside the academy to flow to universities and their researchers.[67]

The Media Lab's description of this program itself offers some interesting ways to think about what it means to be a hub. Consider the description from a web page for potential members whose title is "Getting Value."[68] What's interesting about this description is that it reflects aspects of all our metaphors at once. The Media Lab offers value to its members because it is a source: "By pursuing a range of research that no single company could match the Lab provides an abundance of ideas [and] technologies." The list of potential benefits that follows includes recruitment of students, knowledge transfer, and access to intellectual property. This language makes membership a mechanism for organizations from all over the world to form both formal and informal ties with the lab.

The website also makes the Media Lab sound very much like an anchor. The lab can be a "neutral meeting place for cross-company collaborations" and a location to make important "business connections." In other words, it serves as a meeting ground and a broker. Doing so benefits it both financially and, presumably, intellectually.

The fact that its members are drawn from many industries and locations all over the world makes the Media Lab a place where many different threads of concern come together, a hub. A 2016 listing of member organizations highlights just the kind of reach we would expect to see from a hub organization.[69] The list includes nearly 140 members. They come from all over and represent many different industries and sectors. Parts of the federal government (such as the U.S. Army) are represented, as are prominent nonprofit organizations (such as the Bill and Melinda Gates Foundation, the Ford Foundation, and the Burroughs Wellcome Fund). The corporate members come from a truly impressive range of industries including consumer products (Pepsi, Coca-Cola, Unilever, Estée Lauder), retailers (Target, Ikea), design (IDEO), pharmaceutical and biotech (Biogen, MedImmune, Hoffman–La Roche), information (Google, Twitter), semiconductors and hardware (Intel, Cisco, NEC), media (Viacom, Turner Broadcasting, Sony, 21st Century Fox), auto manufacturing (Jaguar, Mercedes-Benz), and consulting (Boston Consulting Group, Tata Consultancy Services). I haven't exhausted the list, but you get the idea. The Media Lab's membership program demonstrates some of what it can mean for a university to be a hub.

One story about research in the Media Lab offers a useful example.[70] In 2007, a faculty member in the Media Lab named Deb Roy was presenting findings from his research on language acquisition at a conference hosted by the lab. Roy was particularly interested in understanding how social interactions and context shaped young children's acquisition of new words, a process he called "word birth." The method he chose to study this process was interesting. He wired up his house and recorded a comprehensive set of interactions between his son and the adults that were part of his life between ages one and three. The resulting "ultra-dense corpus of audio and video recordings of a single child's life" enabled Roy and his team to "measure the child's experience of each word in his vocabulary."[71]

The research mines thousands of hours of recordings of a single kid's life at home to predict when and how the child will acquire new words. This is fairly long-term, fundamental research that doesn't have an obvious or immediate social or economic payoff. It is precisely the kind of work that a well-funded and patient university researcher might undertake in order to understand a phenomenon of interest. The application of this research to a problem from outside the fields it was initially designed to address was supported by serendipity. Lucky accidents were enabled by a combination of the Media Lab's internal (source) networks and external (hub) networks.

The audience at Roy's 2007 talk included representatives of a "global financial services firm" that then director of the Media Lab Frank Moss calls "the bank."[72] The bankers were interested by Roy's talk, but not because they were fascinated by language acquisition in children. Instead, they saw possibilities in applying the immersive recording system, which Roy called the "speechome," and analytic methods he had developed to study how a child learned words to another problem: understanding how customers and employees interacted in the retail space of banks. As Roy noted: "They pour billions of dollars into designing their retail spaces so that they can get their customers to connect better with their associates, but they have no idea if the space is working for them or not."[73] The collaboration between Roy's group and the bank represents an example of a problem (evaluating the effectiveness of different retail spaces) being brought to a hub where a potential solution (the speechome and associated analytic methods) could be found.

The example deepens, however, with the inclusion of another collaborator who found the project through connections to MIT. A high-level representative from Steelcase, a Media Lab member company and producer of office furniture, was talking with a different faculty member about the company's recent research using ethnographic methods to study how people interact at work. The faculty member, recognizing possible connections between Steelcase's interests and those of the bank and Roy's research team, brokered a meeting. The result was a collaboration where the bank wired up a branch office with Roy's speechome technology and Steelcase employees used that branch to test different configurations of their products in the bank's collaborative spaces.[74]

The new collaboration was made possible by networks internal to the Media Lab that allowed Steelcase's original point of contact to recognize their overlapping interest with Roy and broker a connection. For our purposes here, though, the serendipitous possibilities were turbocharged by the fact that the Media Lab's business model makes it a hub that emphasizes free flow and sharing of information. Steelcase and the bank were both present at the lab. Both were engaged with research being done there, and neither they nor the lab itself attempted to control or prevent the formation of collaborations.

The idea that the lab is a "neutral meeting place" and an opportunity for members to make business connections is evidenced here. We cannot know for certain, but it seems likely that if their joint research uncovered interesting and valuable things, the bank might become a major customer of Steelcase. This is a hub acting as broker. Its ability to do so is a function of its ability to be a source.

The story of Deb Roy and the speechome doesn't end here, however. We can project both backward and forward in time from the period between 2007 and 2009 when the collaboration between Roy, Steelcase, and the bank was getting off the ground. When we reach back in time a short distance, we see that in addition to support from the Media Lab and its membership program, the speechome project was supported by NSF graduate fellowships and by a $50,000 grant from the NSF.[75]

That grant, "Regularities in Children's Word Learning Input: 24/7 Observation and Analysis," was funded by the Behavioral and Cognitive Sciences Division of the Social, Behavioral and Economic Sciences Directorate of the NSF. Within those larger units it was funded by programs in linguistics and cognitive development. So part of what happened in the environment of the Media Lab was that a small federal investment in a project designed to enable deep study of a single child's language acquisition became the seed of a corporate collaboration focused on understanding communication in retail organizations.

The same project also became a start-up that was eventually acquired by yet another Media Lab sponsor, Twitter. In a 2011 TED Talk, Deb Roy describes his research into word birth. He also explained how techniques, which he called "wordscapes," used to trace a child's interactions with people and things as they learned new vocabulary became the basis for a new data science start-up. Bluefin Labs used these tools to analyze social media chatter about television shows and ads.

As is often the case, the turn from language acquisition to "social TV analytics" was driven by the work of a student, Michael Fleischman. Fleischman cofounded the new company with Roy.[76] Bluefin Labs also benefited from an NSF Small Business Innovation Research (SBIR) phase 2 grant for nearly $1 million that was made to Fleischman.[77] After receiving several rounds of venture capital funding, Bluefin was acquired by Twitter in early 2013.[78]

The work Roy and his colleagues did follows a particular, and by now I hope explicable, pattern. An early investment in research that was designed to answer one kind of question, in this case about human development, produces findings, tools, and people that move out into other areas, where they are applied for more or less similar purposes and, as a result, have an economic or social impact. In the case of the speechome we see a research question (and an associated grant) that may seem to have limited immediate application get translated into two very different uses. A detailed study of language acquisition for one child sparked projects designed to improve communications at work and in retail banking transactions. It also supported a platform for social media analytics that helps to shape how advertising and television programming is developed and deployed. I find it very interesting that the same set of discoveries can simultaneously represent innovations in human development, retail, and social media. That they did is in part a result of the fact that the research was done in an organization that is a hub.

Neither of these are cures for cancer or a route to world peace, but what I hope you see by now is that they are neither isolated nor inexplicable incidents. We probably couldn't have predicted that when the NSF linguistics program funded Deb Roy's speechome project in 2005, it would result in a successful start-up acquired by a social media giant in 2013 or a partnership between two big corporations in 2009. But what we can now see is that the grant helped support work done in an infrastructure (in this case, MIT's Media Lab) where networks among researchers enabled discoveries, and partnerships between organizations brought new problems to the table. As a result, the ideas and people produced by academic knowledge work flowed out into other sectors of the economy and society.

At the risk of belaboring a point already made too many times, I am not arguing that every university needs to emulate the Media Lab. Nor do I believe that we should expect every project or every faculty member to follow the path that I describe for the speechome and for Deb Roy. I do want to argue that what we are investing in when we put public resources into research universities is not a particular private return (to, say, Michael Fleischman or to Bluefin's investors) but instead a public good. What our public investments support is a system of research universities that are simultaneously sources, anchors, and hubs. The fact that research, education, and application take place in the system created and maintained by federal and other public investments is what makes research universities an essential part of our society.

What this all means is that we must reclaim the broad language of national interests, general welfare, and public goods that characterized the early debates that set today's system in motion. Those rationales have been minimized and obscured in recent decades. That move endangers our research universities and with them the nation.

When we move from the concrete (a particular university, say MIT or the University of Utah) to the more abstract (research universities as a class of organizations), the unique nature of the system that public investments create and maintain becomes even more clear. A small percentage of universities and colleges perform the lion's share of research. They maintain differently organized knowledge and teaching portfolios, which support varied collaboration networks. They interact with different sets of external partners. As a result, each one offers a slightly different set of possibilities for ideas to develop, get combined with other knowledge, and flow out into the larger world.

The system of universities is why we so often see multiple responses to the same emergent problems. It is what we are investing in when we put significant public funds into our universities. That system helps keeps our society poised to respond to the unexpected and develop the currently unknown.

6 FACING THE FUTURE TOGETHER

DESPITE MY ASPIRATION TO SIMPLICITY, the picture of research universities that I have painted over the last five chapters remains complex. That reflects the challenge of offering a clear, realistic description of some of one exceptionally complicated organization's key workings. Research universities can only be fully understood when we look at them in multiple registers and at multiple levels of analysis. Let's step back and try to integrate the different passes we've taken together.

The kinds of organizations that research universities are, their history, and their complications make them unique homes for generative networks. Those networks depend on public support and on shared resources. They are the key to understanding universities as sources. The same organizational factors make it possible for research universities to act as anchors. Being sources and anchors for many different constituents is what makes them absolutely unique hubs.

These modes of action can amplify or interfere with one another in complicated ways. The larger impact that universities have on the general welfare thus depends on their ability and willingness to preserve and expand their unique roles. They sometimes fall short of their promise, but that doesn't mean the promise isn't there. We should be strengthening their capability to act like universities. Instead, I fear we will dilute or destroy it.

Changing the organization of universities—by diminishing the research component of the knowledge mission in search of greater efficiency for education, or by focusing research on particular fields that seem important now, or by sublimating application through public service to application for private return—will dramatically alter university networks.

I am not suggesting a retreat from responsible stewardship of public resources, nor am I arguing for a return to the institution's monastic origins. Indeed, being a hub requires universities themselves to be amphibious: able to effectively pursue their distinctly public interests in multiple social, political, and economic arenas.

State disinvestment in public institutions and new federal moves to drastically cut research funding[1] make all these imperatives more difficult. More importantly, both moves make universities (especially public universities) less able to create and sustain the on-campus public goods that allow different aspects of the knowledge mission to stay complementary. The result will be a downward spiral driven by the need to trade some of their public missions, some of their openness, and even their productive internal complications for the ability to raise the money necessary to stay afloat.[2]

If universities respond by acting more businesslike and seeking to appropriate the greatest rents from their efforts, then they will become less effective anchors. Instead they are likely to be eight-hundred-pound gorillas whose central role in external networks can stifle rather than support collective ends. Limiting the horizons of significance and more tightly policing the borders of the campus makes it less likely that universities can play the role of information aggregator that was so important in, for instance, the case of UC Davis and Napa Valley.

Diminishing both the source and anchor aspects of a university in pursuit of clarity and ease of management and evaluation also makes our campuses less able to be hubs. As the range of connections that universities make shrink, as campuses close themselves off, and as there are fewer reasons for others to visit, our research institutions become less able to attract, understand, and respond to problems and opportunities that arise outside their walls.

Even if they manage to remain hubs by virtue of the people they teach and the knowledge they produce, shifting the ways universities interact with partners or allowing their internal networks to wither will mean their central positions are less fertile. To the extent that other sectors depend on the things our universities produce, a more barren research university will mean less benefit for all, though the final bill may take quite a long time to come due.

Much of the university's ability to be and to benefit from being a hub is a function of pursuing relationships that serve their interests without being entirely transactional. Relationships with students whose affinity and nostalgia lead them to return as alumni offer one example. Relationships with other organizations and communities that find value in longer-term, "thicker" connections offer another.[3] Positive engagement with municipalities and states that support common interests suggest a third. One key to the research university's contributions is a particular approach to its interactions both internally and externally. Students aren't customers, and corporations, municipal governments, and other organizations aren't clients.

When universities continue to be good sources, their interests and actions allow them to act as anchors and hubs. Doing that lets them help keep our world poised to identify and respond to new challenges and opportunities. The knowledge work that is the research university's hallmark has great value when we need to harness their capabilities to achieve a known end.[4] But their real power lies in creating opportunities we don't currently know exist and in addressing challenges we do not yet know we face.

With tongue only slightly in cheek, one might call this the Rumsfeldian view of the public value of research universities: "there are also unknown unknowns—the ones we don't know we don't know. And if one looks throughout . . . history," these "tend to be the difficult ones."[5] Research universities are a preeminent public means to address unknown unknowns. They do that by filtering, aggregating, and adapting flows of information that reach them because they are hubs. But their ability to be sources means they are not just passive warehouses. Instead they are active contributors capable of bringing to bear a range of capabilities that are combined in no other kind of contemporary organization.

Networks operating at multiple scales can sometimes create new things and the particular kinds of people and organizations necessary to their use. New categories of actors, be they search engine optimization specialists, biotechnology firms, or social movements, are key vectors for innovation and also its result. Universities are, almost by definition, "rich with potential,"[6] but two further steps are needed to capture what it means to say they contribute to the responsiveness of our nation and globe.

First, we need to focus on the characteristics of a rich situation or location. Second, we have to take seriously the idea that the mechanism by which change occurs is the creation of new types of economic and social actors. Universities and the people they help shape have the potential to recombine what exists into something new and appropriate to current needs. The challenge, of course, is that both the need and the opportunity for such innovative work is rare.

Part of what makes universities generative has to do with intersection of networks and institutions.[7] Sociologists Victoria Johnson and Walter Powell highlight just this combination when they describe some of the preconditions for social and economic poisedness. "Inter-related pathways through social and economic structures afford the opportunity for novelty through unanticipated feedbacks across multiple contexts,"[8] a process aided by the "concatenation of social, economic, and political forces that make new forms possible."[9]

Put more simply, networks that span and integrate lots of different institutional arenas enable the movement and application of ideas in unexpected ways. Feedback across different uses can amplify the effects and the reach of an innovation as we saw with the speechome. Many threads of concern converge in stable research institutions. They sustain internal capabilities necessary to innovate. They manifest institutional tendencies toward openness and information sharing, and at least some taste for challenging the current status quo. Universities are precisely these kinds of social locations.

Their work is inextricably tied to the creation of new categories of people, organizations, or other types of social and market actors. Recall that one of the primary things universities do is produce educated people and scaffold a wide range of careers. "New actors" are interesting in that they are both a result of the processes we're been talking about and a key vector for them.

In the last chapter, we talked about how the needs of a particular type of life science innovation (exemplified by BRCA1) combined with the central role of universities helped make possible a new category of actor, the "amphibious" scientific entrepreneur (exemplified by Mark Skolnick). As the role of scientist-entrepreneur has become more common in academe, their presence has shifted both the character of training and the meaning of success in some fields.[10] Here a new type of actor that emerged from academe also changed, in ways both subtle and gross, the processes that make universities sources.

One result of such changes is that many important discoveries become entangled in expensive and challenging conflicts over intellectual property, ownership, and the ability of the institution and its investigators to profit from the products of their work. I am not convinced that this is always bad. But I do believe that these kinds of private returns need to be understood as ancillary benefits of the work rather than its purpose.

Let's consider a brief, recent example of the kind of responsiveness that shows the university's ability to help keep us able to address emergent problems. Then we'll turn to a discussion of how we can make sure our universities stay the kinds of locations that help us deal with unknown unknowns.

An Unexpected Outbreak

Zika is a mosquito-borne virus named after the African forest where it was discovered in 1947 by a scientific expedition that was doing research on yellow fever. Tests with humans in the 1950s and 1960s found that Zika was associated with relatively mild symptoms such as joint pain, fever, and rash. Between 1947 and 2007 (when an outbreak occurred on the Micronesian island of Yap), just fourteen naturally transmitted cases were identified across Asia and Africa.[11] "For all practical purposes, Zika looked like a medical curiosity that posed little if any threat to public health."[12]

Until recently there was "no evidence" of Zika circulation "in the Western Hemisphere."[13] Zika—"an exotic and poorly understood virus" that was "technically difficult to test for" because it could easily be misidentified as two other mosquito-borne illnesses—made a substantial appearance in Brazil. Its presence was confirmed in May 2014.[14] By the middle of 2015 the situation had changed dramatically. Cases of Zika were cropping up all over the Americas, and it had become clear that the virus was more easily transmitted through sexual contact than had previously been believed. Even more important, clear and compelling links had been drawn between Zika infection and Guillain-Barré syndrome, a rare disorder in which the body's immune system targets its own nerves.[15]

More disturbing yet, pregnant women infected with Zika were much more likely to give birth to babies with microencephaly, a condition in which the brain fails to develop properly.[16] In part as a result of these developments, the World Health Organization (WHO) declared Zika a "Public Health Emergency of International Concern" in February 2016. Later that year, in July, U.S. public health officials confirmed the first transmissions of Zika by mosquito bite in a Miami neighborhood.[17]

On August 1, 2016, the U.S. Centers for Disease Control and Prevention (CDC) issued guidance recommending that pregnant women should avoid travel to Miami-Dade County, Florida.[18] Over the course of the outbreak,[19] people in sixty-nine countries were infected with Zika, including more than forty-thousand people living in U.S. states and territories.[20] An obscure disease for which there was no cure, no vaccine, and no reliable diagnostic, and whose effects proved to be much more dangerous than originally imagined, had become a matter of national and international concern.

The response to Zika reached far beyond universities, but some of the roles research universities played highlight one way to understand how these institutions help keep a national and international system poised. I cannot begin to do anything like full justice to the complicated response to Zika, or even to the full range of the scientific response. Instead, I'll offer a few short and illustrative stories.

Zika is a flavivirus, a genus that also includes dengue, yellow fever, and West Nile virus. Because Zika was a relatively obscure disease, "no one noticed" that it had any epidemic potential and, perhaps as a result, very little research specifically targeted the disease until it was clear there was an important outbreak.[21] However, researchers were studying other flaviviruses.

How Zika works has to do with what experts call *host-pathogen interactions*, the biology of how viruses or bacteria live, reproduce, and cause illness in hosts like animals and people. The details of host-pathogen interactions are often important to the development of therapies for infectious diseases. But little was known about Zika. In June 2016, a group of fourteen researchers mostly affiliated with the University of Massachusetts Medical School in Worcester published a paper that used a powerful new gene editing technique called CRISPR[22] to identify key proteins that Zika needed to replicate in human cells. They also identified at least one protein that cells use to protect themselves from attack by Zika and other viruses.[23]

This work happened fast. It took just two months from the time the group received a sample of Zika.[24] As Abraham Brass—the paper's senior author—noted, this speed was possible because of prior work to develop and sustain systems for the study of host-pathogen interactions for other viruses. "Our lab and others in the field have worked hard to develop the systems and infrastructure needed to investigate the genetics underlying how viral pathogens use our own cell's machinery to replicate . . . We plugged Zika Virus into our system and immediately began studying it. What might have taken much longer to build from the ground up, we were able to turn around in just a few short months."[25]

One part of that system was CRISPR screens developed by the Brass lab for use with dengue and influenza. CRISPR also underpinned two related papers, by research teams at Washington University in St. Louis and Stanford, published within a month of the Brass team's work.[26] These papers all used similar whole-genome approaches to "genetically dissect host-pathogen interactions in flaviviruses including Zika and Dengue."[27]

Several things are interesting for us in all of this. First, the three groups all quickly turned existing capabilities and collaborations toward analyses of Zika. Second, all three relied on a new method (CRISPR) that has been characterized as "revolutionary"[28] and "the ultimate weapon" for infectious diseases.[29] The groups' different capabilities and interests led them down distinctive routes. In other words, different recombinations happened in near parallel time in multiple universities in response to an emerging and unexpected crisis. All the groups relied on federal research funding, but each also had support from other sources.[30]

The Massachusetts group led by Brass directed their efforts toward a particular protein (interferon-induced protein 3 or IFITM3), which their earlier work had demonstrated also has the potential to address influenza.[31] Their next steps might include searching for compounds that could amplify the antiviral effects of IFITM3 as a means to treat Zika and other related infectious diseases.

The Washington University group, led by Michael Diamond, was among the first to develop a mouse model for Zika. That allowed them to begin addressing another pressing question: why Zika infection could lead to significant birth defects.[32] Diamond's group used their mouse model to determine that "a lot of Zika's damage occurs at the level of the placenta."[33]

Later work by the group demonstrated that a particular Zika antibody prevents placental infection in mice. It might yield a treatment for pregnant women that could stop the birth defects that result from Zika.[34] It also suggests that Zika vaccines being developed by other groups and organizations might protect fetuses as well as mothers.

This group's move to address Zika was triggered by Diamond's participation in an NIH meeting on chikungunya (another flavivirus) in June 2015. At that meeting, Diamond reports, he "met a number of investigators from Brazil who told me that they were encountering these medical manifestations associated with the Zika virus. . . . Because my laboratory had long-term experience working with flaviviruses . . . we decided to start a program to investigate what was happening."[35] Part of what generated an early response to Zika by the Washington University group was a physical meeting of researchers from many different locations who shared common interests. In this way a recent set of biomedical discoveries can be understood to share something in common with a foundational work of gender theory.

The Stanford group, led by Jan Carette, took yet another tack. They had been working to learn how an antiviral compound initially developed (and then shelved) by pharmaceutical giant GlaxoSmithKline worked.[36] Here CRISPR and an existing therapeutic that researchers thought might hold promise for treating many different viruses offers a potential path to treat Zika.[37] This is another interesting point of contact between one set of stories about Zika and the view of the university we have been developing.

The compound this group has been working with was "discarded" by its corporate developer because its antiviral effects were also associated with cytotoxicity. The potential drug stopped viruses but also killed infected cells. That is bad for patients.[38] The Stanford group's return to that compound represents a small example of how the stability of universities and the fact that their interests are not primarily driven by market returns can add to a larger innovation system.

By pulling on a single thread of the response to an unexpected outbreak we see some of the ways that a system of universities can add to the responsiveness of a nation. None of the approaches that I sketch here have resulted in a cure or vaccine. They may not. There are many responses that I do not discuss. That's part of the point. Capabilities and networks supported by public investments in research universities were quickly repurposed to address a pressing, unexpected problem using a cutting-edge scientific technique. Multiple responses pulled together different pieces of knowledge to generate many routes to a solution. The differences were based in the particular organization of research on different campuses and differences in how each campus connected to partners both national and international. This case of multiple discovery illustrates how a system of research universities helps keep our social and economic system poised.

Explaining, Protecting, and Sustaining Universities

We need to treat research universities as a special case of higher-education institutions, uniquely suited to act as sources, anchors, and hubs. By doing so they help keep us ready to address unexpected problems and benefit from new possibilities, many of which they help create. This form of social insurance rests in the particular organization and institutions of academe and in the networks that public investment allows universities to create and support.

In a time when austerity rhetoric shapes public investments, there are challenges to arguing that increasing (or even simply maintaining) support for research universities is a good bet. The first is that the way discovery works and the way the university has come to be organized and funded make it difficult to calculate a return on any particular investment.

That problem blinds us to the fact that the positive results of research and education are quite often outcomes of collective efforts that span fields over long time frames. As a result, it's difficult to point to a single area of inquiry or particular public investment that was sufficient to create the outcomes we seek. In turn, this means that standard concerns about productive efficiency and efforts to direct research from the top down will be, at best, ineffective and more likely outright destructive.

Examples abound, but skeptics might look no further than the previous section of this chapter for a rebuttal. Isn't it the case, after all, that the three academic responses I described were based in labs that were well funded to study infectious diseases? Yes. Then so what if we didn't see Zika coming and thus didn't invest in research particular to that disease? We certainly know that the potential for pandemics exists and we have put lots of support toward, for instance, research on flaviviruses. Isn't that a reasonably direct connection?

Holding constant the fact that the proposed federal budget for 2018 included dramatic cuts to funding for just this kind of research, the best answer is yes and no. Read this way, disease outbreaks might fall into the category of known unknowns. We are aware they will happen. We prepare for them even though we don't know exactly what the disease might be, or where or how it will manifest. But this response misses the interesting point that all three of the responses to Zika I sketched relied on a common technique (CRISPR) and that each put together a different combination of knowledge.

CRISPR is a recent discovery. The first successful use of this gene-editing technique in human cells can be traced to a 2013 paper[39] by a research group at the Broad Institute.[40] So here too we see something that on its face looks like a pretty direct win. A new technique is described in 2013, and by 2016 it is being broadly used and helps make important strides on a new problem. But the history of CRISPR, at least as told by Broad Institute director Eric Lander, is one of winding, long-term discovery that includes many people, fields, and countries. The story began with a "once-obscure microbial system discovered twenty years earlier in a Spanish salt marsh." Lander continues: "The early heroes of CRISPR were not on a quest to edit the human genome—or even to study human disease. Their motivations were a mix of personal curiosity (to understand bizarre repeat sequences in salt tolerant microbes), military exigency (to defend against biological warfare), and industrial application (to improve yoghurt production)."[41]

I love the fact that a relevant precursor of a key genetic discovery (and thus of the responses to Zika I sketch) implicates techniques to reduce infections in industrial yogurt cultures. It's another example of the fact that you don't have to dig very deep to find something you never would have expected to be important at the outset. The long-term "ensemble act"[42] that supports most discoveries is key to understanding why we need a new way of thinking about how to invest in systems that make these kinds of discoveries and their applications possible. The interdependent, indirect, and lengthy process that supports most important discoveries means we can't invest in particular problems or solutions. We have to invest in systems. Those systems must, at a bare minimum, be national in scope. More realistically, they must be global. U.S. research universities are among their essential components.

All this brings us to a second theme, which has to do with the nature of the discoveries themselves. Understanding what we want to achieve is important to thinking about the system we hope to sustain. Recall the underlying logic of innovation that I described at length in Chapter 3. In outline, most discoveries result from combinations of existing raw materials (bits of existing knowledge, skill, technology, etc.). Those combinations can be more or less typical.[43] Some sets of things are often pulled together to do new things or to do old things in new ways. Other sets of things are rarely or never combined.

More typical combinations are more likely to succeed (in the sense of proof, not market success), but less typical combinations are more likely to be novel and to dramatically change the status quo. Whether we're thinking about field-defining scientific discoveries, creative masterpieces, or really cool new products, radically new things are often the result of successful but atypical combinations. Atypical combinations are also more likely to fail. Successful combinations of this sort are uncommon. The key insight here is that the system we need to understand and sustain must consistently produce rare, risky outcomes that are outside the current status quo.

Because we cannot know what those outcomes are ahead of time, we need to support a system that is robust. It needs to be able to routinely produce multiple solutions to pressing problems. We saw examples of that in the response to Zika and in the discussion of PageRank from Chapter 1. It also needs to be stable and resilient in the face of failure. Resilience and stability are key because (1) the kinds of knowledge work that we should especially value are risky, (2) the results of prior "failures" are often components of future successes, and (3) the ability to consistently challenge the status quo requires some degree of insulation (though not isolation) from day-to-day pressures.

The most important implications, though, reach beyond individual campuses to the system of universities. I have generally drawn examples and arguments from single campuses and discoveries to make these dynamics concrete and visible. But responsiveness results from the collective workings of many research universities, located in diverse places and connected to varied constituencies. When differently located institutions also maintain heterogeneous internal networks, the stage is set for the discoveries we need to address unknown unknowns.

This is why the decentralized research system that is our legacy has come to work so well. It is also a reason why declining public supports stands to damage it. Making it difficult for all but the most elite research universities to maintain their absorptive capacity or engage in more generative and less transactional relationships is egregiously shortsighted. Diversity in the arrangement of research capabilities, anchor possibilities, and hub connections is what makes the system as a whole robust and what allows it to help us stay poised to address and create the future.

The vigorous competition (for students, for faculty, for research support) that characterizes the system has benefits but also detriments that are felt in a highly stratified educational system.[44] One key to the benefits is the drive for individual institutions and even investigators to experiment with new combinations of techniques or new types of organization. Some pockets of innovation we have discussed (for instance, the MIT Media Lab, Stanford's CCRMA, the Broad Institute, and Princeton's Institute for Advanced Study) represent just such efforts to develop new forms of organization that support particular types of scholarship. It is unsurprising, though somewhat depressing, that they are all located at well-heeled private institutions. Regardless, entire campuses can also be test beds for alternative organization, as may be the case with Arizona State's reorganization of research.[45] I am not suggesting that any one of these experiments is the right way to do things, or a template to be broadly imitated. We don't have the capacity to systematically evaluate their utility and effects. We need to expand that capability.

For now, note that experiments with the organization of knowledge and knowledge work in universities adds to the diversity of the system as a whole. Competition among universities is a spur to experimentation. Keeping it from being too destructive requires large investments in public goods. Much as intellectual and institutional monocultures are dangerous for a campus, shared orthodoxies about the best ways to pursue the knowledge mission are dangerous for the system. The key, I suspect, is both to find ways to rigorously understand the effects such experiments have and to ensure that the system as a whole benefits from the mix of stability and experimentation that has always characterized U.S. universities.[46]

What will allow universities to remain a wellspring is new ways to think about support for systems and capabilities rather than better ways to evaluate returns on individual investments. The danger of the latter is that we will rework our institutions to make evaluation easier at the expense of the kinds of productivity we want to see. Instead we must pay close attention to the conditions that produce rare and unexpected outcomes from risky and sometimes unsettling work. We must also attend not just to individual campuses but to (at least) the national system.

There are dangers to thinking this way. Key among them is the fact that research, teaching, and service to the public are unified in our research universities. Asking students and families to bear the lion's share of both the risks and the costs of experimentation is dangerous and immoral. One way to avoid this is to be very clear about the bets we are making as a society and as institutions. That requires reviving the language of public goods that characterized postwar political conflicts. It is another reason we need to think and talk systematically and well about what research universities, in particular, do with and for our nation and the world.

What can we do? As you've probably come to realize, the kinds of answers I'm inclined to offer to seemingly simple questions about research universities emphasize productive complications. This one is no exception. The view I have proposed suggests a set of key changes but few specific prescriptions.

We need to reclaim the language of public goods and add to it a sensitivity to systems and networks. We need to recognize that the public benefit of research universities lies in their being willing and able to act like universities, not like businesses, or venture capitalists, or high schools, or corporate training facilities, or incubators, or any of a number of other alternatives that encompass only a part of their work. We need to turn our best research on ourselves and subject the workings of our institutions and their effects to rigorous, systematic, and public scrutiny. Finally, we need to consider what it would mean, as a nation, to reinvest in the capabilities necessary to keep us poised to face an uncertain future. Let's take each of these ideas in turn.

I think we find ourselves in a dangerous position because we have come to indulge in a few problematic habits of thought. As they have become more and more taken for granted, these ideas exert significant force on our actions and choices. The dominant language we use to talk and think about universities today emphasizes private returns and focuses on the idea that the primary reasons for these institutions to exist is to facilitate a student's or family's trade of (increasingly steep) tuition for a better, more remunerative life. In doing so we have downplayed the unique contributions made by the small number of universities that effectively combine all aspects of the knowledge mission.

In the realm of science policy, a similar move toward justifying investment via return on individual grants or particular fields emphasizes a comparably narrow band of university activity. I hope that by now you see why attempting to account for the work of academic research in such narrow terms is profoundly wrong. Equally dangerous is the recent move to further limit the indirect-cost components of grants. These funds already fail to cover the full costs of research, prompting a dramatic rise in institutional spending on a key aspect of the public mission. There are few good sources for those funds.

When coupled with declines in state support for public universities, reductions in federal investments put a large part of the research enterprise in a desperate bind. Offloading the costs of the shared resources that allow universities to maintain the delicate, abrasive, and ultimately productive balance among their missions onto students and families is wrong. It reinforces the mistakes of thinking on and off campus that are a significant part of our problem.

By failing to consider what research universities contribute to the general welfare, we have disregarded the bargain between these institutions and the public that supports them. Public support allows universities to make necessary contributions to create and respond to a better future for all of us.

We need to take the collective benefits of education, of knowledge aggregation, of discovery, and of capacity building seriously. The primary thing we need our research universities to do is maintain the capabilities that make them a wellspring of public responses to the unknown unknowns that we will face. Our universities do this because of their distinctive organizational and institutional features, their multiple missions, and the networks they sustain and anchor. These are the things that represent investments in our collective future. Most of what we're investing in is the ability to remain poised to take advantage of new possibilities or respond to unexpected problems. That is a matter of national and global importance. No one other than the public has much incentive to pay the freight.

It is, at best, a shell game to try to find ways to make these public investments fit under the rubric of private returns. Important discoveries follow winding paths. Knowledge that may not have had obvious uses when it was developed and projects that seem like failures now can become key to future returns. The need for a system that can routinely generate multiple answers to the problems we face means that we're investing in maintaining a robust, resilient set of capabilities. Trying to fit a justification of those kinds of capabilities into an evaluative framework that starts with the assumption that what matters is measurable returns on individual investments is corrosive.

The conditions under which the system grew were different from those we face today financially, politically, and in almost every other way. As a result it's not safe to simply return to the language of the past. We must adapt to explain what we are investing in. For universities and researchers seeking renewed national or state investment requires more than the "trust us, it'll be great" rationale that too often characterizes conversations about the need for public funding. The effort to reclaim the language of public goods and explain just how research universities fulfill pressing if uncertainly distant public needs thus requires better capabilities for research and explanation.

One key to both the argument about public goods and to ensuring that research universities maintain and expand their ability to be anchors, sources, and hubs lies in the choices executive officers, administrators, and even individual faculty make. An argument on the basis of public goods is difficult to sustain if universities and their occupants seem to be fostering their own private interests at the expense of broader benefits. Even more importantly, we have seen that some of the keys to the public value of these institutions lie in their efforts to maintain diverse portfolios of knowledge, to serve multiple purposes, and to adopt a broad conception of service to the public as a central part of the mission.

Deepening academic commitments to openness and to making the campus as well as what it produces a commons will help. Limiting more transactional approaches to key constituents inside and outside the institution is likewise essential. To be fair, this is difficult under conditions in which public support is in decline and the institution itself is often under attack.

One thing universities and their defenders can do is more clearly articulate the benefits that reach beyond individuals to the communities they occupy, stabilize, and connect. In practical terms this means striving to be anchor tenants in the network sense I describe in Chapter 4. Universities should serve as both a contributor to and convenor of their communities without attempting to exert control. This may mean bringing together otherwise unconnected partners, sharing information as broadly as possible, and serving as an interested but neutral broker and meeting ground. It may also mean emphasizing the benefits of partnerships that increase the institution's ability to be a source by maximizing flows of information and preferring less exclusive (and often less remunerative) arrangements when contracts are necessary.

Universities should strive to serve their legitimate interests and forward their public missions by being engaged institutional citizens in the various spheres their work touches. Doing so can certainly bring benefits, but it represents a departure from the quest for immediate returns.[47] Because the work of universities is so decentralized, these efforts must often proceed from the bottom up as different groups on campus pursue their own intellectual agendas in partnership with various constituencies. One thing that this view of universities suggests quite strongly is that they need not and should not seek a uniform, consistent agenda at the level of the organization as a whole. As we've seen, part of what is generative about universities stems from organized anarchy well contained.

I imagine that the lack of concrete recommendations thus far may be frustrating you. I apologize. With that said, there are reasons why I have not simply tried to author a to-do list for our universities and policy makers. First, the whole of this argument weighs against one-size-fits-all prescriptions. Instead, we need a shared framework that will allow for experimentation and more effective evaluation. Second, and more importantly, we simply do not know enough about how research universities do their work to make the kinds of clear-eyed but difficult decisions that face us. Third, we have more or less quietly lost a once commonly held belief about the public benefits of these institutions. That cannot be reclaimed by fiat; instead it must be cultivated through argument. A framework to guide experimentation, resources to support it, and the data and infrastructure necessary to understand, explain and improve universities' impact are essential.

A Framework for Experimentation

We should find ways to expand and sustain our universities' ability to act as sources, anchors, and hubs. That idea suggests some guiding principles for people and institutions interested in trying new approaches.

Sources

Consider, first, the things that make universities sources. The key is complex, diverse, and balanced networks that span many fields and approaches to problems. Those can be cultivated but not engineered.

Administrators and researchers should think about the many dimensions of proximity that can be leveraged to bring research communities on and across campuses together in distinctive ways. Any such efforts should take place with a clear goal of both providing new opportunities for brokerage and attending to the health of the existing groups that are often essential to "proof work." There are many potential routes to this balance.

Imagine one possibility. Universities might institutionalize the kinds of proximity in physical and knowledge space that some of the examples we have discussed highlight. It might be interesting to create "pop-up" departments that physically co-locate students and faculty interested in similar problems for one to two years. Such arrangements could also include permanent staff or other resources that can serve as a vector for learning across projects.

Rather than blowing up current organizational and institutional arrangements on campus, time-limited experiments might foster new connections and the insights that accompany them. Continued support for promising projects and collaborations that can allow work to continue when investigators return to their permanent homes might offer a route to enhancing the kind of networks I emphasize.

The idea of time limitation is essential here. Too many initiatives on campus become permanent, and some mechanism to sunset experiments must be created. Central to all these efforts should be sustained, well-designed efforts to support evaluation. Universities and funders alike should support efforts to leverage data on the process and products of research to enable the kinds of rigorous analyses that can lead academics to better understand, explain, and improve our efforts.

Institutions must continue to sustain a broad range of research, to develop diverse communities of students and faculty, and to work to ensure the most open flows of knowledge possible both on and off campus. Commitments to open science, replication, and mechanisms to enable researchers to search for solutions and problems are useful targets for experimentation.

At a system level, funders and policy makers too might focus on key principles. The system we need to sustain is decentralized, robust, and varied in that it seats efforts to address similar topics and problems in disparate intellectual contexts and networks. A new measure of success might emphasize attempts to ensure that there will be multiple solutions to any given problem rather than large bets on a single approach.

Second, attention should be paid to the contexts of proposed research. This is already a component of many funding decisions. Instead of simply asking whether local resources are sufficient to enable proposed projects, we might also profitably ask how particular institutions create and sustain distinct possibilities for the kinds of recombinations we hope to see. Here too, attention to existing networks that rely on good data will prove useful. The decentralized and peer-review-driven system that is currently in place should be sustained and augmented.

At both levels these principles should be wedded to a focus on breadth of experience for students and trainees. This might be accomplished by bolstering funding mechanisms (such as fellowships) that make them less beholden to particular faculty projects without isolating them from the successful research efforts that are an essential part of training at the highest levels. I am struck by how often recipients of NSF Graduate Research Fellowships play prominent roles in the cases I examine here. The kind of national support for graduate training that was proposed in 1947 by the Truman Commission offers an even more radical means to accomplish similar goals. Regardless, better data and thorough research to establish the value and appropriate mix of different funding mechanisms is essential.

For now, some research suggests that funding for promising people should be a large part of the arsenal. Longer-term funding directed at individuals such as Howard Hughes Medical Institute investigatorships have been shown to support riskier research profiles for their recipients.[48] There is also emerging evidence that smaller research teams may be more likely to produce discoveries that challenge established technological and research trajectories while larger groups do more to develop them.[49] This suggests the importance of funding mechanisms that shy away from overly concentrating resources in single locations and teams. Again, though, experiments should be coupled with mechanisms that allow academics to transparently turn our best research on ourselves.

Anchors

Stability helps universities be better anchors. So does openness. Approaches to partners that serve universities' interests without imposing control are key. Incentives to support the former are clearly the province of funders and policy makers. The latter is more amenable to work on individual campuses.

Federal research funding, both direct costs and reimbursements for facilities and administration, are essential. Such support accounts for the lion's share of research done in academe. While philanthropic, industrial, and state funding are also important, they cannot close (or, at least, have not closed) the gap that nearly a decade of flat federal funding has opened. Current budget proposals that include substantial cuts to science agency budgets and potentially crippling caps on indirect-cost recovery stand to cause additional damage. State divestment in public institutions only exacerbates the problem.

Uncertainty about funding levels, appropriations, and indirect-cost recovery make it harder for research universities to make the kinds of risky investments in common goods that are so essential to their work as sources. Uncertainty makes it harder for them to serve as anchors because it presses them to squeeze as much immediate return from current relationships as can be had. The very kinds of openness and interested but not expressly transactional partnerships that are the hallmark of anchor tenants both depend on stable streams of support.

A 2014 report from the American Academy of Arts and Sciences makes some good recommendations.[50] They propose aggressive goals to close the funding gap that has opened over the last two decades and deepened in the wake of the Great Recession.[51] Another recommendation emphasizes multiyear appropriations to support research and training in Science, Technology, Engineering and Mathematics (STEM). I would expand that to include all fields, but either way stability enables planning and more experimental investments by universities seeking a competitive edge. Attention to longer-term planning and a new capital investment budgeting process round out the relevant recommendations. Both of those would be grounded in the realization that research investments, particularly substantial capital investments, are an essential component of national infrastructure.[52]

Stable, predictable flows of funding make university investments in costly public goods for their campuses and communities more likely. Competitions for funding adjudicated by expert review focused on capacity building and intellectual merit could provide incentives for the kinds of experiments that I think are necessary.

Hubs

My suggestion that investments in the system include all fields is based in the recognition that the full range of research and training present on today's research campuses is essential to their being hubs. This is particularly important to understanding how our academic research system can ensure our collective future.

Hubs allow problems and solutions to move to and through universities and are inseparable from their anchor roles and source capabilities. Hubs require active work to allow flows of people and ideas to move across the boundaries of campus. The more varied the destinations and sources of those flows, the better. Likewise, the people who come to and leave the universities need to be prepared to recognize problems and possibilities and to make the connections that will help them engage with source networks when they return.

The strong affinities that people feel for their universities are an essential factor in campus "hubness." It's another reason for research institutions to take additional steps to make certain all their residents understand their work and interact with them less like customers and more like community members. It's also a reason to open on campus public goods and opportunities to members of relevant communities. Protecting the boundaries of campus is a bad way to be an anchor and a worse way to be a hub.

Here too, I think experimentation coupled with strong data to support research and evaluation is necessary. In thinking about students, university administrators and faculty might consider relatively simple steps like making it easier for students whose financial aid packages include work-study to use those funds to take jobs that introduce them to research and to the source networks of their universities. Pop-up departments such as those I have suggested might include relevant students and staff or faculty whose work helps them contextualize and learn from their experiences. Such temporary research clusters might also include representatives from relevant partners such as community groups, nonprofits, schools, and corporations. These initiatives might even be supported on a temporary or permanent basis by memberships such as those that define the MIT Media Lab's funding model.

The principles and concrete recommendations for experiments and policies I make here clearly do not exhaust the possibilities. The larger point is that a common framework, commitment to data and evaluation, and the certainty necessary to enable risky bets should guide experiments. Attending to those needs will increase our universities' ability to help the nation and the world remain poised to do well in the face of whatever comes next.

Infrastructure for Research on Research

Which brings us to another necessary component. Research policy lacks a strong evidentiary base. That's not for lack of good studies, but what research there is has tended to be fairly artisanal, featuring high-quality but hard-to-replicate-or-generalize analyses that provide important insights but do not support clear prescriptions. One challenge in the realm I know best, science policy, is that the data necessary to analyze the kinds of systems and outcomes I have been describing have simply not existed.[53] As a result we have been unable to develop the kinds models that might inform policy changes.

The lack is clearest at the federal level, where, as an example, a proposal to alter significant laws pertaining to health care or social security can be evaluated in terms of its potential effects. The work of, for instance, the Congressional Budget Office is certainly not iron clad. Any predictions made about complicated systems are necessarily imperfect. But in many areas of policy making there are at least models that can be deployed with clear assumptions that can be debated. We do not know enough to do the same with the key products of our research universities.[54] We should.

Having read this book, I hope you can see the challenges to that project clearly. Answering even the "simple" questions policy makers face is exceptionally difficult. What are the likely short-, medium-, and long-term effects of, for instance, a 20 percent cut to the budget of the NIH? What is the right percentage of GDP for our nation to invest in research? Is the mix of funding for different fields of inquiry efficient?[55] We simply don't know.[56]

We're on even more challenging terrain when we raise the more complicated questions this book suggests. What effect would cutting funding for social and behavioral sciences have on the public value of research overall? How about eliminating the National Endowments for the Humanities and Arts? How do we conceptualize, explain, and improve less tangible contributions to health, justice, and well-being? Is our system of research universities large, diverse, and appropriately connected enough? How well does the current system respond to unknown unknowns?

Developing answers to these questions requires new data and new institutions, which are just the kinds of things our universities should be uniquely situated to produce. Taking the arguments I have made here seriously would mean developing the capability to examine the whole system of research investment in a way that situates both people and discoveries in collaborative networks that vary across campuses. We'd have to be able to follow the key products of that work (people and ideas) out into the larger society and economy and use the movements to estimate effects over relatively long periods.

The need to focus on rare events, serendipity, and unexpected connections means that we cannot rely on standard statistical methods or data drawn from samples. The view of the university and its work that I propose here suggests the need for a style of research that is simultaneously fundamental, in the sense that it addresses basic questions about the dynamics of large-scale social systems, and applied, in the sense that its findings are of immediate interest for those tasked with making practical decisions about the organization and funding of research. It also requires collaboration and coordination with a wide range of constituents.[57]

Accomplishing that, in turn, requires the commitment and engagement of universities, of the federal government, and potentially of many of the university's key constituencies. Along with collaborators, I am placing a bet on the value of administrative data for analyzing just these questions through a platform called the Institute for Research on Innovation and Science (IRIS).[58] Building a research infrastructure that is sufficient to address the kinds of questions this book raises requires significant commitments to share data from many sources. Such collective, infrastructure-building projects are a necessary corollary to the idea that we need to reclaim the language of public goods as a means to argue for more public support.

I am under no illusions that all experiments will succeed, or that all current endeavors should be sustained and expanded. Right now we have no systematic means to support decisions about what parts of the system should be kept and expanded and which should be shuttered or allowed to fade. Without that possibility, the call for experimentation could be mistaken for a prescription of continuous growth. It is not. Broad, stable, national investments are necessary, but right now our processes for deciding how to make those investments are driven not by knowledge but by political expediency and habit. That needs to change.

One Model for Expanded Support

I recognize that the current financial and political climate makes an argument for federal and state reinvestment a very heavy lift. What is really necessary is an even broader move to revitalize and revise the call for substantial national support first voiced by the Truman Commission. The system view of research universities that I propose here highlights just some of the ways that these institutions speak uniquely to national needs. Contributions to economic growth and social welfare are just two examples.

One response to a call for revitalized public support might be to suggest that the businesses that depend on the work of universities do more to support them. Many of the examples we have discussed demonstrate the substantial private value that is often realized from public investments. The fact that much of that value comes from the purchases of taxpayers who are the ultimate funders of key research makes some kind of return seem sensible. In essence, our current system socializes the risks of publicly funded research and often privatizes the returns, leaving no obvious mechanisms for those who benefit to sustain the kind of work they have depended on.[59]

The ten years since the Great Recession have seen real declines in public support, but industrial investments in academic research have remained flat. Clearly the private sector is not rushing in to feed their golden goose. Even if they were, there is increasing evidence that too-tight industrial connections may push research universities toward projects oriented more toward expanding the current technological status quo.[60] So, if investments from the private sector are to be part of the solution, we must think hard about how to structure them to preserve and even expand the university's independence, which is part of what makes them valuable sources.

I am certainly not the first to call for substantial public reinvestment. Advocates for free college and analysts of the funding model for public universities have done so in different terms, for complementary purposes.[61] But these calls do not attend to the unique contributions and capacity of the academic research system. Public support for our system of research universities is an investment in our collective future on par with social security, health care, physical infrastructure, and K–12 education. It should be treated as seriously.

Some interesting plans and models exist. The basic, though admittedly schematic, proposal is a division of labor whereby research and graduate education become the responsibility of the federal government while undergraduate education (at least on the public campuses that educate the bulk of undergraduates) remains the province of the states.[62] Maintenance-of-effort provisions that spur individual states to at least stabilize levels of support for their public institutions as a condition of federal investments offer one way forward, though that path will have many detractors.[63]

A substantial expansion of this kind of model was recently suggested by the American Academy of Arts and Sciences' Lincoln Project.[64] The plan they proposed involves the creation of a $30 billion national endowment from public and private sources to support ten thousand endowed chairs at public universities across the country. In addition to defraying part of the cost of faculty salaries, the support would cover graduate student stipends and some research support.

This kind of plan has many good features. It stands to stabilize key nodes in the networks of many universities and may incentivize greater risk taking in individual research. It also explicitly makes graduate education across many fields a key part of the national investment. One route to support such an endowment might be to use its creation to incentivize the repatriation of taxable revenue from cash-rich companies whose technologies, employee pipelines, and even business models depend on the work of universities.[65] Regardless, the system of research universities would benefit not just from stabilizing business as usual but also from more forceful arguments for expanded public support. Because they are sources, anchors, and hubs whose work touches nearly every precinct of society, there is a coalition to be built.

While their language is explicitly about public research universities, which current trends put in the most dire situations, the Lincoln Project offers one example of this kind of coalition building: "In the 21st century, public research universities will require support from all sectors—a compact among state and federal governments, universities, businesses and philanthropies to share responsibility for institutions critical to American education, research, culture, and competitiveness."[66] I would be inclined to increase the scale of such support to include all research universities, but realize that the unique features of our private institutions raise complicated challenges. Nevertheless, the essential role that private institutions play in the national research system I have been describing suggests that they too should be the targets of expanded public support.

Nothing less than a broad, comprehensive model for sustained public investment is appropriate and needful for the institutions that are, and must remain, sources, anchors, and hubs. Simple accommodation to current budgetary trends or efforts to squeeze the expansive missions and activities of research campuses into tighter and tighter boxes serve both our campuses and our collective futures poorly.

That is the primary challenge. If we are to think of research universities as public goods in and of themselves and producers thereof, then the correct (if challenging) route to support them is to argue rigorously and well for revitalized public support. That argument may not be successful. But the unique features of our research universities and the dangers posed by allowing them to slowly turn into narrower, more privatized, less open organizations make them well worth the fight.

NOTES

Introduction

1. American Academy of Arts and Sciences, *Public Research Universities: Recommitting to Lincoln's Vision: An Educational Compact for the 21st Century* (Washington, DC: American Academy of Arts and Sciences, 2016).

2. Eric S. Lander and Eric E. Schmidt, "America's 'Miracle Machine' Is in Desperate Need of, Well, a Miracle," *Washington Post*, May 5, 2017, https://www.washingtonpost.com/opinions/americas-miracle-machine-is-in-desperate-need-of-well-a-miracle/2017/05/05/daafbe6a-30e7-11e7-9534-00e4656c22aa_story.html?utm_term=.25834797ef4a.

3. Andrew Rodgers, "Trump's Budget Forgets That Science Is Insurance for America," *Wired*, May 25, 2017, https://www.wired.com/2017/05/trumps-budget-forgets-science-insurance-america/amp.

4. Figures calculated from the Integrated Postsecondary Education Data System (IPEDS).

5. Figures calculated from the NSF Survey of Research and Development Expenditures at Universities and Colleges, accessed via the WebCaspar data system at https://ncsesdata.nsf.gov/webcaspar/.

6. In order to fill out the remaining 10 percent or so of R&D spending reported by NSF, we would need to include an additional 468 campuses. Even if we were to consider every institution reporting R&D spending, we would still only be looking at about 12 percent of degree-granting higher-education institutions.

7. Another view: Nearly 4.4 percent (222) were in the highest-research-activity (115) and higher-research-activity (107) categories of doctorate-granting institutions as rated by the 2015 Carnegie Classification of Higher Education. So, if we are interested in the subset of campuses that are defined by integration of substantial research, graduate training, and undergraduate training across a wide range of fields, we're really looking at somewhere between 2.3 percent (115 very-high-research Carnegie institutions) and 4.4 percent (both high-research-activity and very-high-research-activity Carnegie institutions) of all higher-education institutions. I will use the group defined by research expenditures wherever possible, but in some cases, data limitations require me to use another group such as the Carnegie schools.

8. F. King Alexander, interview with the *Chronicle of Higher Education*, April 27, 2017, http://www.chronicle.com/article/Speaking-Out-in-Troubled-Times/239817.

9. Heidi Ledford, "Keeping the Lights On," *Nature* 515 (2014): 327.

10. Data are drawn from the NSF Higher Education Research Expenditures (HERD) survey, available at https://ncsesdata.nsf.gov/webcaspar/. Data on the detailed sources of all R&D expenditures, not just science and engineering, only began to be tracked by this survey in 2010.

11. Council on Government Relations, "Finances of Research Universities," June 2014, http://www.cogr.edu/sites/default/files/COGR_Research_Finances_JUNE_20 _FINAL.pdf.

12. Ibid., 3.

13. Ibid., 9.

14. Private research universities enroll an additional 840,000 students, bringing the total percentage of students enrolled on research intensive campuses to nearly 35 percent. Data are drawn from the 2015 IPEDS Enrollment Survey for Carnegie high-research-activity and very-high-research-activity campuses, accessed via https://ncsesdata .nsf.gov/webcaspar/.

15. Council on Government Relations, "Finances of Research Universities," 26.

16. Science News Staff, "A Grim Budget Day for U.S. Science: Analysis and Reaction to Trump's Plan," *Science*, March 16, 2017, http://www.sciencemag.org/news/2017/03/ trumps-first-budget-analysis-and-reaction.

17. Lev Facher, "Tom Price Defends Proposed Cuts at NIH, Citing 'Indirect' Expenses," *STAT News*, March 29, 2017, https://www.statnews.com/2017/03/29/tom-price -nih-budget/.

18. Scott Jaschik, "DeVos vs. the Faculty," Inside Higher Education, February 24, 2017, https://www.insidehighered.com/news/2017/02/24/education-secretary-criticizes -professors-telling-students-what-think.

19. Paulina Firozi, "Budget Director: We Can't Ask Coal Miners or Single Moms to Pay for Public Broadcasting," The Hill, March 16, 2017, http://thehill.com/homenews/ administration/324345-budget-director-we-cant-ask-coal-miners-or-single-moms-to -continue-to.

20. See, for instance, Kevin Carey, *The End of College: Creating the Future of Learning and the University of Everywhere* (New York: Riverhead, 2015); Clayton Christianson and Henry Eyring, *The Innovative University: Changing the DNA of Higher Education from the Inside Out* (San Francisco: Jossey-Bass, 2011); Ryan Craig, *College Disrupted: The Great Unbundling of Higher Education* (New York: St. Martin's Press, 2015); Gary Fethke and Andrew Policano, *Public No More: A New Path to Excellence for America's Public Universities* (Stanford, CA: Stanford Business Books, 2012); and Charles Sykes, *Fail U: The False Promise of Higher Education* (New York: St. Martin's Press, 2016).

21. Jeffrey Mervis, "Update: Surprise! Innovation Bill Clears the House, Heads to President," *Science*, December 16, 2016, http://www.sciencemag.org/news/2016/12/ update-surprise-innovation-bill-clears-house-heads-president.

22. Senate Bill 268, "Investing in Student Success Act of 2017," 115th Congress, First Session.

23. Walter McMahon, *Higher Learning, Greater Good: The Private and Social Benefits of Higher Education* (Baltimore: Johns Hopkins University Press, 2009).

24. Mark Granovetter, *Society and Economy: Framework and Principles* (Cambridge, MA: Harvard University Press, 2017.

25. Richard Arum and Josipa Roska, *Academically Adrift: Limited Learning on College Campuses* Chicago: University of Chicago Press, 2011).

26. Elizabeth Armstrong and Laura T. Hamilton, *Paying for the Party: How College Maintains Inequality* (Cambridge, MA: Harvard University Press, 2013); Elizabeth A. Armstrong et al., "Sexual Assault on Campus: A Multilevel, Integrative Approach to Party Rape," *Social Problems* 53, no. 4 (2006): 483–499; Sara Goldrick-Rab, *Paying the Price: College Costs, Financial Aid, and the Betrayal of the American Dream* (Chicago: University of Chicago Press, 2016).

Chapter 1

1. National Science Board, *Science and Engineering Indicators*, NSB 14-01 (Arlington, VA: National Science Foundation, 2014), https://www.nsf.gov/statistics/seind14/.

2. The total figure of more than $67 billion is drawn from the Higher Education Research Expenditures Survey, https://www.nsf.gov/statistics/srvyherd/, accessed May 18, 2017.

3. John Marburger, "Keynote Address," speech given at the 30th Annual AAAS Forum on Science and Technology Policy, Washington, DC, April 21, 2005. https://scisip .weebly.com/uploads/1/6/8/5/1685925/marburger_2005_aaas_keynote.pdf.

4. This is true of all "stimulus" spending and not distinctive for research, though the kinds of economic effects research hiring and spending produce may be different than other types. I address this question in Chapter 4.

5. On the first two, see Nathan Rosenberg, *Inside the Black Box: Technology and Economics* (Cambridge, UK: Cambridge University Press, 1982). On the latter, see Fabio Rojas, *From Black Power to Black Studies: How a Radical Social Movement Became an Academic Discipline* (Baltimore: Johns Hopkins University Press, 1982).

6. Walter W. Powell, Kelley Packalen, and Kjersten Whittington, "Organizational and Institutional Genesis: The Emergence of High-Tech Clusters in the Life Sciences," in *The Emergence of Organizations and Markets*, ed. John Padgett and Walter W. Powell (Princeton, NJ: Princeton University Press, 2012).

7. Mitchell L. Stevens, Elizabeth A. Armstrong, and Richard Arum, "Sieve, Incubator, Temple, Hub: Empirical and Theoretical Advances in the Sociology of Higher Education," *Annual Review of Sociology* 34, no. 1 (2008): 127–151.

8. Robert K. Merton, "Singletons and Multiples in Scientific Discovery: A Chapter in the Sociology of Science," *Proceedings of the American Philosophical Society* 105, no. 5 (1961): 470–486.

9. This reading of multiple discoveries as evidence of robustness runs counter to at least some economists' sense that multiples imply inefficient redundancy. See Partha Dasgupta and Paul David, "Toward a New Economics of Science," *Research Policy* 23, no. 5 (1994): 487–521.

10. Roland Barthes and Annette Lavers, *Mythologies* (New York: Hill and Wang, 1972), 68–71.

11. Peter Galison, *Einstein's Clocks and Poincaré's Maps* (New York: Norton, 2004).

12. Ibid., 41.

13. Freeman Dyson, "Clockwork Science," *New York Review of Books*, November 6, 2003, http://www.nybooks.com/articles/archives/2003/nov/06/clockwork-science/.

14. Stefan Wuchty, Benjamin F. Jones, and Brian Uzzi, "The Increasing Dominance of Teams in Production of Knowledge," *Science* 316, no. 5827 (2007): 1036–1039.

15. Randall Collins, *The Sociology of Philosophies* (Cambridge, MA: Harvard University Press, 2009); Nicholas Mullins, *Theory and Theory Groups in Sociology* (London: Harper and Row, 1973); Michael P. Farrell, *Collaborative Circles: Friendship Dynamics and Creative Work* (Chicago: University of Chicago Press, 1973).

16. Jason Owen-Smith, "Managing Laboratory Work Through Skepticism: Processes of Evaluation and Control," *American Sociological Review* 66, no. 3 (2001): 427–452.

17. Joseph Schumpeter, *Capitalism, Socialism, and Democracy* (London: Routledge, 1943).

18. Felichism W. Kabo et al., "Proximity Effects on the Dynamics and Outcomes of Scientific Collaborations," *Research Policy* 43, no. 9 (2014): 1469–1485.

19. Jake Fisher and Jason Owen-Smith, "How Do Universties Organize Their Science?" working paper, University of Michigan, 2018.

20. Richard C. Levin, "Universities and Cities: The View from New Haven," keynote address at a colloquium at Case Western Reserve University, Cleveland, OH, January 31, 2003, http://community-wealth.org/sites/clone.community-wealth.org/files/downloads/report-baznik.pdf.

21. Ajay Agarwal and Iain Cockburn, "The Anchor Tenant Hypothesis: Exploring the Role of Large, Local, R&D Intensive Firms in Regional Economies," *International Journal of Industrial Organization* 21 (2003): 1227–1253.

22. Jason Owen-Smith and Walter W. Powell, "Knowledge Networks as Channels and Conduits: The Effects of Spillovers in the Boston Biotechnology Community," *Organization Science* 15, no. 1 (2004): 5–21.

23. Powell, Packalen, and Whittington, "Organizational and Institutional Genesis," 439.

24. Stevens, Armstrong, and Arum, "Sieve, Incubator, Temple, Hub," 135.

25. Andrew J. Nelson, "Cacophony or Harmony? Multivocal Logics and Technology Licensing by the Stanford University Department of Music," *Industrial and Corporate Change* 14, no. 1 (2005): 93–118.

26. John F. Padgett and Christopher K. Ansell, "Robust Action and the Rise of the Medici, 1400–1434," *American Journal of Sociology* 98, no. 6 (1993): 1259–1319.

27. Andrew Nelson, *The Sound of Innovation: Stanford and the Computer Music Revolution* (Cambridge, MA: MIT Press, 2015), 12.

28. Google is now officially part of a larger company called Alphabet.

29. In the interests of accuracy, "google" did exist but apparently pertained to a particular breaking bowl in cricket. Thank you, Google.

30. Alphabet, "Investor Relations," https://investor.google.com/corporate/faq.html, accessed July 31, 2014.

31. National Science Foundation, "On the Origins of Google," http://www.nsf.gov/discoveries/disc_summ.jsp?cntn_id=100660, accessed July 31, 2014.

32. NSF Graduate Research Fellowship Program, "Sergey Brin, Google Co-Founder," https://www.nsfgrfp.org/fellows/profiles/sergey_brin, accessed July 31, 2014.

33. U.S. provisional patent application Ser. No. 60/035,205, filed January 10, 1997.

34. Sergey Brin and Lawrence Page, "The Anatomy of a Large-Scale Hypertextual Web Search Engine," paper presented at the Seventh International World-Wide Web Conference, Brisbane, Australia, April 1998, http://ilpubs.stanford.edu:8090/361/, accessed April 24, 2017.

35. This is obviously absurd on both the high and low end. On the low end, many other investments were necessary to go from the grant to the successful firm. On the high end, Alphabet's market capitalization is certainly a woeful underestimate of the social and economic value generated by effective web search. The almost surreal difficulty of talking about return on investment in these terms should make its own point.

36. On the challenges posed by scientific "memory practices," see Geoffrey Bowker, *Memory Practices in the Sciences* (Cambridge, MA: MIT Press, 2006).

37. Steven Levy, *In the Plex: How Google Thinks, Works, and Shapes Our Lives* (New York: Simon and Schuster, 2011); Randall Stross, *Planet Google: One Company's Audacious Plan to Organize Everything We Know* (New York: Free Press, 2008).

38. RankDex is U.S. Patent 5920859. HITS is U.S. Patent 6112202.

39. AnnaLee Saxenian, *Regional Advantage: Culture and Competition in Silicon Valley and Route 128* (Cambridge, MA: Harvard University Press, 1994); David Lampe, *The Massachusetts Miracle: High Technology and Economic Revitalization* (Cambridge, MA: MIT Press, 1988); Martin Kenney and David C. Mowery (eds.), *Public Universities and Regional Growth: Insights from the University of California* (Palo Alto, CA: Stanford University Press, 2014).

40. Brian D. Wright, Kyriakos Drivas, Zhen Lei, and Stephen A. Merrill, "Technology Transfer: Industry-Funded Academic Inventions Boost Innovation," *Nature* 507, no. 7492 (2014): 297–299; David C. Mowery, Richard R. Nelson, Bhaven N. Sampat, and Arvids A. Ziedonis, *Ivory Tower and Industrial Innovation: University-Industry Technology Transfer Before and After the Bayh-Dole Act in the United States* (Palo Alto, CA: Stanford University Press, 2004); Adam B. Jaffe and Josh Lerner, *Innovation and Its Discontents: How Our Broken Patent System Is Endangering Innovation and Progress, and What to Do About It* (Princeton, NJ: Princeton University Press, 2004).

41. Jay R. Ritter, "The Long-Run Performance of Initial Public Offerings," *Journal of Finance* 46, no. 1 (1991): 3–27; Paul A. Gompers and Joshua Lerner, *The Venture Capital Cycle, Second Edition* (Cambridge, MA: MIT Press, 2004).

42. David A. Vise, *The Google Story* (New York: Delta Press, 2008), 40.

43. Barbara Levitt and James G. March, "Organizational Learning," *Annual Review of Sociology* 14 (1988): 319–340.

44. I first heard this analogy drawn by Luigi Orsenigo, an economist working at Bocconi University, Italy.

45. Levy, *In the Plex*, 16.

46. Ibid., 17.

47. Note that the five years that elapsed between the grant being funded and Google's incorporation spans more than two congressional election cycles. In today's political environment it may better to envision that time as spanning five federal budget battles. Computer science is also a "fast" discipline relative to other areas, such as the life sciences, where valuable technologies may emerge from early-stage research.

48. By law, inventors on patents are required to disclose the relevant prior art for their inventions. During the patent examination process, these sources are checked and where necessary others are added by examiners in the U.S. Patent and Trademark Office. The patent system is designed to trade exclusive rights to an invention for a limited time (currently twenty years) for full disclosure of the invention to the public (so that others can draw on and use it). Thus, it is possible to examine the application for a patent that Stanford filed on behalf of Larry Page in order to see what pieces of prior knowledge he cited at the time of application.

49. That patent is U.S. Patent 6285999; the relevant application is U.S. 09/004,827. The prior art references I discuss here were extracted from what is known as the "file wrapper," a compilation of all documents and correspondence pertaining to a patent. That file is available from the U.S. Patent office and contains the original application materials, including the inventor's disclosure of prior art.

50. Mark S. Mizruchi, Peter Mariolis, Michael Schwartz, and Beth Mintz, "Techniques for Disaggregating Centrality Scores in Social Networks," *Sociological Methodology* 16 (1986): 26–48.

51. Beth Mintz and Michael Schwartz, *The Power Structure of American Business* (Chicago: University of Chicago Press, 1987).

52. "NSF by Account," National Science Foundation, http://dellweb.bfa.nsf.gov/NSFHist_constant.htm, accessed April 16, 2017.

53. The fifth NSF investment was a contract with a corporation to develop journal citation ranking measures. I have been unable to determine the amount of that contract and thus do not include it in these calculations.

54. John Padgett and Walter W. Powell (eds.), *The Emergence of Organizations and Markets* (Princeton, NJ: Princeton University Press, 2012).

55. Victoria Johnson and Walter W. Powell, "Poisedness and Propagation: Organizational Emergence and the Transformation of Civic Order in 19th-Century New York City," National Bureau of Economic Research (NBER), working paper 21011, March 2015, http://www.nber.org/papers/w21011.

Chapter 2

1. Enrico Moretti, *The New Geography of Jobs* (Boston: Houghton Mifflin Harcourt, 2012).

2. It is not the newest such description, but an important example can be found in a 2006 report commissioned by then secretary of education Margaret Spellings, which made the point explicit, calling higher education "risk-averse . . . self satisfied . . . and unduly expensive" like the hidebound behemoths that dominated industries such as railroads and steel manufacturing. Those organizations "failed to respond to—or even notice—changes in the world around them" and thus were rendered obsolete and swept

away, a fate increasingly predicted for universities unless drastic changes are made. "A Test of Leadership: Charting the Future of U.S. Higher Education," U.S. Department of Education, 2006, https://www2.ed.gov/about/bdscomm/list/hiedfuture/reports/final -report.pdf.

3. I take the service part of the traditional academic triumvirate of "research, teaching, and service" to refer to service provided to the public through pro bono work off campus rather than to the kinds of on campus administrative service assignments exemplified by faculty committee work.

4. Craig, *College Disrupted.*

5. To cite just one example, in 2011 Florida governor Rick Scott unveiled a proposal to reform the state's colleges and universities. That plan included proposals to shift public support away from degree programs such as anthropology that had few apparent economic prospects. As Scott noted: "If I'm going to take money from a citizen to put into education, then I'm going to take that money to create jobs. So I want that money to go to degrees where people can get jobs in this state." Zac Anderson, "Rick Scott Wants to Shift University Funding away from Some Degrees," *Herald Tribune Politics,* October 10, 2011, http://politics.heraldtribune.com/2011/10/10/rick-scott-wants-to-shift -university-funding-away-from-some-majors/.

6. Clark Kerr, *The Uses of the University,* 5th ed. (Cambridge, MA: Harvard University Press, 2001), xii.

7. For instance, the NSF's "Science and Engineering Indicators" reports that the United States remains the premier destination for internationally mobile undergraduate and graduate students, with 19 percent of all such students enrolling in U.S. colleges. The United Kingdom (the next most popular destination) enrolls 11 percent of internationally mobile students. The U.S. share has declined from 25 percent since 2000 and the composition of students is shifting as more enroll in social science and professional fields. National Science Board, *Science and Engineering Indicators 2014* (Arlington, VA: National Science Board. 2014), 2–43.

8. National Research Council, *Research Universities and the Future of America: Ten Breakthrough Actions Vital to Our Nation's Prosperity and Security* (Washington, DC: National Academies Press, 2012), xi, https://www.nap.edu/catalog/13396/research -universities-and-the-future-of-america-ten-breakthrough-actions.

9. AnnaLee Saxenian, *Regional Advantage: Culture and Competition in Silicon Valley and Route 128* (Cambridge, MA: Harvard University Press, 1994); Walter W. Powell, Kelley Packalen, and Kjersten Whittington, "Organizational and Institutional Genesis: The Emergence of High-Tech Clusters in the Life Sciences," in *The Emergence of Organizations and Markets,* ed. John Padgett and Walter W. Powell (Princeton, NJ: Princeton University Press, 2012); Jason Owen-Smith and Walter W. Powell, "Knowledge Networks as Channels and Conduits: The Effects of Spillovers in the Boston Biotechnology Community," *Organization Science* 15, no. 1 (2004): 5–21; Lee Fleming, Santiago Mingo, and David Chen, "Collaborative Brokerage, Generative Creativity, and Creative Success," *Administrative Science Quarterly* 53, no. 3 (2007): 443–475.

10. Derek Thompson, "Inside Google's Moonshot Factory," *The Atlantic,* November 2017, p. 62.

11. John Gertner, *The Idea Factory: Bell Labs and the Great Age of American Innovation* (New York: Penguin, 2012), 99.

12. Mitchell L. Stevens and Ben Gebre-Medhin, "Association, Service, Market: Higher Education in American Political Development," *Annual Review of Sociology* 42, no. 1 (2016): 121–142.

13. Indeed, German institutions played much the same role as source and hub in the late 1800s that their American counterparts would come to. See, for instance, Johann Peter Murman, *Knowledge and Competitive Advantage: The Co-evolution of Firms, Technology and National Institutions* (Cambridge: Cambridge University Press, 2003). I would argue that they did not serve as effectively as anchors precisely because they did not integrate undergraduate teaching and learning with the research mission.

14. Roger L. Geiger, *The History of American Higher Education: Learning and Culture from the Founding to World War II* (New York: Princeton University Press, 2016).

15. Richard M. Freeland, *Academia's Golden Age: Universities in Massachusetts 1945-1970* (Oxford, UK: Oxford University Press, 1992.)

16. David Larabee, *A Perfect Mess: The Unlikely Ascendancy of American Higher Education* (Chicago: University of Chicago Press, 2017).

17. Roger Geiger, *To Advance Knowledge: The Growth of American Research Universities, 1900-1940* (Oxford, UK: Oxford University Press, 1986).

18. Article three of that document noted, "Religion, morality, and knowledge being necessary to good government and the happiness of mankind, schools and the means of education shall forever be encouraged."

19. Kerr, *Uses of the University*, 38.

20. Stevens and Gebre-Medhin, "Association, Service, Market."

21. Margaret P. O'Mara, *Cities of Knowledge: Cold War Science and the Search for the Next Silicon Valley* (Princeton, NJ: Princeton University Press, 2005), 10.

22. Eric Bennett, *Workshops of Empire: Stegner, Engle, and American Creative Writing During the Cold War* (Iowa City: University of Iowa Press, 2015).

23. Christopher P. Loss, *Between Citizens and the State: The Politics of American Higher Education in the 20th Century* (Princeton, NJ: Princeton University Press, 2012), 13.

24. Larabee, "A Perfect Mess," Kindle location 2667–2669.

25. Fred Block and Margaret Somers, *The Power of Market Fundamentalism: Karl Polanyi's Critique* (Cambridge, MA: Harvard University Press, 2014).

26. President's Commission on Higher Education, *Higher Education for American Democracy*, Vol. 1 (Washington, DC: U.S. Government Printing Office, 1947), v.

27. Ethan Schrum, "Establishing a Democratic Religion: Metaphysics and Democracy in Debates over the President's Commission on Higher Education," *History of Education Quarterly* 47, no. 3 (2007): 281.

28. Julia Reuben and Linda Perkins, "Introduction: Commemorating the 60th Anniversary of the President's Commission Report, *Higher Education for American Democracy*," *History of Education Quarterly* 47, no. 3 (2007): 265–276.

29. President's Commission on Higher Education, *Higher Education for American Democracy*, Vol. 1, p. 8.

30. Ibid., 9.

31. Bill Readings, *The University in Ruins* (Cambridge, MA: Harvard University Press, 1996); Loss, *Between Citizens and the State*, 19.

32. President's Commission on Higher Education, *Higher Education for American Democracy*, Vol. 1, p. 22.

33. Ibid., Vol. 2, p. 88.

34. Jeremy Williams points out the early rhetoric of diversity focused on a diverse set of institutions of higher education necessary to create an ecology that offered broad and equal access in service to democratic goals. In the wake of the civil rights era, the language of diversity shifted to the "identities of students." Jeremy Williams, "Innovation for What? The Politics of Inequality in Higher Education," *Dissent*, Winter 2016, https://www.dissentmagazine.org/article/innovation-for-what-the-politics-of-inequality-in-higher-education.

35. President's Commission on Higher Education, *Higher Education for American Democracy*, Vol. 5, p. 58.

36. Ibid., 57.

37. Ibid.

38. Ibid.

39. Totals calculated using the Bureau of Labor Statistics CPI Inflation Calculator (http://www.bls.gov/data/inflation_calculator.htm accessed 10/18/2016) from proposals made in President's Commission on Higher Education, *Higher Education for American Democracy*, Vol. 5, pp. 59–63. I report figures adjusted for inflation; the actual appropriations proposed by the commission were $284 million and $526 million, respectively.

40. Total federal obligations for R&D in 1952 are extracted from the NSF Survey of Federal Funds for Research and Development via WebCaspar, http://ncsesdata.nsf.gov/webcaspar, accessed May 17, 2017.

41. Maintenance-of-effort provisions such as these seem to have shaped how state legislatures apportion cuts. F. King Alexander, "Make Maintenance of Effort Permanent," *Inside Higher Education*, January 28, 2010, https://www.insidehighered.com/views/2010/01/28/make-maintenance-effort-permanent.

42. Goldrick-Rab, *Paying the Price*, 2016.

43. John R. Thelin, *A History of American Higher Education* (Baltimore: Johns Hopkins University Press, 2011), 269–270.

44. James G. Harlow, "Five Years of Discussion," *Journal of Higher Education* 24, no. 1 (1953): 17–24. See also T. Raymond McConnell, "A Reply to the Critics," *Journal of Educational Sociology* 22, no. 8 (1949): 533–550; and Schrum, "Establishing a Democratic Religion."

45. Reuben and Perkins, "Introduction: Commemorating the 60th Anniversary," 270.

46. Rebecca S. Lowen, *Creating the Cold War University: The Transformation of Stanford* (Berkeley: University of California Press, 1997); O'Mara, *Cities of Knowledge*.

47. Paula Stephan, *How Economics Shapes Science* (Cambridge, MA: Harvard University Press, 2012).

48. Reuben and Perkins, "Introduction: Commemorating the 60th Anniversary," 271.

49. Daniel Kleinman, *Politics on the Endless Frontier: Postwar Research Policy in the United States* (Durham, NC: Duke University Press, 1995).

50. Daniel Kevles, "The National Science Foundation and the Debate over Post-War Research Policy, 1942–1945: A Political Interpretation of *Science—The Endless Frontier*," *Isis* 68, no. 1 (1977): 16.

51. Harley M. Kilgore, "Science and the Government," *Science* 102, no. 2660 (1945): 631.

52. Kleinman, *Politics on the Endless Frontier*, 158.

53. Ibid., 145.

54. The University of Wisconsin–Madison was founded in 1848 and designated a land-grant institution in 1866. The mission called the Wisconsin Idea was first articulated in 1904 by the campus's sitting president. It was written into state law in 1971 with the establishment of the University of Wisconsin System. That legal definition is the one to which Walker and his staff proposed revisions.

55. The amendments are proposed in Section 1111:546 of State of Wisconsin Senate Bill 21, which constitutes the executive budget proposed by the governor for the state.

56. David J. Frank and John W. Meyer, "University Expansion and the Knowledge Society," *Theory and Society* 36, no. 4 (2007): 307.

57. Fethke and Policano, *Public No More*.

58. Philip Selznick, *Leadership in Administration: A Sociological Interpretation* (Berkeley: University of California Press, 1984), 16.

59. There is compelling evidence that the increasing educational attainment of citizens throughout the twentieth century is what made the United States the richest country in the world. So much of what might be called the public-good effect of universities is really the aggregation of private goods that come from individual education. Still, this finding offers little rationale for the costly bundling of research and teaching. That rationale has to come from aspects of public goods produced by universities that reach beyond the sum of individual benefits. Claudia Goldin and Lawrence F. Katz, *The Race Between Education and Technology* (Cambridge, MA: Belknap Press, 2010).

60. John W. Meyer and Brian Rowan, "Institutionalized Organizations: Formal Structure as Myth and Ceremony," *American Journal of Sociology* 83, no. 2 (1977): 340–363; Paul J. DiMaggio and Walter W. Powell, "The Iron Cage Revisited: Institutional Isomorphism and Collective Rationality in Organizational Fields," *American Sociological Review* 48, no. 2 (1983): 147–160.

61. This very idea is hotly contested by scholars who argue that the core benefits of the kind of "liberal education" that has been a distinguishing feature of American higher education for hundreds of years is diminished if we understand it primarily in narrowly instrumental terms.

62. Jonathan R. Cole, *The Great American University: Its Rise to Preeminence, Its Indispensable National Role, and Why It Must Be Protected* (New York: PublicAffairs, 2009).

63. Peter Blau and Otis D. Duncan, *The American Occupational Structure* (New York: Free Press, 1978).

64. Michael Hout, "Social and Economic Returns to a College Education in America," *Annual Review of Sociology* 38 (2012): 380.

65. Mitchell L. Stevens, Elizabeth A. Armstrong, and Richard Arum, "Sieve, Incubator, Temple, Hub: Empirical and Theoretical Advances in the Sociology of Higher Education," *Annual Review of Sociology* 34, no. 1 (2008): 127–151.

66. Enrico Moretti, "Worker's Education, Spillovers, and Productivity: Evidence from Plant Level Production Functions," *American Economic Review* 94, no. 3 (2004): 656–690.

67. Lance Lochner and Enrico Moretti, "The Effect of Education on Crime: Evidence from Prison Inmates, Arrests, and Self Reports," *American Economic Review* 94, no. 1 (2004): 155–189.

68. Stevens, Armstrong, and Arum, "Sieve, Incubator, Temple, Hub."

69. Hout, "Social and Economic Returns to College Education in America," 380.

70. McMahon, *Higher Learning and the Greater Good*.

71. Goldin and Katz, *Race Between Education and Technology*; McMahon, *Higher Learning and the Greater Good*.

72. Goldrick-Rab, *Paying the Price*; Armstrong and Hamilton, *Paying for the Party*.

73. Christenson and Eyring, *The Innovative University*.

74. Kenneth Arrow, "Economic Welfare and the Allocation of Resources for Invention," in *The Rate and Direction of Inventive Activity*, ed. Josh Lerner and Scott Stern (Cambridge, MA: National Bureau of Economic Research, 1962); Partha Dasgupta and Paul David, "Toward a New Economics of Science," *Research Policy* 23, no. 5 (1994): 487–521.

75. Richard R. Nelson, "The Simple Economics of Basic Scientific Research," *Journal of Political Economy* 67, no. 3 (1959): 297–306.

76. This argument is made explicitly in *Public No More* (2012) by Gary Fethke and Andrew Policano, who propose, among other things, that independent business schools or auxiliary units like intercollegiate athletics or hospitals should become the model for academic units in a university that is resolutely public no more.

77. This description is so simple as to be a caricature. In reality, universities vary dramatically in the extent to which they implement RCM and in the details of particular implementation. The general insight that RCM is a means to decentralize decision making in the university. The concern that it mitigates against investments in interdisciplinary collaboration, in important subjects for which there might be less demand such as foreign languages, and in campuswide public goods is a common one.

78. Indirect or facilities and administration (F&A) costs are audited amounts that are added to the direct costs of federal grants to help universities recover the costs of investments necessary to support funded research. The AAU recently produced a useful infographic that summarizes the uses to which direct and indirect costs are put. "Costs of Research Infographic," Association of American Universities, May 26, 2017, https://www.aau.edu/key-issues/costs-research-infographic.

79. This, combined with the fact that federal grants generally do not pay the full cost of the research they support, has prompted at least one analyst of public research university budgets to argue that less research-intensive and more teaching-intensive

areas of the university such as the humanities and social sciences subsidize the work of the scientific fields that rely more heavily on federal funding. Christopher Newfield, *The Great Mistake: How We Wrecked Public Universities and How We Can Fix Them* (Baltimore: Johns Hopkins University Press, 2016).

80. As the economy has financialized, firms like Chrysler are increasingly making a greater profit off their financing arms than they do from their physical products. In this regard, see Greta Krippner, *Capitalizing on Crisis: The Political Origins of the Rise of Finance* (Cambridge, MA: Harvard University Press, 2011).

81. Some good data is available about the cost of university research libraries. The Association of Research Libraries (ARL) publishes statistics based on a survey of some 115 member institutions. They found that the mean university library cost just under $30 million in the 2013–2014 academic year. See Martha Kyrillidou, Shaneka Morris, and Gary Roebuck, *ARL Statistics 2013–2014* (Washington, DC: Association of Research Libraries, 2014), 25. The Department of Education's IPEDS survey has also started collecting data on research library expenditures, which allows us to characterize library costs in per-student terms to allow comparisons. On this measure, a large public research university, the University of California, Berkeley, spent $1,620 per student on its library in 2014. At the very high end, Harvard, a rich, private institution, spent more than $8,500 per student on library operations.

82. Michael Cohen and James March, *Leadership and Ambiguity: The American College President* (New York: McGraw-Hill, 1974), 117.

83. David Stark, *The Sense of Dissonance: Accounts of Worth in Economic Life* (New York: Princeton University Press, 2009).

84. Ibid.

85. Ibid., 11.

86. Kerr, *Uses of the University*, 105.

87. Jeffrey Williams, *How to Be an Intellectual: Essays on Criticism, Culture, and the University* (New York: Fordham University Press, 2014).

Chapter 3

1. I realize that there is a complicated (and to my mind overly scholastic) argument to be had about the relative meanings of the terms *innovation, invention*, and *discovery*. I basically choose to ignore it here in order to make headway on what I take to be a more important question.

2. Joseph Schumpeter, *Capitalism, Socialism, and Democracy* (New York: Harper Brothers, 1942).

3. Thomas Kuhn, *The Structure of Scientific Revolutions,* 3rd ed. (Chicago: University of Chicago Press, 1996); Peter Galison, *Einstein's Clocks and Poincaré's Maps* (New York: Norton, 2004).

4. Joseph Schumpeter, "The Creative Response in Economic History," *Journal of Economic History* 7, no. 2 (1947): 151.

5. Joseph Schumpeter, *The Theory of Economic Development: An Inquiry into Profits, Capital, Credit, Interest, and the Business Cycle* (Cambridge, MA: Harvard University Press, 1934), 66.

6. Ecclesiastes 1:9 (King James Version).

7. Robert K. Merton, *On the Shoulders of Giants: A Shandean Post-Script* (New York: Free Press, 1965).

8. Richard R. Nelson and Sidney Winter, *An Evolutionary Theory of Economic Change* (Cambridge, MA: Belknap Press, 1982), 130.

9. For this, among other reasons, I find the common distinction between basic and applied research, which depends wholly on the intentions of funders and performers, to be unhelpful in describing the university. The same piece of knowledge can be basic at one point, applied at another, or both at the same time.

10. Steve Cichon, "Everything from This 1991 Radio Shack Ad You Can Now Do with Your Phone," *Huffington Post*, January 16, 2014, http://www.huffingtonpost.com/steve-cichon/radio-shack-ad_b_4612973.html.

11. A web page developed by the Association of American Universities highlights many academic contributions to the smartphone. See "Universities Made Your Smartphone Smart," Association of American Universities, September 19, 2017, https://www.aau.edu/research/smartphone.aspx.

12. "Apple Reinvents the Phone with iPhone," press release, January 9, 2007, http://www.apple.com/pr/library/2007/01/09Apple-Reinvents-the-Phone-with-iPhone.html.

13. Samuel Hurst and James E. Parks, "Electrical Sensor of Plane Coordinates," U.S. Patent 3,662,105, filed May 21, 1970, issued May 9, 1972.

14. Wayne Westerman, "Hand Tracking, Finger Identification, and Chordic Manipulation on a Multi-touch Surface," PhD diss., University of Delaware, 1999.

15. Juliana Reyes, "How I Sold My Company to Apple: Jeff White Former Finger-Works CEO [Q&A]," *Technically Philly*, January 9, 2013, http://technical.ly/philly/2013/01/09/jeff-white-fingerworks-apple-touchscreen/.

16. For more on this general dynamic, see Mariana Mazucatto, *The Entrepreneurial State: Debunking Public vs. Private Sector Myths* (New York: PublicAffairs, 2015). Mazucatto also devotes substantial time to a more detailed analysis of the smartphone than I provide here.

17. NSF graduate research fellowship recipients can be identified using a search engine at "Award Offers and Honorable Mentions List," FastLane Graduate Research Fellowship Program, https://www.fastlane.nsf.gov/grfp/AwardeeList.do?method=loadAwardeeList, accessed May 10, 2017.

18. Schumpeter, "The Creative Response in Economic History," 150.

19. Michael D. Cohen, James G. March, and Johan P. Olsen, "A Garbage Can Model of Organizational Choice," *Administrative Science Quarterly* 17, no. 1 (1972): 1–25.

20. FACA Database, http://facadatabase.gov, accessed December 23, 2015.

21. Brian Uzzi, Satyam Mukherjee, Michael Stringer, and Ben Jones, "Atypical Combinations and Scientific Impact," *Science* 342, no. 6157 (2013): 468–472.

22. Wesley M. Cohen and Daniel A. Levinthal, "Innovation and Learning: The Two Faces of R&D," *Economic Journal* 99, no. 397 (1989): 5569–5596.

23. Wesley M. Cohen and Daniel A. Levinthal, "Absorptive Capacity: A New Perspective on Learning and Innovation," *Administrative Science Quarterly* 35, no. 1 (1990): 131.

24. César A. Hidalgo and Ricardo Hausmann, "The Building Blocks of Economic Complexity," *Proceedings of the National Academy of Science* 106, no. 20 (2009): 10570–10575.

25. Fiona Murray and Scott Stern, "Do Formal Intellectual Property Rights Hinder the Free Flow of Scientific Knowledge? An Empirical Test of the Anti-Commons Hypothesis," *Journal of Economic Behavior and Organization* 63, no. 4 (2007): 648–687.

26. Russell J. Funk and Jason Owen-Smith, "A Dynamic Network Measure of Technological Change," *Management Science* 63, no. 3 (2017): 791–817.

27. Stark, *Sense of Dissonance.*

28. Walter W. Powell, "Neither Market nor Hierarchy, Network Forms of Organization," *Research in Organizational Behavior* 12 (1990): 295–336.

29. Charles Kadushin, *Understanding Social Networks* (New York: Oxford University Press, 2012), 11.

30. Scott E. Page, *The Difference: How the Power of Diversity Creates Better Groups, Firms, Schools, and Societies* (New York: Princeton University Press, 2008).

31. Scott E. Page, *The Diversity Bonus: How Great Teams Pay Off in the Knowledge Economy* (Princeton, NJ: Princeton University Press, 2017).

32. Nikolas Zolas et al., "Wrapping It Up in a Person: Exploring Employment and Earnings Outcomes for Ph.D. Students," *Science* 350, no. 6266 (2015): 1367–1371.

33. Ibid.

34. The Census Bureau economic data we examined are at the establishment level of analysis. Companies can be single- or multi-establishment. In keeping with my earlier invocation of the iPhone, Apple is a company, and your local Apple store is one of its establishments.

35. Scott L. Feld, "The Focused Organization of Social Ties," *American Journal of Sociology* 86, no. 5 (1981): 1015–1035.

36. Cohen and Levinthal, "Absorptive Capacity."

37. Joel Podolny, "Networks as the Pipes and Prisms of the Market," *American Journal of Sociology* 107, no. 1 (2001): 33–60.

38. Mark Granovetter, "The Strength of Weak Ties," *American Journal of Sociology* 78, no. 6 (1973): 1360–1380; Fritz Heider, "Attitudes and Cognitive Organization," *Journal of Psychology* 21, no. 1 (1946): 107–112.

39. For several excellent introductions to different conceptions of social capital, see Pierre Bourdieu and Loïc Wacquant, *An Invitation to Reflexive Sociology* (Chicago: University of Chicago Press, 1992); Ronald Burt, *Structural Holes: The Social Structure of Competition* (Cambridge, MA: Harvard University Press, 1992); Nan Lin, *Social Capital: A Theory of Social Structure and Action* (Cambridge: Cambridge University Press, 2001); Alejandro Portes, *The Economic Sociology of Immigration: Essays on Networks, Ethnicity, and Immigration* (New York: Russell Sage, 1998); and Robert Putnam, *Bowling Alone: The Collapse and Revival of American Community* (New York: Simon and Schuster, 2000).

40. James S. Coleman, "Social Capital in the Creation of Human Capital," in "Organizations and Institutions: Sociological and Economic Approaches to the Analysis of Social Structure," supplement, *American Journal of Sociology* 94 (1988): S95–S120.

41. Ronald Burt, "Structural Holes and Good Ideas," *American Journal of Sociology* 110, no. 2 (2004): 349–399.

42. David Obstfeld, "Social Networks, the *Tertius Iungens* Orientation, and Involvement in Innovation," *Administrative Science Quarterly* 50, no. 1 (2005): 100–130.

43. Russell Funk, "Making the Most of Where You Are: Geography, Networks, and Innovation in Organizations," *Academy of Management Journal* 57, no. 1 (2014): 193–222.

44. Burt, "Structural Holes and Good Ideas," 393.

45. Morten T. Hansen, "The Search-Transfer Problem: The Role of Weak Ties in Sharing Knowledge Across Organization Subunits," *Administrative Science Quarterly* 44, no. 1 (1999): 82–111.

46. Robert K. Merton, "The Matthew Effect in Science," *Science* 159, no. 3810 (1968): 56–63.

47. Jason Owen-Smith, "Managing Laboratory Work Through Skepticism: Processes of Evaluation and Control," *American Sociological Review* 66, no. 3 (2001): 427–452.

48. Harry Collins, *Changing Order: Replication and Induction in Scientific Practice* (Chicago: University of Chicago Press, 1992).

49. Coleman, "Social Capital in the Creation of Human Capital"; Powell, "Neither Market nor Hierarchy."

50. John Lombardi, *How Universities Work* (Baltimore: Johns Hopkins University Press, 2013), 8.

51. Leon Festinger, Kurt Back, and Stanley Schachter, *Social Pressures in Informal Groups: A Study of Human Factors in Housing* (Stanford, CA: Stanford University Press, 1951).

52. Heider, "Attitudes and Cognitive Organization"; Dorwin Cartwright and Frank Harary, "Structural Balance: A Generalization of Heider's Theory," *Psychological Review* 63, no. 5 (1956): 277–293; Norman P. Hummon, and Patrick Dorien, "Some Dynamics of Social Balance Processes: Bringing Heider Back into Balance Theory," *Social Networks* 25 (2003): 17–49.

53. Linus Dahlander and Daniel McFarland, "Ties That Last: Tie Formation and Persistence in Research Collaborations over Time," *Administrative Science Quarterly* 58, no. 1 (2013): 69–110.

54. When inflation is taken into account, this is about $20 billion in 2013 dollars.

55. Peter Galison, *Image and Logic: A Material Culture of Microphysics* (Chicago: University of Chicago Press, 1997), 820 and more generally Chapter 4. For a short and accessible piece on how collaboration in the wartime laboratories altered the culture of physics, see David Kaiser, "Shut Up and Calculate," *Nature* 505 (2014): 153–155.

56. Craig Rawlings, Daniel McFarland, Linus Dahlander, and Dan Wang, "Streams of Thought: Knowledge Flows and Intellectual Cohesion in a Multidisciplinary Era," *Social Forces* 93, no. 4 (2015): 1687–1722.

57. Festinger, Bach, and Schachter, *Social Pressure in Informal Groups*.

58. Felichism W. Kabo et al., "Proximity Effects on the Dynamics and Outcomes of Scientific Collaborations," *Research Policy* 43, no. 9 (2014): 1469–1485; Felichism Kabo,

Yongha Hwang, Margaret Levenstein, and Jason Owen-Smith, "Shared Paths to the Lab: A Sociospatial Network Analysis of Collaboration," *Environment and Behavior* 47, no. 1 (2015): 57–84.

59. Judith Butler, *Gender Trouble: Feminism and the Subversion of Identity* (New York: Routledge, 1990). I thank Wendy Espeland for suggesting Butler's work as a case study for this discussion and Paul Vicinanza for impressive research assistance in developing it.

60. Claire B. Potter, "Books that Matter: Twenty-Five Years of Gender Trouble," Society for U.S. Intellectual History, January 1, 2016, http://s-usih.org/2016/01/books-that-matter-gender-trouble.html.

61. Moya Lloyd, *Judith Butler: From Norms to Politics* (Malden, MA: Polity Press, 2007); Isa Leshko, "Who Did You Say You Are? An Interview with Riki Anne Wilchins," *Gay Community News* 22, no. 1 (1996): 29.

62. Leslie Camhi, "Masculine Feminine: Rrose Is a Rrose Is a Rrose: Gender Performance in Photography," *Village Voice*, February 4, 1997, https://www.mutualart.com/Article/Masculine-feminine/26A238CB74765952; Molly Fischer, "Think Gender Is Performance? You Have Judith Butler to Thank for That," *New York Magazine*, June 13, 2016, http://nymag.com/thecut/2016/06/judith-butler-c-v-r.html.

63. Vicki Schultz, "Reconceptualizing Sexual Harassment," *Yale Law Journal, Faculty Scholarship Series* 107 (1998): 1683–1805.

64. Arlene I. Lev, "Disordering Gender Identity: Gender Identity Disorder in the *DSM-IV-TR*," *Journal of Psychology and Human Sexuality* 17, no. 3–4 (2006): 35–69.

65. In the course of writing this book I have read broadly beyond my own areas of specialization. *Gender Trouble* seems no more notably difficult for a nonspecialist to read than, for instance, a stem-cell biology article.

66. Judith Butler, "A 'Bad Writer' Bites Back," *New York Times*, March 20, 1999, http://query.nytimes.com/gst/fullpage.html?res=950CE5D61531F933A15750C0A96F958260.

67. Judith Butler, "Speaking Up, Talking Back: Joan Scott's Critical Feminism," in *The Question of Gender: Joan W. Scott's Critical Feminism*, ed. J. Butler and E. Weed (Bloomington: Indiana University Press, 2011), 20.

68. Lila Abu-Lughod, Yasmine Ergas, Donna Haraway, Evelyn Fox Keller, Dorinne Kondo, Rayna Rapp, Carroll Smith-Rosenberg, and Louise Tilly.

69. Sara Ahmed, "Interview with Judith Butler," *Sexualities* 19, no. 4 (2016): 487.

70. Higher Education Research and Development Survey, 2014, https://ncsesdata.nsf.gov/webcaspar/.

71. There is some very compelling evidence from the life sciences that more certain, longer-term funding aimed at supporting the research programs of individuals yields higher-impact discoveries than the sorts of project-oriented funding I describe here. See, for instance, Pierre Azoulay, Joshua Graff-Zivin, and Gustavo Manso, "Incentives and Creativity: Evidence from the Academic Life Sciences," *RAND Journal of Economics* 42, no. 3 (2011): 527–554.

72. On peer review, see Daryl E. Chubin and Edward J. Hackett, *Peerless Science: Peer Review and U.S. Science Policy* (Albany: State University of New York Press, 1990).

On hypercompetition in biomedicine, see Bruce Alberts, Marc W. Kirschner, Shirley Tighlman, and Harold Varmus, "Rescuing US Biomedical Research from Its Systematic Flaws," *Proceedings of the National Academy of Sciences* 111, no. 16 (2014): 5773–5777.

73. See, for example, Jane Maienschein, *Whose View of Life? Embryos, Cloning, and Stem Cells* (Cambridge, MA: Harvard University Press, 2003); and Charis Thompson, *Good Science: The Ethical Choreography of Stem Cell Research* (Cambridge, MA: MIT Press, 2013)

74. See, for example, Christopher T. Scott, Jason Owen-Smith, and Jennifer B. McCormick, "We Must Reverse the Bush Legacy of Stem Cell Problems," *Nature* 460 (2009): 33; and Jason Owen-Smith, Christopher T. Scott, and Jennifer B. McCormick, "Expand and Regularize Federal Funding for Human Pluripotent Stem Cell Research," *Journal of Policy Analysis and Management* 31, no. 3 (2012): 714–722).

75. Michael J. Shamblott et al., "Derivation of Pluripotent Stem Cells from Cultured Human Primordial Germ Cells," *Proceedings of the National Academy of Sciences* 95, no. 23 (1998): 13726–13731; James A. Thomson et al., "Embryonic Stem Cell Lines Derived from Human Blastocysts," *Science* 282, no. 5391 (1998): 1145–1147. Thomson's group had earlier demonstrated the derivation of embryonic stem cells in rhesus monkeys and, on the strength of that NIH-funded work, the Wisconsin Alumni Research Foundation (WARF) had applied for a patent on primate embryonic stem cells. WARF and Thomson also patented the process for deriving human embryonic stem cells.

76. Christopher Scott, Jennifer McCormick, and Jason Owen-Smith, "And Then There Were Two: Use of hESC Lines," *Nature Biotechnology* 27, no. 8 (2009): 696–697; Christopher T. Scott et al., "Federal Policy and the Use of Pluripotent Stem Cells," *Nature Methods* 7 (2010): 866–867; Christopher T. Scott et al., "Democracy Derived? New Trajectories in Pluripotent Stem Cell Research," *Cell* 145, no. 6 (2011): 820–826.

77. Jeffrey L. Furman, Fiona Murray, and Scott Stern, "Growing Stem Cells: The Impact of Federal Funding Policy on the U.S. Scientific Frontier," *Journal of Policy Analysis and Management* 31, no. 3 (2012): 661–705.

78. Donald E. Stokes, *Pasteur's Quadrant: Basic Science and Technological Innovation* (Washington, DC: Brookings Institution Press, 1997).

79. Timothy Caulfield et al., "The Stem Cell Research Environment: A Patchwork of Patchworks," *Stem Cell Reviews and Reports* 5, no. 2 (2009): 82–88.

80. Passaging is the process by which stem cell scientists create new generations of cells from existing cultures for their work.

81. Patterning is the process by which stem cell scientists induce pluripotent cells to turn into specific types of tissues found in the adult human body, such as neurons.

82. The exact language of the relevant NIH restriction reads, "NIH-funded research with this line is limited to research consistent with the following language from the informed consent document: 'These cells will be used to study the embryonic development of endoderm with a focus on pancreatic formation. The long-term goal is to create human pancreatic islets that contain ß cells, the cells that produce insulin, for transplantation into diabetics.'" NIH Human Embryonic Stem Cell Registry, http://grants.nih.gov/stem_cells/registry/current.htm?id=40, accessed February 20, 2016.

Chapter 4

1. Mitchell Stevens makes a similar point with regard to the physical plant of selective colleges. Campuses, the weight of tradition their buildings and grounds represent, and the geographic associations that define athletic and often academic rivalries anchor the institutions in place. Mitchell Stevens, *Creating a Class: College Admissions and the Education of Elites* (Cambridge, MA: Harvard University Press, 2009) 254–255.

2. Blake Gumprecht, *The American College Town* (Amherst: University of Massachusetts Press, 2008).

3. Zoltan Acs, *Innovation and the Growth of Cities* (Cheltenham, UK: Edward Elgar, 2002), 3–5; John M. Quigly, "Urban Diversity and Economic Growth," *Journal of Economic Perspectives* 12, no. 2 (1998): 127–138.

4. Scott Andes, "140 Billion Reasons Why Cities Should Care About Federal R&D in Their Backyards," Brookings Institution, January 12, 2017, https://www.brookings.edu/blog/metropolitan-revolution/2017/01/12/140-billion-reasons-why-cities-should-care-about-federal-rd-in-their-backyards/.

5. Dean Gatzlaff, Stacy Sirmans, and Barry Diskin, "The Effect of Anchor Tenant Loss on Shopping Center Rents," *Journal of Real Estate Research* 9, no. 1 (1994): 99–110.

6. B. Peter Pashigian and Eric D. Gould, "Internalizing Externalities: The Pricing of Space in Shopping Malls," *Journal of Law and Economics* 41, no. 1 (1998): 116.

7. Ajay Agrawal and Iain M. Cockburn, "The Anchor Tenant Hypothesis: Exploring the Role of Large, Local R&D-Intensive Firms in Regional Innovation Systems," *International Journal of Industrial Organization* 21 (2003): 1227–1253.

8. Maryann Feldman, "The Locational Dynamics of U.S. Biotechnology Firms: Knowledge Externalities and the Anchor Hypothesis," *Industry and Innovation* 10, no. 3 (2003): 311–329.

9. Ibid.

10. Jason Owen-Smith and Walter W. Powell, "Knowledge Networks as Channels and Conduits: The Effects of Spillovers in the Boston Biotechnology Community," *Organization Science* 15, no. 1 (2004): 5–21. See also Jason Owen-Smith and Walter W. Powell, "Accounting for Emergence and Novelty in Boston and Bay Area Biotechnology," in *Cluster Genesis: Technology-Based Industrial Development*, ed. Maryann Feldman and Pontus Braunerhjelm (Oxford, UK: Oxford University Press, 2006).

11. Walter W. Powell, Kelley Packalen, and Kjersten Whittington, "Organizational and Institutional Genesis: The Emergence of High-Tech Clusters in the Life Sciences," in *The Emergence of Organizations and Markets*, ed. John Padgett and Walter W. Powell (Princeton, NJ: Princeton University Press, 2012). 439.

12. Internal Revenue Service, "Exemption Requirements—501(c)(3) Organizations," https://www.irs.gov/charities-non-profits/charitable-organizations/exemption-requirements-section-501-c-3-organizations, accessed December 26, 2016.

13. Burton Weisbrod, Jeffrey P. Ballou, and Evelyn D. Asch, *Mission and Money: Understanding the University* (Cambridge: Cambridge University Press, 2008).

14. Burton Weisbrod, *The Nonprofit Economy* (Cambridge, MA: Harvard University Press, 1991).

15. Internal Revenue Service, "Organizational Test—Internal Revenue Code Section 501(c)(3)," https://www.irs.gov/charities-non-profits/charitable-organizations/organizational-test-internal-revenue-code-section-501c3, accessed December 26, 2016.

16. Gumprecht, *American College Town*, 66.

17. Ibid., 63.

18. Arik Lifschitz, Michael Sauder, and Mitchell L. Stevens, "Football as a Status System in U.S. Higher Education," *Sociology of Education* 87, no. 3 (2014): 204–219.

19. Jane Jacobs, *The Death and Life of Great American Cities* (New York: Random House, 1961), 267.

20. The architecture of technology firms, largely structured as suburban campuses, owes much to their historical connection to universities, their overwhelming need to attract skilled people trained by universities, and the history of federal investments that led early technology companies to locate outside established urban cores. Margaret P. O'Mara, *Cities of Knowledge: Cold War Science and the Search for the Next Silicon Valley* (Princeton, NJ: Princeton University Press, 2005).

21. Daniel F. Chambliss and Christopher Takacs, *How College Works* (Cambridge, MA: Harvard University Press, 2014), 102.

22. See, for instance, O'Mara's description of town-and-gown conflicts surrounding Stanford's economic efforts in the 1970s. O'Mara, *Cities of Knowledge*.

23. John Sedgwick, "The Last Boola-Boola," *GQ*, April 1994, p. 182.

24. Thomas Kaplan, "Levin at 15 Years: Yale's Greatest?" *Yale Daily News*, October 2, 2008, http://yaledailynews.com/blog/2008/10/02/levin-at-15-years-yales-greatest/.

25. Shiri M. Bresnitz, *The Fountain of Knowledge: The Role of Universities in Economic Development* (Palo Alto, CA: Stanford University Press, 2014), particularly chap. 4.

26. Ibid., 60.

27. Ibid., 65.

28. The story I summarize here differs from others in the details, but it is far from unique. Wayne State University has undertaken significant work to revitalize midtown Detroit. Carnegie Mellon University and the University of Pittsburgh have played important roles in the resurgence of Pittsburgh, to name just two examples.

29. Bresnitz, *Fountain of Knowledge*, 65.

30. Ibid., 71.

31. Ibid., 68.

32. Davarian Baldwin, "When Universities Swallow Cities," *Chronicle of Higher Education*, July 30, 2017, https://www.chronicle.com/article/When-Universities-Swallow/240739.

33. Richard C. Levin, "Universities and Cities: The View from New Haven," Yale University Inaugural Colloquium, January 30, 2003, https://web.archive.org/web/20030219103735/http://www.yale.edu/opa/president/case_western_20030130.html.

34. For a set of detailed and sensitive portraits of several university community relationships, see David Maurrasse, *Beyond the Campus: How Colleges and Universities Form Partnerships with Their Communities* (New York: Routledge, 2002).

35. Paul Krugman, "Increasing Returns and Economic Geography," *Journal of Political Economy* 99, no. 3 (1991): 483–499; Feldman, "Locational Dynamics of U.S. Biotechnology Firms."

36. See, for instance, CampusPhilly (http://campusphilly.org), a nonprofit organization that works with businesses, government, colleges, and universities in the Philadelphia area to introduce students to the city in hopes of enticing them to remain and work there after graduation.

37. Nathaniel Goldschlag et al., "Research Funding and Regional Economies," NBER, working paper 23018, January 2017, http://www.nber.org/papers/w23018.

38. Bruce Weinberg et al., "Science Funding and Short Term Economic Activity," *Science* 344, no. 6179 (2014): 41–43.

39. Zolas et al., "Wrapping It Up in a Person."

40. Yulia Chhabra, Margaret Levenstein, and Jason Owen-Smith, "Local Fiscal Multiplier on R&D and Science Spending: Evidence from the American Recovery and Reinvestment Act," working paper, University of Michigan, 2018.

41. See, among many others, Adam B. Jaffe, Manuel Trajtenberg, and Rebecca Henderson, "Geographic Localization of Knowledge Spillovers as Evidenced by Patent Citations," *Quarterly Journal of Economics* 108, no. 3 (1993): 577–598; Stefano Breschi and Francesco Lissoni, "Knowledge Spillovers and Local Innovation Systems: A Critical Survey," *Industrial and Corporate Change* 10, no. 4 (2001): 975–1005; and Lynne G. Zucker, Michael Darby, and Jeff Armstrong, "Geographically Localized Knowledge: Spillovers or Markets," *Economic Inquiry* 36, no. 1 (1998): 65–86.

42. F. Dacunto and L. Yang, "Financial Advice and the Entrepreneurial Spillovers of Basic Research," paper presented at the meeting of the American Economic Association, Chicago, Illinois, January, 2017.

43. Sunil Iyengar and Ayanna Hudson, "Who Knew? Arts Education Fuels the Economy," *Chronicle of Higher Education*, March 10, 2014. https://www.chronicle.com/article/Who-Knew-Arts-Education-Fuels/145217.

44. Richard Florida, *The Rise of the Creative Class, Revisited* (New York: Basic Books, 2012), 310–311.

45. See Bresnitz, *Fountain of Knowledge*; Owen-Smith and Powell, "Knowledge Networks as Channels and Conduits"; Owen-Smith and Powell, "Accounting for Emergence and Novelty"; and Powell, Packalen, and Whittington, "Organizational and Institutional Genesis," to name a few.

46. Christopher Henke, *Cultivating Science, Harvesting Power: Science and Industrial Agriculture in California* (Cambridge, MA: MIT Press, 2008).

47. Fred Turner, *From Counterculture to Cyberculture: Steward Brand, the Whole Earth Network, and the Rise of Digital Utopianism* (Chicago: University of Chicago Press, 2006).

48. George Taber, *The Judgment of Paris: California vs. France and the Historic 1976 Paris Wine Tasting That Revolutionized Wine* (New York: Scribner, 2005).

49. Ibid., 1.

50. James Lapsley and Daniel Sumner, "We Are Both Hosts: Napa Valley, UC Davis, and the Search for Quality," in *Public Universities and Regional Growth: Insights from the*

University of California, ed. Martin Kenney and David Mowery (Palo Alto, CA: Stanford University Press, 2014).

51. Dorothy J. Gaiter, "The Warren Winiarski Interview," *Grape Collective*, March 24, 2016, https://grapecollective.com/articles/the-warren-winiarski-interview.

52. Taber's book *The Judgment of Paris* makes the connection between the university and the wine industry in the region very clear. For other, more detailed discussions, see James Lapsley, *Bottled Poetry: Napa Winemaking from Prohibition to the Modern Era* (Berkeley: University of California Press, 1997); and Jerry Patchell, *The Territorial Organization of Variety: Cooperation and Competition in Bordeaux, Napa, and Chianti Classico* (New York: Ashgate, 2011).

53. Lapsley and Sumner, "We Are Both Hosts."

54. Fiona M. S. Morton and Joel Podolny, "Love or Money? The Effects of Owner Motivation in the California Wine Industry," *Journal of Industrial Economics* 50, no. 4 (2002): 431–456.

55. Lapsley and Sumner, "We Are Both Hosts," Kindle location 3413.

56. Data extracted from the NSF Survey of Research and Development Expenditures at Universities and Colleges/Higher Education Research and Development Survey, https://ncsesdata.nsf.gov/webcaspar/index.jsp?subHeader=WebCASPARHome, accessed May 17, 2017.

57. Linda Bisson et al., "The Present and Future of the International Wine Industry," *Nature* 418 (2002): 696–699.

58. Lapsley and Sumner, "We Are Both Hosts."

59. For a very different example of the co-evolution of industries and universities, see Murmann's detailed analysis of nineteenth-century German dyestuffs. Johann P. Murmann, *Knowledge and Competitive Advantage: The Coevolution of Firms, Technology, and National Institutions* (Cambridge: Cambridge University Press, 2003).

60. Lapsley and Sumner, "We Are Both Hosts," Kindle location 3514–3516.

61. Ibid., Kindle location 3695–3687.

62. Ibid., Kindle location 3354–3356.

63. The idea that cooperation and competition coexist in and improve the work of regional industrial clusters is now commonplace. See, for instance, Walter W. Powell, "Neither Market nor Hierarchy, Network Forms of Organization," *Research in Organizational Behavior* 12 (1990): 295–336; and Michael Porter, "Clusters and the New Economics of Competition," *Harvard Business Review* 76, no. 6 (1998): 77–90. Porter uses Napa as an example, noting that "a host of local institutions is involved with wine, such as the world renowned viticulture and enology program at the University of California at Davis" (78).

64. Lapsley and Sumner, "We Are Both Hosts," Kindle location 3350-3352.

65. Owen-Smith and Powell, "Knowledge Networks as Channels and Conduits"; Owen-Smith and Powell, "Accounting for Emergence and Novelty"; Kjesten Bunker Whittington, Jason Owen-Smith, and Walter W. Powell, "Networks, Propinquity and Innovation in Knowledge Intensive Regions," *Administrative Science Quarterly* 54, no. 1 (2009): 90–122.; Powell et al., "Organizational and Institutional Genesis."

66. Lapsley and Sumner, "We Are Both Hosts," Kindle location 3845.

67. Ibid., Kindle location 3837.

68. Ibid.

69. Lapsley and Sumner, "We Are Both Hosts," Kindle location 3637.

70. A type of aphid that feeds on the roots of particular species of grapes, killing them.

71. To be fair, the outbreak of this insect was, at least in part, also a result of early work done by Davis to develop and test a particular type of rootstock called AxR1. During the 1970s planting boom, Davis researchers and extension personnel recommended AxR1 to vineyards in the region, leading some to argue that Davis had failed Napa winemakers. See George Gale, *Dying on the Vine: How Phylloxera Transformed Wine* (Berkeley: University of California Press, 2011), particularly chap. 8.

Chapter 5

1. Martin L. Weitzman, "Recombinant Growth," *Quarterly Journal of Economics* 113, no. 2 (1998): 331–360.

2. "ATL Fact Sheet," Hartsfield-Jackson Atlanta International Airport, http://www .atl.com/about-atl/atl-factsheet/, accessed February 19, 2017.

3. Anming Zhang, "An Analysis of Fortress Hubs in Airline Networks," *Journal of Transport Economics and Policy* 30, no. 3 (1996): 293–307.

4. Mitchell L. Stevens, Elizabeth A. Armstrong, and Richard Arum, "Sieve, Incubator, Temple, Hub: Empirical and Theoretical Advances in the Sociology of Higher Education," *Annual Review of Sociology* 34, no. 1 (2008): 135.

5. Raj Chetty et al., "Mobility Report Cards: The Role of Colleges in Intergenerational Mobility," working paper, July 2017, http://www.equality-of-opportunity.org/ papers/coll_mrc_paper.pdf.

6. Andrew Abbott, *The System of Professions: An Essay on the Division of Expert Labor* (Chicago: University of Chicago Press, 1988); Steven Brint, *In an Age of Experts: The Changing Role of Professionals in Politics and Public Life* (Princeton, NJ: Princeton University Press, 1994).

7. In the next chapter I will explicitly discuss the need for investments in new types of data to enable better analyses to understand, explain, and improve the public value of academic research.

8. Baxter Pharmaceuticals, for instance, was a key source of corporate leaders in the early years of the biotechnology industry. Monica Higgins, *Career Imprints: Creating Leaders Across an Industry* (New York: Jossey-Bass, 2005).

9. Helena Buhr and Jason Owen-Smith, "Networks as Institutional Support: Law Firm and Venture Capitalist Relationships and Regional Diversity in High-Technology IPOs," *Research in the Sociology of Work* 21 (2010): 95–126.

10. Christoper D. McKenna, *The World's Newest Profession: Management Consulting in the Twentieth Century* (Cambridge: Cambridge University Press, 2006).

11. Andrew Hargadon and Robert I. Sutton, "Technology Brokering and Innovation in a Product Design Firm," *Administrative Science Quarterly* 42, no. 4 (1997): 716–749.

12. Andrew Hargadon, "Brokering Knowledge: Linking, Learning and Innovation," *Research in Organizational Behavior* 24 (2002): 41–85.

13. Stefan Wuchty, Benjamin F. Jones, and Brian Uzzi, "The Increasing Dominance of Teams in Production of Knowledge," *Science* 316, no. 5827 (2007): 1036–1039.

14. Erin Leahey, "From Sole Investigator to Team Scientist: Trends in the Practice and Study of Collaboration," *Annual Review of Sociology* 42 (2016): 82.

15. Benjamin F. Jones, Stefan Wuchty, and Brian Uzzi, "Multi-University Research Teams: Shifting Impact, Geography, and Stratification in Science," *Science* 322, no. 5909 (2008): 1259–1262; see also Jonathon Cummings and Sara Kiesler, "Collaborative Research Across Disciplinary and Organizational Boundaries," *Social Studies of Science* 35, no. 5 (2005): 703–722.

16. Wesley Shrum, Joel Genuth, and Ivan Chompalov, *The Structures of Scientific Collaboration* Cambridge, MA: MIT Press, 2007); Walter W. Powell and Eric Giannella, "Collective Invention and Inventor Networks," in *Handbook of the Economics of Innovation*, ed. Bronwyn Hall and Nathan Rosenberg, vol. 1 (Amsterdam: Elsevier, 2010), 575–605.

17. The data I present here are drawn from Table 5-27 in National Science Board, *Science and Engineering Indicators 2016*, NSB-2016-1 (Arlington, VA: National Science Foundation, 2016), 5-104.

18. It's important to get the denominator right when talking about these kinds of proportions. So here's what I've done. In all cases, I'm taking as a baseline the number of co-authored papers from each sector that involved a researcher from at least one other sector. Papers authored by researchers at two different universities or two different companies don't count in this tally. Researchers from a university working with researchers from a federal agency would. When I report a percentage, it is the proportion of all multisector co-authorships that involve an academic, university-affiliated researcher.

19. Jeff M. Hall et al., "Linkage of Early-Onset Familial Breast Cancer to Chromosome 17q21," *Science* 250, no. 4988 (1990): 1684–1689.

20. Natalie Angier, "Fierce Competition Marked Fervid Race for Cancer Gene," *New York Times*, September 20, 1994, http://www.nytimes.com/1994/09/20/science/fierce-competition-marked-fervid-race-for-cancer-gene.html?pagewanted=all. For a more detailed journalistic treatment of the "race," see Kevin Davies and Michael White, *Breakthrough: The Race to Find the Breast Cancer Gene* (New York: Wiley, 1996). Another useful point of introduction is Rachel Nowak, "Breast Cancer Gene Offers Surprises," *Science* 265, no. 5180 (1994): 1796–1799.

21. Yoshio Miki et al., "A Strong Candidate for the Breast and Ovarian Cancer Gene BRCA1," *Science, New Series* 266, no. 5182 (1994): 67–71.

22. I'm using this example as a means to illustrate some of the things that I mean when I say a university is hub. I cannot and do not try to do justice to the complex business, ethical, and legal questions that have been raised by the patenting of BRCA1 and challenges to it, the development of genetic tests by Myriad, and their application to the preemptive treatment of breast cancer. For more details see, for instance, Shobita Parthasarathy, *Building Genetic Medicine: Breast Cancer, Technology, and the Comparative*

Politics of Health Care (Cambridge, MA: MIT Press, 2012). Indeed many of the details that I draw on in this section come from legal documents filed in the course of a long and contentious court case that eventually ended with the Supreme Court ruling that Myriad's patents on human genes were invalid. See, for instance, Shobita Parthasarathy, *Patent Politics: Life Forms, Markets, and the Public Interest in the United States and Europe* (Chicago: University of Chicago Press, 2017), for an excellent discussion of many of the important controversies surrounding gene patenting.

23. Walter W. Powell, Kenneth Koput, and Laurel Smith-Doerr, "Interorganizational Collaboration and the Locus of Innovation: Networks of Learning in Biotechnology," *Administrative Science Quarterly* 41, no. 1 (1996): 116–145.

24. Benjamin Jones, "The Burden of Knowledge and the 'Death of the Renaissance Man': Is Innovation Getting Harder?" *Review of Economic Studies* 76, no. 1 (2009): 283–317.

25. Harry Collins, *Gravity's Shadow: The Search for Gravitational Waves* (Chicago: University of Chicago Press, 2004); Paul N. Edwards, *A Vast Machine: Computer Models, Climate Data, and the Politics of Global Warming* (Cambridge, MA: MIT Press, 2010).

26. See, for instance, Martha L. Slattery, and Richard A. Kerber, "A Comprehensive Evaluation of Family History and the Risk of Breast Cancer: The Utah Population Database," *Journal of the American Medical Association* 270, no. 13 (1993): 1563–1568.

27. This represents another case of multiple (or near-multiple) discoveries. Large multi-institutional and often multisectoral teams of researchers anchored at Berkeley, at the University of Michigan, and at Imperial College London were also deeply involved in the race to identify BRCA1. While the Utah team is the focus of this discussion, other groups assembled a similar mix of resources in different ways, further cementing the idea that there are multiple routes to being a hub.

28. Gregory A. Patton and Reed M. Gardner, "Medical Informatics Education: The University of Utah Experience," *Journal of the American Medical Informatics Association* 6, no. 6 (1999): 457–465.

29. Ricki Lewis, "Founder Populations Fuel Gene Discovery," *The Scientist*, April 16, 2001, http://www.the-scientist.com/?articles.view/articleNo/13337/title/Founder-Populations-Fuel-Gene-Discovery/.

30. Declaration of Dr. Mark Skolnick, December 21, 2009, Case 1:09-cv-04515-RWS, Document 172, filed December 23, 2009, 2.

31. Ibid.

32. Quoted in Davies and White, *Breakthrough*, 184.

33. "About Us," Utah Cancer Registry, http://healthsciences.utah.edu/utah-cancer-registry/about/, accessed March 10, 2017.

34. Declaration of Dr. Mark Skolnick, 3.

35. "Utah Population Database," University of Utah, https://healthcare.utah.edu/huntsmancancerinstitute/research/updb/, accessed May 17, 2017.

36. Declaration of Dr. Donna Shattuck, December 21, 2009, Case 1:09-cv-04515-RWS, Document 173, filed December 23, 2009, 4.

37. Declaration of Dr. Mark Skolnick, 4. See also Davies and White, *Breakthrough*, 187.

38. Declaration of Dr. Mark Skolnick, 5.

39. Davies and White, *Breakthrough*, 194.

40. Battelle Technology Partnership Practice, "Preparing for the Future: Utah's Science, Technology, Talent, and Innovation Plan," Spring 2012, https://business.utah.gov/wp-content/uploads/Utahs-Science-Technology-Talent-and-Innovation-Plan.pdf.

41. As many commentators and researchers have noted, this kind of commercial endeavor is not an unambiguous good from the perspective of "public" science; I leave those debates to one side for now, as the point for our purposes is about the central role the university can play in key research and organizational developments in a wide range of fields.

42. This description is drawn from a declaration that is part of a major lawsuit against Myriad that sought (successfully, as it turns out) to invalidate patents on BRCA1 and a second breast cancer gene, BRCA2, so it should be taken with a grain of salt. Declaration of Dr. Mark Skolnick, December 21, 2009, Case 1:09-cv-04515-RWS, Document 172, filed December 23, 2009, 5.

43. Walter W. Powell and Kurt Sandholtz, "Amphibious Entrepreneurs and the Emergence of Organizational Forms," *Strategic Entrepreneurship Journal* 6, no. 2 (2012): 94–115.

44. Ibid., 95.

45. This project was funded by the NSF and depended heavily on the work of graduate research assistants including Helena Buhr, Natalie Cotton-Nessler, Mariana Craciun, and Russell Funk as well as the efforts of a rotating cast of more than forty undergraduate research assistants.

46. For more details, see Jason Owen-Smith, Natalie Cotton-Nessler, and Helena Buhr, "Network Effects on Organizational Decision Making: Blended Social Mechanisms and IPO Withdrawal," *Social Networks* 41 (2015): 1–17.

47. Larry Page, University of Michigan Commencement Address, 2009, http://googlepress.blogspot.com/2009/05/larry-pages-university-of-michigan.html.

48. We looked at technology firms in five high-tech industrial sectors starting when they filed IPO prospectuses and every subsequent year they filed an annual report with the SEC. The tranche of data I describe here comes from a random sample of 684 companies that filed for an IPO in industries related to computer hardware, information and software, drug development, medical devices, and analytic services between 1993 and 2006. With the help of a team of undergraduate research assistants my graduate students and I content-coded information about the alliances companies reported, the biographies and organizational affiliations of corporate officers and directors, and the characteristics of significant minority owners. The result is a pretty comprehensive sense of the most visible network connections, both formal and informal, linking high-profile technology firms to other organizations.

49. For more details see Russell J. Funk and Jason Owen-Smith, "A Dynamic Network Measure of Technological Change."

50. Edwin Mansfield, "Academic Research Underlying Industrial Innovations: Sources, Characteristics, and Financing," *Review of Economics and Statistics* 77, no. 1 (1995): 55–65.

51. Lynn Zucker, Michael Darby, and Marilynn Brewer, "Intellectual Capital and the Birth of U.S. Biotechnology Enterprises," *American Economic Review* 88, no. 1 (1998): 290–306; Bronwyn Hall and Rosemarie Ziedonis, "The Patent Paradox Revisited: An Empirical Study of Patenting in the U.S. Semi-Conductor industry," *RAND Journal of Economics* 32, no. 1 (2001): 101–128.

52. Mark C. Suchman and Mia L. Cahill, "The Hired Gun as Facilitator: Lawyers and the Suppression of Business Disputes in Silicon Valley," *Law and Social Inquiry* 21, no. 3 (1996): 679–712; Mark C. Suchman, "Dealmakers and Counselors: Law Firms as Intermediaries in the Development of Silicon Valley," in *Understanding Silicon Valley: The Anatomy of an Entrepreneurial Region*, ed. Martin Kennedy (Palo Alto, CA: Stanford University Press, 2000); Helena Buhr and Jason Owen-Smith, "Networks as Institutional Support: Law Firm and Venture Capitalist Relations and Regional Diversity in High-Technology IPOs," *Research in the Sociology of Work* 21 (2010): 95–126.

53. Mansfield, "Academic Research Underlying Industrial Innovations."

54. Peter Thiel, *Zero to One: Notes on Start Ups or How to Build the Future* (New York: Crown Business Press, 2014).

55. For a recent, detailed look at the whole field of higher education in the San Francisco Bay Area and its relationship to high-technology industries, see W. Richard Scott and Michael W. Kirst, *Higher Education and Silicon Valley: Connected but Conflicted* (Baltimore: Johns Hopkins University Press, 2017).

56. The numbers are similar when we expand our view to include both highest-research and very-high-research universities. Slightly less than 93 percent of these 222 institutions have at least one ROTC program. Just under 35 percent have ROTC programs for all the service branches.

57. This number varies pretty dramatically from service to service. More than 50 percent of Army officers were commissioned through ROTC, but only slightly more than 5 percent of Marine Corps officers were. Office of the Under Secretary of Defense, Personnel and Readiness, *Population Representation in the Military Services: Fiscal Year 2015. Table B-31 Active Component Commissioned Officer Corps, FY2015: By Source of Commission, Service, and Gender*, 2016, http://www.cna.org/research/pop-rep.

58. For the broader sample of 222 high-research and very-high-research universities, that figure is just over 50 percent.

59. All data about judges is drawn from the Federal Judicial Center Biographical Directory of Federal Judges, http://www.fjc.gov/history/home.nsf/page/judges.html, accessed March 23, 2017.

60. Gueorgi Kossinets and Duncan J. Watts, "Empirical Analysis of an Evolving Social Network," *Science* 311, no. 5757 (2006): 88–90.

61. Matthew S. Kraatz and Emily S. Block, "Organizational Implications of Institutional Pluralism," in *The Sage Handbook of Organizational Institutionalism*, ed. Royston Greenwood, Christine Oliver, Roy Suddaby, and Kerstin Sahlin-Andersson (Thousand Oaks, CA: Sage, 2008), 243.

62. Kerr, *Uses of the University*, 8.

63. Chambliss and Takacs, *How College Works*; Armstrong and Hamilton, *Paying for the Party*; Amy Binder and Kate Wood, *Becoming Right: How Campuses Shape Young*

Conservatives (Princeton, NJ: Princeton University Press, 2013); Neil Gross, *Why Are Professors Liberal and Why Do Conservatives Care?* (Cambridge, MA: Harvard University Press, 2013); Peter Kauffman and Kenneth A. Feldman, "Forming Identities in College: A Sociological Perspective," *Research in Higher Education* 45, no. 5 (2004): 463–496; Lauren Rivera, *Pedigree: How Elite Students Get Elite Jobs* (Princeton, NJ: Princeton University Press, 2015).

64. "About the Lab. Mission and History," MIT Media Lab, https://www.media.mit.edu/about/mission-history/, accessed March 31, 2017.

65. In particular I draw on two books written about the lab soon after its founding and more recently: Stewart Brand, *The Media Lab: Inventing the Future at MIT* (New York: Viking Adult, 1987); and Frank Moss, *The Sorcerers and Their Apprentices: How the Digital Magicians of the MIT Media Lab are Creating the Future* (New York: Crown Business Press, 2011). Both of these books make much of the Media Lab's physical, social, and intellectual organization. In keeping with this chapter's focus on understanding a university's connections to its larger environment, I pay very little attention to these aspects of the lab. However, in choosing this example I am not advocating for universities to emulate particular features of the lab. Instead, I am using it to illustrate some of the key aspects of what it means to be a hub on a scale that is more concrete and easier to grasp than the university as a whole.

66. Moss, *The Sorcerers and Their Apprentices*, 4.

67. In one interesting example, Moss frames Lego's sponsorship of a particular research group in the lab by suggesting that the company informs the group's research rather than directing it. In other words, the sponsorship becomes an explicit mechanism for problems and concerns that the company considers important to flow to academic researchers.

68. "Media Lab Membership Getting Value," MIT Media Lab, https://www.media.mit.edu/members/getting-value/, accessed March 31, 2017.

69. "MIT Media Lab Members," MIT Media Lab, https://dam-prod.media.mit.edu/x/2017/01/12/members1016.pdf, accessed March 31, 2017.

70. Much of this description is adapted from Moss, *The Sorcerers and Their Apprentices*, chap. 4.

71. Brandon C. Roy et al., "Predicting the Birth of a Spoken Word," *Proceedings of the National Academy of Sciences* 112, no. 41 (2015): 12663.

72. Moss, *The Sorcerers and Their Apprentices*, 93.

73. Ibid.

74. Ibid., 96.

75. "SGER: Regularities in Children's Word Learning Input: 24/7 Observation and Analysis," BCS-0554772, National Science Foundation, https://www.nsf.gov/awardsearch/showAward?AWD_ID=0554772&HistoricalAwards=false, accessed April 1, 2017. See also an early conference paper describing the speechome project, which acknowledges this grant. Deb Roy et al., "The Human Speechome Project," *Proceedings of the 28th Annual Cognitive Science Conference*, Vancouver, Canada, 2006.

76. Deb Roy, "The Birth of a Word," *Huffington Post*, February 7, 2013, http://www.huffingtonpost.com/deb-roy/the-birth-of-a-word_b_2639625.html.

77. NSF IIP-0923936, "Semi Automated Sports Video Search," 2009. This grant was a part of the American Recovery and Reinvestment Act (ARRA) stimulus package.

78. Ali Rowghani, "Welcoming Bluefin Labs to the Flock," Twitter, February 5, 2013, https://blog.twitter.com/2013/welcoming-bluefin-labs-to-the-flock.

Chapter 6

1. Paul Basken, "How Threats to Indirect Research Payments Could Make Universities Less Willing to Gamble on Science," *Chronicle of Higher Education*, April 7, 2017, https://www.chronicle.com/article/How-Threats-to-Indirect/239736.

2. Christopher Newfield, *The Great Mistake: How We Wrecked Public Universities and How We Can Fix Them* (Baltimore: Johns Hopkins University Press, 2016), makes a similar argument from different premises. For a negative case of just such an effort, see Gaye Tuchman, *Wannabe U: Inside the Corporate University* (Chicago: University of Chicago Press, 2009).

3. Walter W. Powell, "Neither Market nor Hierarchy: Network Forms of Organization," *Research in Organizational Behavior* 12 (1990): 295–336; Andrew Schrank and Josh Whitford, "The Anatomy of Network Failure," *Sociological Theory* 29, no. 3 (2011): 151–177.

4. Significant directed investment aimed toward particular ends has proven successful in the past. The Manhattan Project, the Apollo missions, and the Human Genome Project offer just a few examples. Daniel Sarewitz, "Saving Science," *New Atlantic* 49 (2016): 4–40.

5. "Secretary of Defense Donald Rumsfeld: DoD News Briefing," February 12, 2002, http://archive.defense.gov/Transcripts/Transcript.aspx?TranscriptID=2636.

6. Ibid.

7. Jason Owen-Smith and Walter W. Powell, "Networks and Institutions," in *The Sage Handbook of Organizational Institutionalism*, ed. Royston Greenwood, Christine Oliver, Roy Suddaby, and Kjerstin Sahlin-Anderson (Thousand Oaks, CA: Sage, 2008), 596–624.

8. Victoria Johnson and Walter W. Powell, "Organizational Poisedness and the Transformation of Civic Order in Nineteenth-Century New York," in *Organizations, Civil Society and the Roots of Development*, ed. Naomi Lamoreaux and Joseph Wallis (Chicago: University of Chicago Press, 2017), 179.

9. Ibid., 38.

10. Jason Owen-Smith and Walter W. Powell, "Careers and Contradictions: Faculty Responses to the Transformation of Knowledge and Its Uses in the Life Sciences," *Research in the Sociology of Work* 10 (2001): 109–140; Walter W. Powell and Kurt Sandholtz, "Amphibious Entrepreneurs and the Emergence of Organizational Forms," *Strategic Entrepreneurship Journal* 6, no. 2 (2012): 94–115.

11. "One Year into the Zika Outbreak: How an Obscure Disease Became a Global Health Emergency," World Health Organization, May 5, 2016, http://www.who.int/emergencies/zika-virus/articles/one-year-outbreak/en/.

12. Ibid., 2.

13. Scott C. Weaver et al., "Zika History: History, Emergence, Biology, and Prospects for Control," *Antiviral Research* 130 (2016): 70.

14. "One Year into the Zika Outbreak," 1.

15. "Guillain-Barré Syndrome Fact Sheet," National Institutes of Health, https://www.ninds.nih.gov/Disorders/Patient-Caregiver-Education/Fact-Sheets/Guillain-Barr%C3%A9-Syndrome-Fact-Sheet, accessed April 18, 2017.

16. Jmej Mlakar et al., "Zika Virus Associated with Microcephaly," *New England Journal of Medicine* 374 (2016): 951–958; Sonja A. Rasmussen et al., "Zika Virus and Birth Defects: Reviewing the Evidence for Causality," *New England Journal of Medicine* 374 (2016): 1981–1987.

17. Lena H. Sun and Brady Denis, "U.S. Confirms Florida Zika Cases Are First Local Transmission in Any State," *Washington Post*, July 20, 2016, https://www.washingtonpost.com/news/to-your-health/wp/2016/07/29/florida-announces-zika-is-likely-spreading-by-mosquitoes-in-the-continental-u-s-2/?utm_term=.2f2820465286.

18. "CDC Guidance for Travel and Testing of Pregnant Women and Women of Reproductive Age for Zika Virus Infection Related to the Investigation for Local Mosquito-borne Zika Virus Transmission in Miami-Dade and Broward Counties, Florida," CDCHAN-00393, U.S. Centers for Disease Control and Prevention, August 1, 2016, https://emergency.cdc.gov/han/han00393.asp.

19. I date the end of the outbreak to November 2016, when WHO declared the end of the Public Health Emergency of International Concern. "Fifth Meeting of the Emergency Committee under the International Health Regulations (2005) Regarding Microcephaly, Other Neurological Disorders and Zika Virus," World Health Organization, November 18, 2016, http://www.who.int/mediacentre/news/statements/2016/zika-fifth-ec/en/.

20. Ibid.

21. World Health Organization,"One Year Into the Zika Outbreak," 2.

22. The story of CRISPR/Cas9 itself replicates many of the features of universities we are interested in. Multiple discoveries spread quickly to revolutionize work in several fields. The lead-up to the discovery was long and spanned continents, types of research, and institutional locations. There's also a very hotly contested patent fight. Unfortunately, the space we have here does not allow us to pursue the juicy details. But see Eric S. Lander, "Heroes of CRISPR," *Cell* 164 (2016): 18–28. This article makes a good starting point, though note that Lander is the director of one of the organizations embroiled in the patent conflict.

23. George Savidis et al., "Identification of Zika Virus and Dengue Virus Dependency Factors Using Functional Genomics," *Cell Reports* 16 (2016): 232–246.

24. "Scientists Offer First Look at How Our Cells Can 'Swallow Up and Quarantine' Zika," June 3, 2016, https://www.sciencedaily.com/releases/2016/06/160604051001.htm, accessed March 8, 2018.

25. "Scientists Use CRISPR to Discover Zika and Dengue Weaknesses," Phys.org, June 21, 2016, https://phys.org/news/2016-06-scientists-crispr-zika-dengue-weaknesses.html.

26. Caleb D. Marceau et al., "Genetic Dissection of *Flaviridae* Host Factors Through Genome-Scale CRISPR Screens," *Nature* 353 (2016): 159–163; Rong Zhang et al., "A CRISPR Screen Defines a Signal Peptide Processing Pathway Required by Flaviviruses," *Nature* 353 (2016): 164–168.

27. M. Doerflinger et al., "CRISPR/CaS9—The Ultimate Weapon to Battle Infectious Diseases?" *Cellular Microbiology* 19 (2017): e12693, 5.

28. Lander, "Heroes of CRISPR."

29. Doerflinger et al., "CRISPR/CaS9."

30. The grants acknowledged in these papers all preceded, often by years, the announcement of more than $1 billion to support responses to Zika in September 2016. The lion's share of those special funds were devoted to vaccine development, which I do not discuss here.

31. Aaron R. Everett et al., "IFITM3 Restricts Mortality and Morbidity Associated with Influenza," *Nature* 484 (2012): 519–523.

32. Helen Lazear et al., "A Mouse Model of Zika Virus Pathogenesis," *Cell Host and Microbe* 19, no. 5 (2016): 720–730.

33. Marla Vacek Broadfoot, "Forging a Path for Zika Vaccines, Therapies, and Diagnostics: A Q&A with Michael Diamond," Burroughs Wellcome Fund, https://www .bwfund.org/newsroom/newsletter-articles/forging-path-zika-vaccines-therapies-and -diagnostics, accessed April 21, 2017.

34. Gopal Sapparapu et al., "Neutralizing Human Antibodies Prevent Zika Virus Replication and Fetal Disease in Mice," *Nature* 540 (2016): 443–447.

35. Broadfoot, "Forging a Path for Zika Vaccines," 1.

36. Richard M. Deans et al., "Parallel shRNA and CRISPR-Cas9 Screens Enable Antiviral Drug Target Identification," *Nature Chemical Biology* 12 (2016): 361–366.

37. Nathan Hurst, "The Story of a Resurrected Antiviral Could Hold Lessons for Combating Zika," *Smithsonian Magazine*, September 8, 2016, http://www .smithsonianmag.com/science-nature/story-resurrected-antiviral-lessons-combatting -zika-180960325/.

38. Ibid.

39. L. Cong et al., "Multiplex Genome Engineering Using CRISPR/Cas Systems," *Science* 339 (2013): 819–823.

40. Broad is a joint venture of Harvard and MIT, a research institute founded to capitalize on advances in genetic research stemming from the Human Genome Project.

41. Lander, "Heroes of CRISPR," 26.

42. Ibid. *Ensemble* is, to me, another way to say *network*.

43. Brian Uzzi, Satyam Mukherjee, Michael Stringer, and Ben Jones, "Atypical Combinations and Scientific Impact," *Science* 342, no. 6157 (2013): 468–472.

44. Recall that there are also negative consequences of hypercompetition, a situation that may only be exacerbated by continuing cuts to public support. In other arenas, increasing competition breeds a kind of conservativism that is dangerous for research institutions, which we need to be able to paddle against the stream of the status quo. Because stability and a long view of impact are essential, competition that has the po-

tential to destroy the less successful is also contraindicated. David Larabee, *A Perfect Mess: The Unlikely Ascendancy of American Higher Education* (Chicago: University of Chicago Press, 2017).

45. Michael Crow and William Dabars, *Designing the New American University* (Baltimore: Johns Hopkins University Press, 2015).

46. Larabee, *A Perfect Mess*.

47. Gaye Tuchman, *Wannabe U: Inside the Corporate University* (Chicago: University of Chicago Press, 2009).

48. Pierre Azoulay, Joshua Graff-Zivin, and Gustavo Manso, "Incentives and Creativity: Evidence from the Academic Life Sciences," *RAND Journal of Economics* 42, no. 3 (2011): 527–554.

49. Lingfei Wu, Dashun Wang, and James A. Evans, "Large Teams Have Developed Science and Technology; Small Teams Have Disrupted It," working paper, 2017, https://arxiv.org/pdf/1709.02445.pdf.

50. American Academy of Arts and Sciences, *Restoring the Foundation: The Vital Role of Research in Preserving the American Dream* (Cambridge, MA: American Academy of Arts and Sciences, 2014).

51. Ibid., 21.

52. Ibid., 20.

53. Julia Lane, Jason Owen-Smith, Rebecca Rosen, and Bruce Weinberg, "New Linked Data on Research Investments: Scientific Workforce, Productivity, and Public Value," *Research Policy* 44, no. 9 (2015): 1659–1671.

54. Kaye Husbands Fealing, Julia Lane, John H. Marburger III, and Stephanie Shipp (eds.), *The Science of Science Policy: A Handbook* (Stanford, CA: Stanford University Press, 2011).

55. Paula Stephan, *How Economics Shapes Science* (Cambridge, MA: Harvard University Press, 2012).

56. John H. Marburger III, "Wanted: Better Benchmarks," *Science* 308 (May 5, 2005): 1087.

57. Julia Lane, "Big Data for Public Policy: The Quadruple Helix," *Journal of Policy Analysis and Management* 35, no. 3 (2016): 708–715.

58. See http://iris.isr.unich.edu for a description of the Institute for Research on Innovation and Science (IRIS), a consortium of research universities which share data that are integrated with restricted data maintained by the U.S. Census Bureau and information on research productivity. The resulting linked, appropriately de-identified data are made available for researchers to use with restrictions that protect privacy and confidentiality. The first data release from this project is Institute for Research on Innovation & Science (IRIS) UMETRICS Initiative (Universities: Measuring the Impacts of Research on Innovation), Documentation for UMETRICS 2016Q3a Dataset (Ann Arbor, MI: IRIS, 2017). Along with me, the co-PIs of the project are Julia Lane, Bruce Weinberg, Ron Jarmin, Barbara McFadden Allen, and James Evans.

59. Mazzucatto, *The Entrepreneurial State*.

60. Funk & Owen-Smith, "A Dynamic Network Measure of Technological Change."

61. Goldrick-Rab, *Paying the Price*; Newfield, *The Great Mistake.*

62. Paul Courant, James Duederstadt, and Edie Goldenberg, "Wanted: A Plan to Save Public Research Universities," *Chronicle of Higher Education*, January 3, 2010, http://www.chronicle.com/article/A-Plan-to-Save-Americas/63358/.

63. King, "Making Maintenance of Effort Permanent."

64. American Academy of Arts and Sciences, *Public Research Universities: Recommitting to Lincoln's Vision: An Educational Compact for the 21st Century* (Washington, DC: American Academy of Arts and Sciences, 2016).

65. Ibid., 24.

66. Ibid., 28.

INDEX